first-time parents

Dr. Miriam Stoppard

LONDON, NEW YORK, MELBOURNE,
MUNICH, DELHI

For Ed and Amie

Produced for Dorling Kindersley by
Cooling Brown
Designer Tish Jones
Editor Jemima Dunne
Creative Director Arthur Brown
Technical Support Peter Cooling

Dorling Kindersley
Consultant Editor Jinny Johnson
Managing Editor Esther Ripley
Senior Editor Emma Woolf
US Editors Shannon Beatty, Beth Hester
US Medical Consultant Aviva Schein, MD
Managing Art Editor Marianne Markham
Senior Art Editor Nicola Rodway
Senior Production Editor Jenny Woodcock
Creative Technical Support Sonia Charbonnier
Production Controller Hema Gohil
Jacket Design Charlotte Seymour
Special Photography Vanessa Davies
Art Direction for Photography Anne Fisher

First American Edition, 1998
This revised edition published in 2009 by
Dorling Kindersley Publishing,
375 Hudson Street
New York, New York 10014
A Penguin Company
10 11 10 9 8 7 6 5 4 3
FD177—03/2009

A catalog record for this book is available from the
Library of Congress.
ISBN 978-0-7566-4422-2

DK books are available at special discounts when
purchased in bulk for sales promotions, premiums,
fund-raising, or educational use.
For details, contact: DK Publishing Special Markets,
375 Hudson Street, New York, New
York 10014 or SpecialSales@dk.com.
Printed and bound in Singapore by Tien Wah Press

Discover more at
www.dk.com

Contents

Introduction

Today's new parents have many advantages over their predecessors, but they also face many new challenges. Knowledge of the way babies grow and develop both before and after birth has increased enormously in the past few years. This knowledge in itself creates new pressures, worries, and anxieties for parents. If you are a couple thinking of starting a family, how do you know where to turn? I hope that this book will help you to find out what best suits you and will make you feel comfortable and confident enough to follow your own instincts.

There's much evidence to indicate that the unborn baby benefits from having a relaxed, calm mother who can take obstacles in her stride. Other research demonstrates that the most important factor in determining whether a pregnant woman is tranquil or not is a caring, interested, supportive partner. And here we have come to the reason for my writing this book. It is not just for first-time mothers, but for couples—mothers and fathers. I've included basic advice on caring for your baby during his first year of life, but it's just as important to emphasize how a baby will affect your relationship.

The impact on your relationship

Few couples think about the impact their new baby will have on their lives, their work, their emotions, and their feelings for one another. With the care of their baby a top priority, parents can easily give too little consideration to themselves.

Both new mothers and new fathers will find their world turned upside down by the arrival of a baby. This may create tensions and strains, which, if unspoken and unresolved, could drive a wedge between them. It's a huge leap from being a couple to becoming a family. A man is very different from a father, and different things are expected of him.

If they're honest, most men admit to experiencing difficulties in making the transition to fatherhood. By the same token, a mother is a very different person from a woman, who was probably self-confident and independent before she became pregnant. Now she may be apprehensive and come to feel isolated. She has to cope with a baby who is completely dependent upon her, which can bring with it a perceived loss of identity. This in turn may lead to confusion, resentment, and irritation toward her partner.

The good news is that it's possible for both of you to pick your way through this minefield of new feelings and responsibilities. But it isn't always easy and it requires a lot of give and take to smooth the path. Perhaps now, more than at any other time, each of you has to be aware of and sensitive to the needs of the other and actively look for ways of showing you care.

Advice and reassurance

While my main aim is to give new parents the confidence to follow their own instincts in fashioning their particular brand of family life, and to be open and loving with one another so that their relationship is enriched by their new baby, there's no doubt that first-time parents find bits of advice quite useful. So I've tried to be helpful in matters with which most young families have problems.

Issues such as how to stay healthy during pregnancy, where to have your baby, what to expect during labor, how to establish breastfeeding and cope with broken nights or an inconsolable crying baby are all covered. While love for your baby can begin from the moment of birth, his care is a skill that you'll be learning throughout his first year, and understanding how he develops is a crucial part of it. All new parents feel anxious and inept to begin with, but if you both share the worries as well as the joys, you're less likely to strain your relationship.

Making room for fathers

Throughout the book, I approach pregnancy, birth, and babycare as a joint venture. Fathers figure on every page because mothers and babies need involved, active fathers. Men are as good at fathering as women are at mothering; there's no qualitative difference between the two. Fathering instincts are strong and need only a little encouragement to flower. Babies love being nurtured by fathers as well as mothers; it follows that parenting should be equal and shared.

On the face of it, following this principle may seem fraught with obstacles, but it need not be so. Parents can share all the elements of babycare with a little planning and a generous heart. After all, babycare means loving and encouraging your baby, teaching your baby, watching your baby grow

and develop, and establishing bonds with your baby that in all probability will be the strongest you ever make with anyone. Who in their right mind would miss out on it?

Men should try not to allow themselves to be deprived of this unique relationship. And when they're fully involved with their baby, a little miracle occurs along the way: their relationship with their baby's mother flourishes, too.

Making parenting a partnership

To help both parents become fully involved, I've included special panels that give the mother's point of view on one side of the page and the father's point of view on the other. Arranging information in this way has a special purpose: it can help you gain insight into what your partner may be feeling about a particular topic, or might want to say, but is reluctant to make demands. Looking at this information together may help you to get a discussion going. Communication is the key to a successful relationship. I hope the panels will enable you to talk things through and be generous about different ways of looking at things.

Above all, couples whose relationships are on a sound footing and who enter into parenthood as a true partnership are doing the best for their baby, who will grow up secure in the love of both parents. Shared care means there'll be time for your baby, time for yourselves, and time when, as well as being a family, you're just a couple—but with the knowledge that together you have produced and nurtured a wonderful baby.

Dr. Miriam Stoppard

Deciding on parenthood

When you decide to have a baby, you're also making the decision to become a parent. This is probably the most important step you'll ever take in your life, because bringing a child into the world isn't something that you can simply add on to your current lifestyle. You're creating a completely new person, and taking on a responsibility that is lifelong. You're also creating a new unit—from being two individuals, you're becoming a family—something that both cements and puts strains on your existing relationships, with each other, your friends, and your family. This is equally true if you're a lone parent and, even if you have children from a previous relationship, your new baby is going to create a new family grouping. So it's well worth looking at all the implications of parenthood and the different forms that the modern family takes, and to ask yourselves some searching questions about how you see parenting, and how it's going to affect your everyday needs as well as your emotions.

The changing family

Having a baby creates a whole new social unit. Instead of being just two people, you become a family. Families give babies constant care and protection and, though family groupings may vary, babies know only the quality of care, interest, and love that they receive.

How roles are changing

At their most basic, the terms "mother" and "father" describe a range of biological facts. A mother produces eggs and gives birth to children. A father's sperm fertilizes the eggs and contributes half his children's genes. But these are obviously not the only differences. Human beings belong to a species with clear distinctions between male and female. Traditionally, the physical differences between men and women meant that men (being bigger and stronger) were seen as protectors of women.

No need for brute strength

For thousands of years, men used their biological role to claim authority over women, but today, the traditional roles of mother and father are no longer relevant. Modern technology has done away with the need for brute strength, and nowadays women and children generally don't need men to protect them.

Involving men in parenting

Since the 1970s, it has been increasingly recognized that men should be more involved in the upbringing of their children. This is sometimes seen as a spin-off from the women's movement, but this misses the point. The equal sharing between men and women in the care of their children isn't just the result of women's changing thoughts, but also the outcome of men's need to be involved in the nurture, guidance, and raising of their children.

How it used to be

Until two or three generations ago, the family was usually based on the extended model. People were part of a large grouping of three or four generations, extending outward to include cousins. When people's lives were less mobile, and they lived and worked in one small area, face-to-face contact was possible on a daily basis. This larger family unit could act as a support group for its members, particularly in the case of child rearing.

The family today

In the past 50 years, the extended family has largely broken down. Rapid technological change produced a labor market that demanded mobility; people wanted to go where the jobs were, or were forced to do so through economic necessity. Leaving home meant leaving the extended family network and possibly settling where there were no relations at all to lean on for financial and emotional support. At the same time, increased prosperity allowed people to set up their own homes, whereas in the past they may have remained in the family home, even when married. This broad social movement saw the rapid spread of the isolated nuclear family—just mother, father, and children. Even when embedded within an extended family, this unit can be a hothouse of troubled emotions; on its own, its long-term survival is more likely to be precarious.

New family groupings

Since the 1960s, women have increasingly developed a degree of financial independence, which has made them less likely to hang on to the last remnant of a marriage just because they didn't think they could provide for themselves and their children on their own. Liberal attitudes to welfare have also played their part in the transformation of the traditional family; as the nuclear family—detached from its older members or more tenuous branches—became the norm rather than the exception, so the divorce rate increased, giving rise to less orthodox family structures.

Divorce and remarriage

Many divorced or separated people haven't turned their backs on marriage or partnership as such, but only on the one they found intolerable, and there are a growing number of families in which one partner or both partners have children from a previous relationship. As with the nuclear family, the stepfamily has been around for a long time (and hasn't always had a good image), but its recent growth in numbers has been dramatic.

Single parents

The one-parent family is a much maligned institution. It's true that it has often grown out of unhappy situations and the pressures, not least financial, on the lone parent are great. But many single-parent families are thriving, vigorous units that are bound by particularly close ties and offer the children involved continuity, stability, and happiness (see p. 140).

A new kind of parenting

Fathers used to be seen as protectors, having little direct involvement in day-to-day childcare, but their importance as equal partners is now recognized—side by side with women's increasing role as equal or even primary financial provider. And in some families the father cares for home and family by choice, while his partner earns the daily bread (see p. 176). One reason why such families are often strong and successful units is that they take account of both partners' talents and, generally, are a result of careful discussion and planning. But whatever the practicalities of any individual family unit, providing a stable, loving, and open environment in which to bring up children is probably the only important constant.

BABY IN THE FAMILY If your partner has a child from a previous relationship, a new baby can cause tensions. Encourage your stepchild to develop a relationship with the baby. Reassure her that you still love her and there is time and space for everyone.

What is a father?

No one has a problem defining a mother's role. A mother's role is to care for children: mothers feed, comfort, and dress; they encourage, teach, carry, undress, and put to bed. We know this because it's what we experienced as children. Defining the father's role can be more difficult.

Finding a role model

Much as you may love your father, you may want your relationship with your own children to be different to the one that you had with your father. Men are constantly encouraged to become fully involved in nurturing their children, but few have any role model to demonstrate what this actually means. What we really need is for fathers to be more like mothers.

Babies don't mind

Babies and young children don't mind whether they are cared for by their mother or father. They experience comfort, warmth, and security from their parents and, though they soon learn to tell them apart, they don't make value judgments based on what mothers and fathers ought to do. Apart from breastfeeding, there's nothing a man can't do for his baby.

The need for parenting

Babies don't need mothering and fathering, they need parenting. They need the most important adults in their lives to be models of what parents do for their children. A child will only separate her expectations of each parent if this is what she learns from her experiences.

Why be a parent?

✳ JUST FOR MOM

It's worth questioning your own ideas about parenthood, and whether what you think of as a mother's role isn't just as applicable to fathers.

Attitudes to fathering

✳ Traditionally, fathers came home from work expecting the home to be clean, the children ready for bed, and a meal on the table. Today, it's hard to believe that many modern mothers would stand for this.

✳ At one time women expected their partners to handle all of the family finances, sometimes to their disadvantage. Nowadays most couples find a fairer way to share their financial burdens.

✳ It's often assumed that men do all the heavy work. However, while a man must do this when his partner is pregnant and the baby is young, women are stronger than they used to be, and these tasks can be shared.

✳ Women still tend to take on the chores while their partners play with the baby, even when both parents work. It's much better, though, if both of you play with your baby, and share the housework equally.

✳ Try to agree on attitudes to discipline for your family and make sure you both apply them consistently (see p. 181).

You may never do anything more important than bring up a child. However satisfying your career, whatever sports or leisure goals you've achieved, you'll find parenthood is a role that is rewarding in a way that is unlike anything else.

Following your instincts

The instinct to bear children is a strong one, and luckily the joy and fulfillment felt by most parents far outweigh some of the inconveniences and compromises that they may have to accept. Although this isn't always so, making the decision to have a child usually comes from within a close, loving relationship between two people who decide that they would like to express their mutual affection in having a baby. This is just as well—you're unlikely to make the decision because you're attracted by the idea of reduced free time, never being able to put yourself first, sleeplessness, and forking out for designer infant clothes! If you think carefully about the changes brought about by parenthood, you'll realize that it's your genes that are pushing you relentlessly towards recreating yourselves in the form of children. Nowadays, people don't like to admit that they might be at the beck and call of basic urges, and tend to dress them up as something more refined. That's fine, so long as we remember that we can also push back and say no to parenthood. For some, that can be the best decision, because having a baby is a commitment like no other.

More than just nature

Aside from biological reasons, people also want to have a baby for fulfillment and personal achievement. Human beings are social animals, and the way they think and act always has a social element. This is shown most clearly in human parenthood in the case of adoption where (usually) two people voluntarily make a commitment to assume all the rights and duties of natural parents, while being genetically unrelated to the child (see p. 142). Adoption also illustrates the depth of the emotional need that people feel to nurture, educate, and, above all, love a child. What you give to your children in time, love, understanding, and teaching will constantly be repaid as you watch them grow and develop over the years. Every child is genetically the sum of his parents, but he is also a unique personality in his own right, and knowing that you have been the primary influences and educators in allowing that personality to take shape and mature is deeply enriching as well as being a major achievement.

Social and economic pressures

In a society where everyone goes to school, everyone expects to go to school. Similarly, when everyone except a small minority has children, people expect to have children. It's as though a person has to have a reason for remaining childless, rather than the opposite. In the past, when families tended to live close together, in the same street or village if not actually in the same house (see p. 10), there were quite important economic reasons for having children. As soon as they were old enough to work, children made a vital contribution to the family's economic welfare, and parenthood was also a guarantee of being cared for in old age.

Changing demands

In the much more fragmented society in which we live today, children aren't expected to contribute to the family income (at least not until they have finished their education), and the government has taken over some of the basic responsibilities for the elderly, or people make their own provision for old age. As a result, the economic demands of the family are now directed downward, from parents to children, instead of the other way around. Bringing up children today can be a costly business, and not just financially. For the first time in history, large numbers of women can achieve a whole range of satisfactions outside parenthood and the home; and with safe methods of contraception, they can also choose whether and when they want to have children. This doesn't mean that large numbers of women are opting out of motherhood, though some are; but what they are doing is fitting having and bringing up children into lives in which work and a career are also seen as theirs by right.

A question of upbringing

Having begun to consider parenthood seriously, the first thing to realize before you go further is that having a baby is just the overture to bringing up a child. It isn't too difficult to imagine having a baby—the excitement, the celebrations, the delighted grandparents, the supportive friends and family. It's almost impossible to visualize bringing up a child if you haven't done it. The demands in time, energy, and emotion are almost limitless, unless of course the first thing you're going to teach your toddler is how to use the remote control for the TV and VCR. This isn't an option for most people because, even before you become parents, you'll have some idea of the kind of people you hope your children will grow up to be, and of the upbringing that will make this idea a reality.

A firm foundation

Upbringing begins from the moment of birth. For a baby or young child, everything is a learning experience, so how you care for your baby is influential from day one. It's worth looking at the background of someone you know who is independent but has a large capacity to love and interrelate with others, who is effective and confident, who recognizes that there is such a thing as the general good, and wants to contribute to it. You'll probably discover that person found the world an accepting, loving, encouraging, reasonable, and respectful place from birth. His parents made him feel that way, and the foundation for everything he has become was provided by them in his first year of life.

✳ JUST FOR DAD

It's a good idea to be clear about your own attitude to parenting to make sure it doesn't reinforce traditional stereotypes about mothers and fathers. What you may think of as a mother's role can be just as applicable to fathers.

Attitudes to mothering

✴ While it's still true that it's mostly women who stay at home, many are now returning to work within months of their baby's birth. Also, more and more men are becoming stay-at-home dads (see p. 176).

✴ Recent surveys show that women, even full-time working mothers, still do most of the chores in the home. Ask yourself if this is fair—there's no reason why cooking and cleaning can't be shared.

✴ Tasks such as dealing with caregivers and teachers and taking the kids to school used to be seen as a mother's responsibility. But more fathers are fitting daily activities like the school run or taking their child to the doctor into their working day.

✴ It used to be thought that mothers put children to bed, but most fathers enjoy the bedtime routine, especially if they've been away from their children all day.

✴ The idea—prevalent not so long ago—that it was somehow demeaning for a man to push a stroller is now laughable. Men are glad to be seen doing this and are also more than happy to take their children out without their partners.

Timing it right

Your attitude to parenting

Parenting is not an exact science. However right the decision to have a child may seem at the time, it may be helpful to ask yourselves the following questions. If you answer "yes" to more than five, you may need to think more about your attitude to parenting:

✳ Do you already have ambitions for your child's future?

✳ Are you uncertain about how parental actions affect children?

✳ Do you still need to work out some of your views on parenting?

✳ Do you think that after the birth, instinct will take over and you'll know exactly how to behave toward your child?

✳ Are you worried that you and your partner have different ideas about parenting?

✳ Do you believe in a strict routine for a newborn baby?

✳ Do you think a baby would benefit from such a routine?

✳ Can you spoil a young baby?

✳ Do you believe that babies cry for no reason?

✳ Will you leave investigating childcare until after the birth?

✳ Are your views on babycare at odds with those of your partner?

✳ Will you find it hard to tolerate all the disorder of a new baby?

✳ Do you foresee any conflict with family members about the way you intend to care for your baby?

It's rare for a couple to feel that everything is just right and that the perfect moment has arrived to have a child, but now that we have control over our fertility, it gives time for all the options to be considered carefully.

Making the decision

For many people, finances and accommodation may be the most pressing issues when making the decision whether or not to become parents. Others may look at their personal freedom, and how having a child may affect it. In today's society, where more and more women are finding satisfaction in the progress of their careers, making the decision to take time off and have a child can be extraordinarily difficult. Although many companies—and countries—are providing increasingly generous maternity leave and benefits, this may not compensate for the fact that having a baby could delay your career prospects, especially if you want to spend more than a few months at home with your baby. This is one reason why many women, particularly those with satisfying or high-powered jobs, are now waiting to start a family at least until their 30s, when they feel that they've reached a level of achievement that enables them to stand back from their careers for a while with confidence.

Making space for parenthood

Men also need to think about how their work commitments may impact their relationship with their children. Many older men who become parents for a second time in a new relationship have acknowledged that they regretted having missed out on their first family's childhood because pressures of work effectively separated them from their children. Childhood passes quickly and you only have one chance with any child, so think about how much time you will be able to give to her.

Practical considerations

You can bring up a child in anything from a two-room apartment on up—if there's a separate space for the baby, that's ideal. If you're thinking of moving into a larger home to accommodate future children, try to move before you become pregnant; otherwise it's best to wait until after your baby is born. You don't want the double pressure of a new baby and moving. No one pretends there isn't a financial implication in parenthood, but the cost of having a baby is largely dependent on what a couple sees as essential. Be assured that no baby in a secondhand crib with one or two loving parents ever lay awake wondering why she didn't have an expensive new crib with Brahms' lullaby wafting from the attached electronic music box. Nevertheless, it makes good sense to make the best of what's available. Look at your likely overall income and expenditure once the baby is born, taking account of available benefits (see p. 184), and plan accordingly. Whenever your budget allows you to shop, invest in the basic minimum (see p. 74); leave luxuries until you can really afford them.

Partnership or marriage

If you're in a long-term stable relationship, but are unmarried, you probably had good reason for choosing this kind of partnership. Now that you're considering parenthood, is there a case for reconsidering your position? Do either or both of you have anything to gain from marrying and, more importantly, does your prospective child? One of the reasons most commonly given by prospective parents for marrying before the birth of a baby is to ensure the father is the legal parent of his child, but in some countries the law states that a father named on the birth certificate has equal parental rights, even if not married to the mother. Clearly neither of you would want to encounter problems in gaining access to your child in the event of your relationship breaking down. However unlikely this may seem at present, no one can see into the future, and most couples would want to guarantee that their baby always has the equal benefit of both parents, even if at some time they may not live together anymore.

Changing relationships

Sometimes new parents haven't bargained for the fact that their relationships with family and friends will change. More importantly perhaps, the dynamics of their own relationship will also change. No time is better spent before you even start trying for a baby than in exploring together what these differences might be (see p. 128).

Grandparents You both know the personalities of the grandparents, and you may see difficulties ahead if their views are not the same as yours. You'll find later that agreement with grandparents about how you're going to set limits for your child is invaluable. It's also a good idea to agree that both parents will gently but firmly resist any attempt by them to dictate methods of parenting to you. You can, however, ask them to help you to implement yours. But it's also wise to listen to their views, or you may be passing up good advice based on real experience.

Your friends Once you have children you may not be available to your friends as much as you were before, so they'll appreciate it if you retain your identity as a friend rather than a parent while you're with them. Bear in mind also that you'll meet other parents with whom you'll forge friendships, based on the shared experience of new parenthood.

The impact at work Try also to rehearse in advance what difference the advent of the baby may have at work. You may never have clock-watched in your life before now, but it's difficult not to when you're aching to get back to your baby—and this is just as true for fathers as it is for mothers. However, your colleagues, no matter how sympathetic, have the right to assume that you'll be as good at your job as you were before. If you can see possible pitfalls, be up-front and negotiate; you won't always be a new parent, and lost trust is difficult to reestablish.

Questioning your reasons

Even if you think you both really want a baby, it's still sensible to think about all the issues. The following questions don't have right or wrong answers, but provide what I hope will be a useful starting point for you:

✱ Does the idea of having a baby seem to be the instinctive next step for you both?

✱ Have you always taken it for granted that you would have children?

✱ Do you just want a child, or do you want a child specifically with your partner?

✱ Does one of you want this baby more than the other? If so, what effect has this had on your relationship?

✱ Do you want to have a baby because you think it will strengthen your relationship with your partner?

✱ What images do you see when thinking about life with your baby? Do they include sleepless nights and dirty diapers?

✱ What will you miss most about being a couple rather than a trio?

✱ Do you have any firm personal ambitions that could be compromised by having a baby?

✱ Do you want a baby to make up for areas in your life that you find unsatisfactory?

✱ Is any part of your motivation to please family members, such as grandparents?

✱ Are you and your partner very clear about the commitment each of you will make to the baby?

Preparing for parenthood

Pregnancy is an exciting time for you both, but your excitement can also be tinged with apprehension, uncertainty, and—if the pregnancy is a surprise—even dismay. Each person's reaction to the knowledge that he or she is going to become a parent is different, but luckily nature has made sure that there is plenty of time to get used to the idea during the 40 or so weeks from conception to birth. Pregnancy is not an illness, but it does put a lot of strain on a woman's body. So if you're planning to become parents it makes sense to think about your fitness well before you conceive, and to take care of yourself during the pregnancy. Once the pregnancy is confirmed, you will both feel happier if you follow its progress by attending prenatal appointments together and finding out as much as possible about how your baby develops in the womb. It will help you both to understand the minor discomforts and emotional ups and downs that a pregnant woman sometimes feels, and to face the slight possibility of something unexpected happening.

Plan for pregnancy

Your due date will be calculated as 40 weeks from the first day of your last period, so you need to take that into account when planning your pre-pregnancy fitness.

Why fitness is important

There are a number of physical changes during pregnancy. Here are a few: the womb increases in volume (muscle) 1,000 times; the womb increases in weight (protein) 30 times; the work done by a mother's heart increases 50 percent; the volume of her blood increases by one-third; her kidneys filter 50 percent more blood.

Preventing anemia

If you're anemic, your heart is overworked, which can affect your baby. A blood test would reveal anemia, and it may be necessary to take iron supplements.

Avoiding birth defects

Folic acid reduces the risk of some birth defects like spina bifida. It's a good idea to start increasing folic acid intake three months before you stop contraception, and for three months after you conceive. Good food sources are green leafy vegetables, cereals, and bread, or you can take supplements.

Preexisting medical problems

If you regularly take drugs for a medical condition, let your doctor know before you try for a baby, as the dose may have to be changed once you're pregnant.

When you decide to become parents, it makes sense to prepare yourselves in advance. To have a healthy baby, research shows that by far the most important factors are your own and your partner's fitness and nutrition.

Timing of the birth

Ideally you should begin to think about it at least a year before the time you'd like your baby to be born. It's a good idea to allow at least three months to get your bodies to peak pre-conception fitness (see opposite). There are other issues you may want to take into account as well. If you're planning to move, or know that work commitments are going to take you away from home at a specific time of year, you'll want to avoid allowing these to clash with the possible arrival of your baby. Some parents may want to take into account whether their baby is born in winter or summer. Most education systems involve an autumn start to the academic year and there is evidence to suggest that some children born in the summer, the youngest in their school year group, may not achieve as well academically as the older and more mature children who are born in the winter.

✳ Routine health precautions

What to look at	What to do
Smoking	Smoking reduces fertility, especially in men as it lowers their sperm count. Give up before you try for a baby; smoking during pregnancy—directly or secondhand—harms your unborn child.
Alcohol	Alcohol can damage both sperm and the egg (ovum), so prospective parents should consume no more than five units a week for women, ten for men. (One unit = one small glass of wine or an 8-oz glass of beer.)
Drugs and medication	Many medicinal and street drugs affect fertility. In particular, marijuana reduces sperm production; the effects can take months to wear off. Consult your doctor if you're taking regular medication.
Pre-pregnancy screening	Well before trying for a baby, ask your obstetrician if there are any tests you should have before becoming pregnant;in the United States, some doctors recommend screening for certain genetic diseases.
Environmental factors	Make sure you avoid X-rays, hot saunas, and pollutants such as dioxins and PCBs in household products.

Delaying parenthood

More women are now delaying childbearing into their 30s or even early 40s. A pregnant woman over 35 will be monitored more closely, but women's general health and fitness have improved so much that the older pregnant mother is no longer likely to have the same risks of earlier generations. In addition, couples starting a family in their 30s are more likely to have planned the baby, be in a stable relationship, and be financially secure. But leaving conception until later does increase the time you might have to wait to conceive—an average of six months when you're 35, as opposed to four months when you're 25 (see p. 20).

When to stop contraception

If you've been using straightforward barrier methods, such as the condom or diaphragm, you can safely conceive as soon as you stop using them. However, some doctors recommend at least one normal period after ceasing other forms of contraception before you try to conceive.

The pill It's best to stop the pill three months beforehand, but a month would do, as long as you have one normal period before conceiving.

Intra-uterine device (IUD) The same timescale would apply to an IUD, so have it removed three months before you intend to get pregnant. Wait until you've had at least one normal period before stopping all contraception—use a barrier method in the meantime.

How fitness helps you both

As a prospective mother, your body undergoes a great deal of physical change (see box opposite). The fitter you are, the more easily your body will cope. But fitness and lifestyle may also change a man's ability to father a child, by affecting sperm production (see box above). Think about your health and lifestyle at least three months before you plan to stop contraception. As well as improving your fitness, it will increase your chances of conceiving without delay and of having a healthy baby.

A healthy diet

Adjusting your diet shouldn't require uncomfortable changes. Include good-quality carbohydrates, such as whole-wheat bread, rice, and potatoes. Keep your animal fat intake down and use olive or sunflower oil for cooking. Eat lots of fresh fruit and vegetables every day (see p. 36). Don't skip meals, avoid processed foods, outlaw the liquid lunch, and eat a hearty breakfast, though not a fried one. Start taking folic acid at least three months before you're planning to conceive.

Exercise

Exercise makes a contribution to becoming a healthy potential parent, so if you don't already do so, start following a gentle exercise program together, such as jogging, swimming, or gym sessions. Try for 20 minutes' exercise that increases your heart rate at least three times a week. However, bear in mind that very strenuous training or dieting may reduce fertility.

✳ JUST FOR DAD

Your partner's fitness and lifestyle obviously have a bearing on her ability to conceive, but your own fitness is also a crucial factor. If you aren't healthy, you may not donate the best genetic material to your child in your sperm.

Why your lifestyle matters
Male fertility not only depends on the number of sperm produced, but also on the health of that sperm. This is affected by all sorts of lifestyle factors, such as smoking, alcohol, and drugs (see left), and also stress. Try to reorder your life if it's stressful, and look at your diet and fitness.

✳

Genetic counseling

Seek advice and have tests in advance if a genetic disorder, such as cystic fibrosis, muscular dystrophy, thalassemia, or hemophilia, runs in your family.

What happens in counseling
The counselor explains the condition and your family background and shows you the pattern of inheritance through past generations. Not all carriers of a defective gene get the condition. If it's recessive it can be masked by a healthy version, whereas a dominant gene will always show up. With a dominant gene, the chances of your baby being affected are one in two; with a recessive gene they are one in four.

Conception

Conceiving a baby is the ultimate expression of a loving sexual relationship between partners. You could conceive within a few months of deciding to have a baby, especially if you have intercourse when you're most fertile.

Increasing chances of conception

The following tips might help you conceive more quickly:

✳ Try to have intercourse during your most fertile period (see right). This period is signalled by the texture of your cervical mucus, which becomes clear, thin, and slippery, making it easier for the sperm to swim up through your cervix. Ovulation usually occurs 24 hours after this type of mucus is at its most profuse.

✳ Avoid lovemaking for a couple of days before your fertile period to help build up sperm numbers.

✳ The "missionary position" (man on top) may be most effective for conception, particularly if the woman lies down for half an hour afterward.

✳ Cut down on caffeine. It may interfere with the embryo's ability to implant in the wall of the uterus.

When you're fertile

A woman is fertile only when she is ovulating—when an egg has been released from her ovary. For women with a 28-day cycle, this is nearly always 14 days after the first day of the last menstrual period. You can therefore predict ovulation by tracking your periods in a diary, or you can do an ovulation test on your urine, which may be helpful if you don't have a regular 28-day cycle. Three-quarters of couples who have unprotected intercourse will conceive within nine months, and 90 percent in 18 months. But from about age 25, the fertility of both men and women starts to wane.

What happens when you conceive

Since the egg can survive for 36 hours and sperm for 48 hours, your fertile period can last for about three days. When ovulation and intercourse overlap, sperm swim up through the cervix and uterus to meet the egg, and fertilization with one sperm usually happens in the upper end of the Fallopian tube. It then takes three to four days for the fertilized cell (called a zygote) to reach the uterus and implant in the endometrium—the specially prepared uterine lining. The process of implantation is called nidation; the fertilized egg, now called a blastocyst, burrows into the lining and quickly forms a primitive placenta; seven days after fertilization, the blastocyst is embedded and growing.

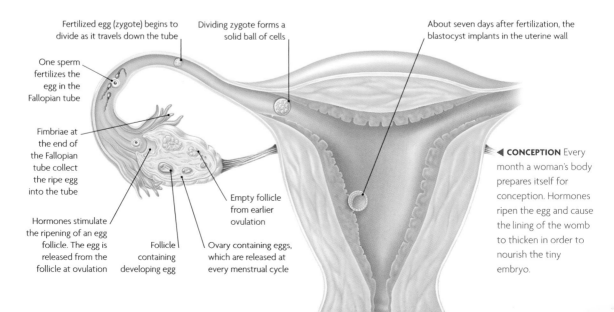

Fertilized egg (zygote) begins to divide as it travels down the tube

Dividing zygote forms a solid ball of cells

About seven days after fertilization, the blastocyst implants in the uterine wall

One sperm fertilizes the egg in the Fallopian tube

Fimbriae at the end of the Fallopian tube collect the ripe egg into the tube

Hormones stimulate the ripening of an egg follicle. The egg is released from the follicle at ovulation

Follicle containing developing egg

Empty follicle from earlier ovulation

Ovary containing eggs, which are released at every menstrual cycle

◀ **CONCEPTION** Every month a woman's body prepares itself for conception. Hormones ripen the egg and cause the lining of the womb to thicken in order to nourish the tiny embryo.

Finding out if you're pregnant

Many women suspect that they are pregnant within days of conception, but the single most obvious indicator is a missed period, and anyone who has a regular menstrual cycle will realize something has happened once they are three or four days late. Other women may not realize for two or three weeks, especially if they continue to have so-called "withdrawal" bleeding, where pre-pregnancy hormones still present in the body cause a weak menstrual bleed. They may, however, suspect that they are pregnant from other physical signs (see below). Either way, you'll probably want to confirm it as soon as possible with a pregnancy test. You can buy pregnancy test kits that confirm whether or not you are pregnant from the day your period is due. If you can wait a day or two longer, you'll get a more reliable result; you may wrongly test negative if you try too early. You can also ask your doctor to do the test.

Other signs of pregnancy

* Tender, heavy breasts that may tingle a little. Your bra may seem a touch too tight, the veins on your breasts more prominent than usual, and your nipples and areolae may seem redder than usual.
* A feeling of nausea. Although often called "morning sickness," it may happen at any time of the day.
* A super-sensitive sense of smell, and a metallic taste in your mouth.
* The need to pass urine more frequently than usual.
* Feeling incredibly tired, especially in the evening.

Waiting a long time to conceive

If you've been trying to conceive for 12 months without success (or eight months if you're over 35), you could approach your doctor to talk about being referred for investigations into your fertility. Finding out that you are unable to conceive without help can be very stressful, but many couples discover that taking this first step is in itself an antidote to stress, and they may go on to conceive even before talking to a specialist.

Preparing yourselves for fertility investigations
The test process can be long and difficult, so both partners must enter willingly into the investigation. Before you embark on it, you should think carefully about the strain (including

perhaps financial) of what you are about to do. Many relationships have crumbled under the stress of infertility investigations, and living with the uncertainty, and the unpleasant and invasive tests, can be extremely hard.

Sharing the responsibility
Be aware that your ability as a couple to conceive—your fertility—is the sum of both your fertilities. Investigations may indicate a problem that will probably be treatable, and it's worth remembering that in as many as half of infertile couples, the problem lies with the man. Infertility is nobody's fault, you share the problem. Don't apportion blame, feel resentment or guilt, or you'll drive a wedge between you that may make conception even more elusive.

Boy or girl?

Nature does a good job of maintaining a balance of about 103 boys to 100 girls, and I'm not in favor of trying to interfere with that. With ultrasound and fetal cell investigations, you may be able to find out the sex of your baby during pregnancy—if you want to.

What determines a baby's sex?
Men produce sperm with 22 chromosomes plus either one X (female) or one Y (male) sex chromosome. Women's eggs also have 22 corresponding chromosomes, but they produce only an X sex chromosome. A zygote fertilized by an X sperm grows up to be a girl; a Y sperm results in a boy.

Is it possible to influence a baby's sex?
Although no method with any scientific validity has been developed, by noting the different characteristics of X and Y sperm, it's possible to suggest a way of increasing your chances of conceiving the gender you want:

* X sperm are larger and slower than Y sperm, and X sperm live longer than Y sperm.

* To increase the chances of a girl, intercourse should be two to three days before ovulation, as only X sperm survive long enough to meet the egg when it's finally released.

* There's a higher chance that a Y sperm will fertilize an egg on the day of ovulation because it will reach the egg more quickly, and the baby will be a boy.

* Frequent ejaculation lowers the proportion of Y sperm, so a girl is likely. Infrequent sex increases the proportion of Y sperm and the chances of a boy.

Adjusting to pregnancy

Pregnancy after miscarriage

A miscarriage, stillbirth (see p. 35), or even a termination in the past, can affect how you both feel about your current pregnancy.

Rekindling grief

Even if your earlier pregnancy or pregnancies were some time ago, being pregnant again may rekindle the grief. Talk things over with your partner or a close friend.

Reliving the past

If you had a miscarriage, you'll both find it difficult to be relaxed about the new pregnancy. Take heart from the fact that most women who miscarry go on to have a healthy child the next time.

After a termination

If you had a termination due to abnormality, you're likely to be offered diagnostic tests in this pregnancy as soon as practically possible. Again, take heart from the fact that many such problems are extremely unlikely to recur. If your termination was for other reasons, you may suffer feelings of guilt that you're going ahead with this pregnancy. It's important to talk about this rather than bottling up feelings that may affect your relationship with your new baby.

After a stillbirth

If you had a stillbirth, you'll probably be wondering whether or not this baby is alive and find the end of your new pregnancy almost unbearable. Although you'll be monitored carefully, talk to your healthcare provider—you may be able to have the baby days or even weeks before the due date.

Becoming a parent is one of the most profound experiences you'll ever have. It's an essentially positive and deeply satisfying experience—but you're going to find it disruptive, exhausting, and incredibly hard work too.

Thinking ahead

Your pregnancy is a time to ponder on the changes ahead—for each of you as individuals and for you as a couple. In many ways it's impossible to describe exactly what's ahead in pregnancy until you're there, but it's certainly true that you can be as prepared as it's possible to be by asking questions, reading, and talking to friends who've already gone through it.

Your differing reactions

Men and women often respond differently to the news of pregnancy; elation may fade into fear, anxiety, or depression at the thought of the responsibilities looming, and the changes that are unavoidable. Changes in relationships can be threatening at the best of times. Those that take place in early pregnancy are particularly taxing because they have to be played out when the mother is feeling tired and possibly anxious, and the father may be feeling ambivalent about the new situation (see p. 24). Use the months ahead to prepare, as much as possible, for what's in store, but try to enjoy your pregnancy, too. Life will, after all, never be the same again. If you can, go away for a weekend or take a vacation when you're between four and seven months pregnant—it will give you plenty of time and space to share your feelings together.

Feelings about pregnancy

At first, the physical changes common to most pregnant women may color your view of the pregnancy. Many women find the physical discomforts of the first three months—tiredness, nausea, tender breasts—begin almost as soon as the pregnancy has been confirmed, sometimes within a few days of missing a period (see p. 21). This can take couples by surprise, turning initial delight into apprehension and uncertainty. However, this reaction is usually temporary, lasting about 12 weeks; after this you'll suddenly realize that you're not waking up with nausea and a fuzzy head, that you're full of energy, and that instead of just looking thicker around the waist, you're developing a recognizable "bump" that announces your pregnancy to the world, and of which you can be proud!

Planned or unplanned

Whether the pregnancy was planned or not has a bearing on your attitude to it. An unplanned pregnancy may be welcomed by one partner more than the other (and this is often the father rather than the mother), or both of you could be ambivalent about it, especially if you have financial worries. Whether your pregnancy is planned or unplanned, there may well be implications for your career, especially if you work for a company that doesn't have a sympathetic attitude to parenthood, even though they have to stand by their legal obligations. This is more important for working women than men, but experience shows that it is possible to resume a career even when you've had a long break for birth and childcare (see p. 170). Once you know you're pregnant, talk to your employer about your options as soon as possible to find out what maternity leave is available (see p. 184). This will help to allay any fears you have about your career.

If your pregnancy was assisted

Your attitude to your pregnancy is bound to be affected if you've had to wait a long time to conceive, and perhaps had treatment to assist conception. You'll feel an enormous sense of relief that your longed-for baby is at last on the way, but may worry about doing anything that may lead to miscarriage, so there may be a tendency to treat the pregnancy like an illness. Try to avoid this; most specialists in assisted conception will hand their patients over to the normal maternity services once the pregnancy is established—if anything is going to go wrong, it is most likely to happen in the first eight to ten weeks, and you'll have been warned about this. Even if you've had to endure quite lengthy and invasive treatments to achieve the pregnancy, try not to dwell on them and look forward instead to the birth of your healthy baby.

Spreading the news

You might want to tell everyone right away that you're having a baby; on the other hand, you might want to hug your secret to yourself for a while. You may surprise yourself at how the news comes out, depending on who you're telling, because many people find admitting they are about to become parents to a third party seems to make it real for the first time. The support of friends and family can help to overcome any feelings of doubt; alternatively you may find yourself confessing to your closest friend your ambivalence to the whole thing, even though on the surface you appear to be delighted. Bear in mind that in the event of a miscarriage, the more people you've told, the more distressing it may be for you if you have to explain that you've lost the baby (see p. 35).

Pre-birth bonding

Although it's wonderful to be able to see your baby moving when you have your first scan (see p. 29), many women feel that the bonding process really begins once they feel it. Though this may not happen until about 20 weeks in a first pregnancy, it's an advantage you have which your partner lacks— so share your feelings as much as possible and encourage him to feel your belly. First sensations of movement often coincide with a change in energy levels, so you'll probably be feeling better about yourself and the baby than you ever thought possible to start with.

✳ JUST FOR DAD

The physical changes of pregnancy can affect how your partner feels about it. Preparing for this should help you deal with any low moments she may have.

Your partner's feelings

✳ Exhaustion is common in early pregnancy—it's probably caused by all the hormones that her body suddenly has to deal with. Encourage your partner to take things easy, and look forward to the middle months when she'll probably feel incredibly energetic and wide awake. The "bloom" of pregnancy at this time will make your partner look wonderful—so make sure you tell her!

✳ The effect of pregnancy hormones combined with the whole idea of becoming a parent could make her much more emotional than usual. Be supportive and sympathetic.

✳ She may worry about the fact that she'll inevitably be gaining weight. Don't draw attention to this. Be positive about how she looks and compliment her. It's a very bad idea to diet during pregnancy, but she doesn't need to eat for two either. Encourage her with the fact that most of the fat gained in pregnancy is stored to nourish breastfeeding, and is burned off remarkably quickly once she starts nursing (see p. 78).

✳ Your partner may feel that she's lost control of her life because there's always someone else with ideas on what's best for her. Don't add to this—she knows her body best and when it comes to decisions about it, she should have the last word.

The expectant father

JUST FOR MOM

Your relationship with your partner will change before the baby is born, so it will help to be prepared for this.

Understanding your partner

✳ It's very easy for men to feel left out so, make sure you involve your partner as much as possible.

✳ Expecting a baby is an external experience for your partner and it may be very difficult for him to empathize with the invisible changes taking place within you. Remember, his day-to-day life will stay much the same until after the baby is born.

✳ Talk to your partner about how you're feeling. You may have big mood swings and go through periods of feeling insecure and unattractive. Sit down with your partner and explain how you're feeling.

Affection and sex

✳ Your partner may be anxious about your well-being and treat you as if you're sick. This kind of attention can be suffocating, so tell your partner if you don't like it. Also, remind him that you're as eager as he is not to do anything to harm the baby. Equally, if your partner isn't giving you enough attention, tell him.

✳ Your desire to have sex may well change at different stages of your pregnancy. If you don't want intercourse, tell your partner.

✳ Talk candidly to your partner about sex so that it does not become an issue between you.

One of the most exciting moments of your life will probably be when you find out that you're going to be a father. The emotional impact is just as real for you as for your partner, so talk about your feelings and get involved in the pregnancy and birth plans.

Understanding your conflicting emotions

The pregnancy may not seem real for the first couple of months—not least because your partner will physically look the same. Don't worry if you feel differently than she does about the pregnancy; it's an internal experience for her and an external one for you, and you don't suddenly become one person with one set of feelings just because you are having a baby together. However, once you see your partner's body begin to change and, later, when you have felt the baby move, the idea of having a baby will become more real. It is at this time that your feelings of joy and excitement may be replaced by fears and worries; whatever your family setup, it's normal for a man to begin to worry about being able to provide for his family. Be open about your feelings and express your concerns.

Having a child can be an extra financial burden, especially if your partner is going to give up her job, but try not to make life-changing decisions, such as seeking promotion. It's difficult to know whether you'll want that extra responsibility once you are a parent. Remember, as a father, you have more than material possessions to offer your child.

How you can participate

Being an expectant father is one time in your life when you're quite likely to feel out of control. This feeling of being an outsider will not be helped by the way other people treat you—well-meaning female friends and relatives may unconsciously push you out of what they see as their territory. You may also find that healthcare providers such as obstetricians and midwives direct their conversations at your partner more than you.

Take the initiative

Don't step back and allow your female relatives and friends to be more involved than you. Tell your friends and colleagues your news—you may be subject to a certain amount of teasing, but people may also view you as more responsible. Try to find out as much as you can about the pregnancy so that you can understand the changes taking place in your partner's body.

Plan for the birth together

You will need to discuss with your partner the type of birth that she wants (see p. 26) and decide what your involvement will be. Be involved in all arrangements and plans for the birth. Go to prenatal appointments so that you can hear your baby's heartbeat. If possible go to birthing classes too.

Taking an active role

What to do	How it can help you
Talk to your partner	The best way to understand how your partner is feeling, and what is going on in her body, is to talk to her. Ask her what it feels like to feel the baby move; discuss your plans for the birth together; find out if she's got particular discomforts. She'll appreciate your interest.
Go to birthing classes	If you go to birthing classes (especially the father-only sessions), you'll have an opportunity to learn about the birth and talk through your own concerns. This will help you work out the best way to support your partner and enable you to be more involved in birth choices.
Talk to other fathers	Get to know the other expectant fathers at birthing classes—they will probably be feeling the same as you and be glad to have someone to talk to. Talk to friends and colleagues who already have babies; find out what their experiences were like and ask them for advice.
Read about pregnancy and parenting	Read pregnancy and parenting books and any leaflets you're given. The more you understand about what's going on during the pregnancy, the more familiar it will become, and it can help you to understand how your partner is feeling. It will also enable you to ask the right questions.
Ask questions	Go to prenatal appointments with your partner so that you can meet the healthcare providers and be present at the examinations. As a first-time parent, there will be things you don't understand and need to know about. If you ask questions of professionals, they are more likely to involve you.

Prenatal bonding

Babies can hear sounds outside the womb by five or six months; if you talk to your baby, he will bond to your voice and, in fact, he can hear your low-pitched voice more clearly than his mother's. To help you to bond with your baby:

* Gently massage your partner's belly and feel your baby move.

* Talk to your baby, and nuzzle him through your partner's skin.

* Use the inner tubes of paper-towel rolls to listen to the heartbeat.

* Go to scans with your partner to see your baby develop (see p. 29).

Visit the hospital and delivery room with your partner. If possible, go with her to the scans so that you can see your baby developing and watch him move on the ultrasound monitor. Talk about the fact you're going to be a father, and ask as many questions as you want—most of all, enjoy it! You will also need to talk to your employer about taking time off to go to the prenatal appointments as well as the birth.

The birth plan

Contribute to the birth plan. Discuss the issues raised by the birth plan (see p. 27) with your partner, but don't impose your views. If your partner feels strongly about issues such as a drug-free labor (see p. 43), respect her feelings, but talk about the advantages and disadvantages, too. Look forward to being present at the birth. Remember, being at your child's birth is probably one of the most poignant experiences you'll ever have, and holding your baby in the first seconds after the birth is proven to help you bond with your child.

▲ **SHARE THE PLANNING** Get as involved as you can in the planning of the birth and give your partner plenty of love and support.

Options for prenatal care

Prenatal classes

Prenatal and birthing classes are helpful and supportive for you both.

What classes do

They will help explain a lot of the choices available before, during, and after the birth and will tell you about labor, birth, and babycare. You'll also meet other expectant parents with due dates near yours.

Where to find classes

If you're planning a hospital delivery, hospital-based classes can be useful since they'll help familiarize you with procedures and will include a tour of the labor and delivery ward. Some women opt instead for Birthing Centers, which are affiliated with a hospital and physically close enough to allow a woman to be transferred if she needs medical intervention. Most prenatal classes are held in the hospital or birthing center where a woman plans to deliver. The sessions may be run by a midwife, nurse, or other medical professional.

There's now a huge choice in maternity care, although how wide the choice is will depend on what's available in your area.

Who can deliver care?

Once you know you're pregnant, your first call will probably be to your obstetrician/gynecologist (OB/GYN) or family practitioner. She will tell you about options for prenatal care in your area, and you can also talk through where the baby will be born. Don't feel you have to decide on any of these issues immediately—go away and think before finalizing details.

OB/GYN Your gynecologist can transition to the role of obstetrician and provide prenatal care as well as delivering your baby. She may be in a solo practice or a group, in which case you will likely be seen by all members of the group for prenatal visits so you are familiar with whoever is on call when it comes time to deliver your baby. This is the most common option.

Family physician Family physicians are trained and licensed to provide prenatal care and deliver babies, although they may not be comfortable taking care of high-risk or complicated pregnancies.

Midwife Licensed midwives or certified nurse-midwives provide prenatal care and deliver babies. The American College of Obstetricians and Gynecologists (ACOG) endorses midwifery. Most states require midwives to practice under the supervision of a doctor, who may or may on-site. Midwives will generally refer complicated pregnancies to an OB/GYN.

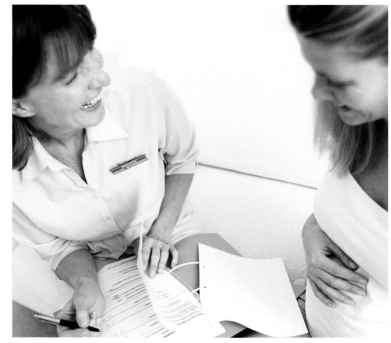

▶ **INDEPENDENT MIDWIVES** If you want to be cared for solely by midwives, you might want to consider hiring an independent one. This is expensive, but it does allow you to arrange your care, labor, and birth exactly as you want it.

Hospital care You'll be cared for by hospital-based doctors and midwives. The care may lack the informality of other options, but if you have any complications, have an existing medical condition, or are having twins, it's probably the wisest and safest choice.

Where to have your baby

Thinking about prenatal care also means deciding where you want your baby to be delivered: in a hospital, at a birthing center, or at home.

Hospital birth

Having a first baby in a hospital feels right to many couples. There's plenty of backup on hand and access to a wide range of pain relief.

Advantages Choosing a hospital birth doesn't necessarily mean opting for high-tech—some hospitals have special birthing rooms where patients are free to walk around during labor and intervention is kept to a minimum. Hospitals offer access to advanced medical care (including on-site pediatricians to resuscitate a baby after a complicated delivery) and pain relief. Most hospitals have tried to make their labor floors feel less clinical and give parents more control over decision-making in delivery.

Disadvantages Having a baby in the hospital does mean accepting policies that may cramp your style. You may, for example, be given electronic fetal monitoring, at least for a time, which may make it difficult for you to stay active and upright, but this is no longer routine for low-risk mothers. Some hospitals require an intravenous line (IV) in case of emergency.

Home birth

Although they are not common in the United States, most midwives and some doctors are happy to attend a home birth unless there are good reasons why it may not be safe.

Advantages Home is a more relaxed place to have a baby than in a hospital. You're far less likely to need emergency treatment if you remain active as far into labor as you can. Your chances for a straightforward, problem-free delivery at home are good, even if this is your first child.

Disadvantages You don't have immediate access to emergency treatment, so if anything unexpected happens or your labor fails to progress, you might need to be transferred to a hospital. You also won't have access to pain relief such as an epidural (see p. 43), though you can have some narcotic pain relievers (such as demerol).

Delivery in a birthing center

Birthing centers are usually sited in or near hospitals, but are self-contained and designed to have a less-medical feel. The staff may consist of obstetricians and midwives or only midwives, and staff members may wear their own clothes instead of uniforms. You'll probably be given your own room in which to labor, give birth, and recover after the delivery. These centers can provide an excellent halfway house, giving you the informality of a home birth with the safety net of high-tech care nearby.

Your birth plan

Once you've considered all your prenatal care and birth options, it's worth preparing a simple birth plan in consultation with your doctor or midwife. This should be kept with your hospital notes. Wait until you're about 32–36 weeks pregnant, as by that time you'll probably have discovered whether there are any special factors in your pregnancy that might affect some of your requests. You also need to be prepared to be flexible, because things may not go according to plan on the day. Your birth plan might include the following:

✷ Who you want to be present at the birth with you.

✷ Your views on interventions such as induction, the artificial speeding up of labor (see p. 50), and electronic fetal monitoring (see p. 44).

✷ Your views on active labor, and whether you would like the option of using a birthing pool (see p. 43).

✷ Your preferences for pain relief (see p. 43), and the use of breathing and relaxation techniques.

✷ Whether you mind student doctors or midwives being present during your labor and birth.

✷ What position you might adopt to deliver your baby (see p. 46).

✷ Whether you would prefer not to have an episiotomy (see p. 46).

✷ Whether you mind if the delivery of your placenta is speeded up with pitocin or whether you'd prefer it to be delivered naturally (see p. 48).

Your prenatal care

The physical examination

At every prenatal appointment, various checks will always be done to rule out potentially dangerous medical conditions.

Blood pressure
A rise in blood pressure could mean you're at risk of pre-eclampsia (see p. 35).

Urine test
Your urine will be tested for the presence of protein, which could mean an infection or, later, pre-eclampsia; glucose or sugar, which could signal diabetes; and ketones, chemicals that indicate you're not eating enough.

Abdominal check
The doctor or midwife will feel your abdomen to check the size of your uterus. She'll also listen to your baby's heartbeat, using either a stethoscope or an electronic fetal monitor, a stethoscope that amplifies sound of the baby's heartbeat so you can hear it (see below).

▲ **YOUR BABY'S HEARTBEAT** It's a thrill the first time you hear your baby's heartbeat amplified through a fetal monitor.

In general, prenatal checks are to ensure that all is going well with your pregnancy—that you are healthy, and that your baby is growing properly.

Your first appointment

The first prenatal session may be quite long, lasting as much as an hour. It will usually take place at your doctor's or midwife's office. She will take a detailed medical history, and will ask questions about your general health, your family's health, and your gynecological and obstetric history. She will also ask whether or not this baby was planned, how long ago you stopped using contraceptives or what contraceptive you were using when you got pregnant, and the date of the first day of your last menstrual period. The doctor or midwife will also ask you how you feel and talk to you generally about your pregnancy. She'll offer advice on issues like diet and exercise. You can discuss what kind of delivery you'd like, though you don't have to decide at this time unless you're absolutely sure (see p. 27).

Your routine prenatal checkups will generally be shorter than your initial appointment. Between appointments, it's a good idea to write down any questions you may want to ask your midwife or doctor and keep them with your maternity notes so you remember to ask them. You'll probably be asked to provide a urine sample at each appointment.

The blood tests

You'll probably have some blood taken, which will be sent to the laboratory for analysis. Ask your doctor or midwife exactly what your blood will be checked for and why; it's routinely checked for iron content, blood group and rhesus status, rubella immunity, blood sugar levels, and sexually transmitted diseases, including HIV. Other tests, such as one to check whether you've been exposed to toxoplasmosis (a parasitic disease that may affect your unborn baby) may be available. Blood isn't usually tested at every appointment, but in certain situations you'll be asked to give blood again at later appointments (see opposite), and most doctors test at 28 weeks for anemia, blood group antibodies, and diabetes.

Ultrasound scans

Ultrasound is now offered routinely to almost all pregnant women, as it enables the baby's age to be measured very accurately and can also detect visible abnormalities. Many doctors offer two scans, one at about 12 weeks and the other at 16 to 20 weeks.

The ultrasound scans will be carried out at the doctor's office or hospital, and your partner should be allowed into the examination room with you; this is a wonderful opportunity for a father to relate to his growing baby, since he'll be able to see it moving.

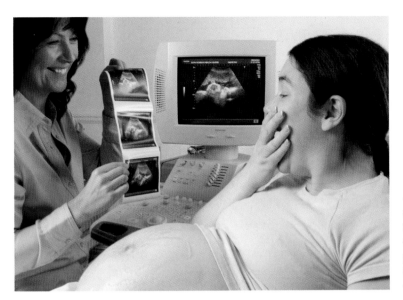

◀ **HAVING AN ULTRASOUND** The operator slowly scans across your abdomen with a handheld instrument called a transducer, which detects sound waves bounced off your uterus and your baby's body. These are transmitted to a computer and monitor for visual interpretation.

Specialist screening and diagnostic tests

If you're offered any of the screening or diagnostic tests for abnormalities (see chart below), it's helpful to ask yourselves what you'd do if you found your baby did have Down's syndrome or spina bifida. If the answer is that you wouldn't do anything, but continue with the pregnancy, it may not be worth having the tests. If you know you would have a termination, or wouldn't be able to decide until you had the information, then you may want to go ahead. Before any test, find out exactly what your baby is being tested for and whether there are any risks. You also need to know how accurate the test is, what information it will actually provide, and whether there's an alternative to having the test.

Test	How it is done	What it can tell you
Nuchal scan	A non-invasive scan at 11–13 weeks, measuring the thickness of the "nuchal pad" in the baby's neck. Often combined with a blood test.	A thick nuchal pad may indicate a higher risk of chromosomal defects, so you'll be offered a test such as CVS or amniocentesis later.
Triple screen	A blood test that screens you for the risk of Down's syndrome. It is done at 15–16 weeks along with a scan to confirm dates.	Hormone levels indicate the risk of your baby being affected; if it is greater than one in 250, you'll be offered amniocentesis.
AFP test	A screening blood test that checks the level of alpha-fetoprotein (AFP) at about 15–18 weeks.	A higher or lower level than usual may indicate Down's syndrome or spina bifida.
Chorionic villus sampling (CVS)	A diagnostic test, in which a cannula (tube) is passed through the cervix at about 10–12 weeks to take cells from the developing placenta.	The cells are examined to check the baby's chromosomes for any abnormalities. CVS carries a one percent risk of miscarriage.
Amniocentesis	A diagnostic test done at about 15 weeks. Guided by ultrasound, a needle takes a sample of amniotic fluid through the abdominal wall.	Chromosomes in fetal cells can be checked for abnormalities, such as Down's syndrome. There's a small risk (one in 200) of miscarriage.
Fetal blood test (cordocentesis)	This rare diagnostic test is carried out after about 18–20 weeks. It takes blood from the umbilical cord.	Blood is tested for abnormal chromosomes or infections. There's a miscarriage risk of about one to two percent.

The progress of pregnancy

Coping with common complaints

✳ Nausea is most common in the first three months. It may happen in the morning, but by no means always, and you may also vomit. Eating small amounts often, rather than big meals, helps. If you're vomiting incessantly, consult your doctor.

✳ You're more likely to get cramps in your legs or feet. It's not known exactly why, but you can relieve cramping by pulling your toes up hard toward your knee.

✳ Constipation is a common problem, caused by the presence of hormones that slow down the workings of the large intestine. Eat plenty of fiber, exercise regularly, and drink plenty of water. Iron pills may make it worse.

✳ Later in pregnancy, you may suffer from indigestion or heartburn, because your enlarging womb is pressing on your stomach. Prevent this by eating smaller meals more often, sitting up straight when eating, and avoiding spicy foods. Sipping milk, especially at night, can help if you have heartburn.

✳ Hemorrhoids—swollen varicose veins that protrude from the anus—can occur in pregnancy due to pressure from the baby, especially if you're constipated. Eat plenty of fiber and avoid standing for long periods. Check with your doctor if they become very painful.

Having a baby growing inside you is like being part of a real-life miracle. Sometimes you'll pat your bump and feel you can hardly believe your child is in there. Take time to ponder the wonder of what's happening; you'll both be laying the foundations for a baby who feels secure and wanted.

Following your pregnancy

No part of a woman's body escapes when she's carrying a baby, and you both need to keep that in mind. For instance, tender breasts that are getting ready for breastfeeding need to be treated gently by a father when he caresses them; the growing uterus pressing on your internal organs means that you must never be too far from a toilet during the last three months of pregnancy. The guide that follows is only a brief outline of the complex changes going on inside your body.

What's happened by three months

The first three months of pregnancy (the first trimester) are tremendously important in laying the foundations of your baby's healthy development. In spite of this, there are few visible signs of your baby's phenomenal growth, except that you may have been suffering morning sickness (p. 21).

You at three months Your pregnancy is well established now:

✳ You'll really start to gain weight regularly; any morning sickness will soon disappear.

✳ The uterus is rising out of the pelvis and can now be felt.

✳ The risk of miscarriage is almost zero by this time.

✳ Your heart is working hard and will continue to do throughout the rest of your pregnancy.

Your baby at three months She is fully formed, but needs to mature.

✳ She has a fully formed body, complete with fingers, toes, and ears.

✳ Her eyes move, though her eyelids are closed.

✳ Her body is covered with fine hair.

✳ She wriggles if poked—her muscles are growing.

What's happened by six months

The period from about the third to the sixth month (the second trimester) is when morning sickness ends, your baby really grows, and you begin to feel her move. You're brimming with energy, vitality, and well-being.

You at six months You'll notice the following signs:

✳ You're putting on about 1 lb (0.5 kg) in weight per week.

✳ Your uterus is a good 2 inches (5 cm) above the pelvis.

✳ You may have bouts of indigestion.

✳ From about 20 weeks, you'll feel your baby move.

AT SIX MONTHS You'll gain weight regularly each week and will feel healthier and more energetic.

FULL TERM Not long to wait now. Soon you and your partner will meet your new baby for the first time.

Your baby at six months He's well developed and growing:

* His hearing is acute, he can recognize your voice.
* He's becoming better proportioned—his body is now catching up with his head.
* He's well muscled, but thin. He'll start to put on fat now.
* His lungs are growing and maturing fast.

What's happened by nine months (full term)

The final 12 weeks or so of pregnancy, known as the third trimester, are when the baby puts on fat in preparation for birth and the body and lungs mature in preparation for independent life.

You in the last weeks of your pregnancy You may have to visit your doctor or midwife more often and you may notice the following signs:

* You may feel a "lightening" as your baby's head drops into the pelvis.
* It's more difficult to find a comfortable position for sleep.
* Your breasts secrete clear-colored nutritious colostrum.

Your baby in the last weeks of your pregnancy He's preparing to be born:

* He weighs about 6–8 lbs (2.7–3.5 kg) and he measures 14–15 inches (35–38 cm) from crown to rump.
* His head is "engaged," lying just on top of your cervix.
* The placenta is 8–10 inches (20–25 cm) across, 1-inch (3-cm) thick, and there are 2 pints (1.1 liters) of amniotic fluid.
* His breasts may be swollen due to the action of your hormones.

Pregnancy at a glance

It's useful to be able to visualize what is happening by the end of each of the three phases, or trimesters, of pregnancy. By the end of the first trimester, your baby is recognizably human but tiny. The second trimester is a period of rapid growth, and during the third trimester the baby gets longer and heavier.

✱ JUST FOR DAD

Although you're experiencing the pregnancy secondhand, following its progress helps you to become emotionally attached to your baby.

The progress of pregnancy

✱ Accompanying your partner to prenatal appointments (see p. 28) enables you to find out together how your baby is growing.

✱ Remember that the baby is part of you as well as your partner. It's amazing to think that a single cell created from your sperm and your partner's egg (see p. 20) can develop so rapidly.

✱ Understanding and learning about the impact of the growing baby and uterus on your partner's body helps you to be sympathetic when she suffers the inevitable discomforts.

Hearing is developed; he may respond to noise. Skin is red and thin, with little fat beneath it

By full term, the baby is usually positioned with his head downward.

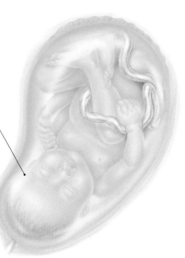

The fetus is recognizably human, and all his internal systems are in place

▲ **AT THREE MONTHS** Your uterus is about the size of a grapefruit and can just be felt above the pubic bone. Your baby's organs are formed and are now resistant to potential dangers, such as an infection and medication.

▲ **AT SIX MONTHS** Your baby's organs are fully formed, his face is that of a newborn, and he sucks his thumb. Your uterus is poised for labor. You may notice Braxton Hicks contractions (see p. 42).

▲ **AT NINE MONTHS (FULL TERM)** You'll find you get breathless because your baby is now so big. His eyes can open and he's fat and healthy. If your baby is a boy, his testes have descended.

Difficult pregnancies

✳ "Small for dates"

After reviewing the date of your last period and your expected date of delivery, both your heights, and scans of the baby, your pregnancy may be pronounced "small for dates." Don't worry, but doctors will keep an eye on you by:

✳ Giving you scans every two weeks for a while to ensure all's well and to check the placenta.

✳ Checking on the baby's heart rate for any sign of strain.

✳ Discussing with you the possibility of inducing your baby or delivering by Cesarean section (see p. 52). to prevent the baby having to go through a vaginal delivery.

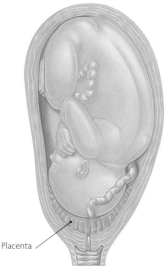

Placenta

▲ **PLACENTA PREVIA** The placenta embeds close to or across the cervix. Pressure from the baby may cause bleeding.

Although the majority of pregnancies proceed without incident, occasionally things don't go according to plan. When something unexpected causes concern, you're both going to feel extremely worried about it, especially if all has gone well up to this point. It helps enormously to face what's ahead together and to get as much information as you can.

Pregnancy and pre-existing medical conditions

Any existing long-term medical condition means that your pregnancy will be carefully monitored. Medical conditions like asthma, epilepsy, heart disease, or kidney disease don't in themselves make pregnancy and labor difficult, but they may increase the risk of complications. If you take care of yourself, have meticulous prenatal supervision, and prepare yourself for in-patient hospital care in the last ten weeks of pregnancy, the chances are you'll be able to have a normal birth.

Diabetes

Sugar—a sign, but not proof, of gestational diabetes—may appear in your urine at any time in pregnancy. The most common reason for this is a change in the way the kidney handles sugar in pregnancy. You will be screened for gestational diabetes in your third trimester, and if positive, may be treated with diet, insulin, or both. Pre-existing diabetes needs strict supervision because your insulin needs may change. Babies of diabetic mothers tend to be large, so you may be induced early or you may need to have a Cesarean section (see p. 52).

Vaginal bleeding

Never ignore vaginal bleeding at any stage of your pregnancy. Although it's always worrying, close medical supervision can help avoid serious problems.
Bleeding in the first three months Bleeding in early pregnancy doesn't mean you'll lose your baby. You may not yet have high enough hormone levels to subdue your periods. You may have a condition such as cervical erosion or polyps, neither of which are likely to interfere with your pregnancy. Contact your doctor or midwife as soon as possible so you can be referred for a scan; if the heart is beating well, bleeding will probably stop and the pregnancy will continue normally. You'll need to rest and forgo sex for a while.
Bleeding in later pregnancy It's rare to bleed late in pregnancy, but it's serious since it may indicate problems with the placenta, such as placenta previa or approaching placental abruption. Placenta previa means the placenta is positioned in the lower part of the womb, possibly across the cervix (see left). Placental abruption means that the placenta is

Multiple pregnancy

Carrying more than one baby will undoubtedly mean you have more professional attention and more prenatal appointments during your pregnancy. The diagnosis of twins, triplets, or more will be confirmed with an ultrasound. The news may take time to get used to, but there's a lot of help and support for you both.

How you may feel

Nausea Multiple pregnancies often cause severe nausea, even vomiting, in the first three months. Eat little and often, and drink plenty of fluids—drinks containing glucose or glucose tablets may boost energy levels if you feel too sick to get calories from food.

Increasing size You get bigger faster than a mother with one baby because, as well as carrying two babies, you produce more amniotic fluid.

Backache Be careful about posture and avoid carrying or lifting heavy weights, because the additional levels of pregnancy hormones mean your pelvic ligaments can soften and stretch, and become painful.

Fatigue You'll tire very easily, and this may be made worse by anemia. Rest, eat meat, and take folic acid and iron.

Indigestion This may be worse than in a single pregnancy (see p. 30) because your stomach is squashed against your diaphragm. Have nourishing drinks and soups and eat frequent small meals.

▶ **HOW TWINS LIE** Twins normally lie both head down, or one breech and one head down. How they lie may affect the way your delivery is managed (see p. 51).

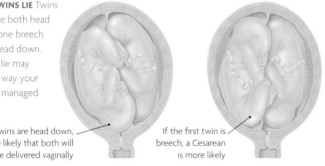

If both twins are head down, it's more likely that both will be delivered vaginally

If the first twin is breech, a Cesarean is more likely

beginning to separate from the uterine wall. Both conditions can be confirmed by ultrasound scanning, and hospital admission for observation and subsequent Cesarean delivery (see p. 52) will be necessary.

Pre-eclampsia

This is a potentially serious condition that affects one in ten women, especially first-time mothers and women carrying more than one baby. It can start at any time in the second half of pregnancy. It's not known precisely what causes it, but it tends to run in families. There are no symptoms, but raised blood pressure and protein in the urine may signal its presence. It affects the placenta, so your baby may grow more slowly than normal. The pregnancy can't be restored to normal, but delivery of the baby and placenta ends the disease; this may need to be arranged as a matter of urgency before serious complications arise. The birth of the baby usually reverses all the effects of pre-eclampsia on the mother.

Losing your baby

No one can imagine the grief of losing a baby. Seek counseling so that you can grieve fully and come to terms with your loss.

Early miscarriage

A miscarriage in the first few weeks is more common than you might think—in fact one in three of first pregnancies. It usually happens because there was something amiss with the fetus or perhaps it had not implanted correctly. Early miscarriage may not be accompanied by much pain, although you may suffer severe period-like cramps. You may have to deal with sudden hormonal changes that can make you very emotional and you'll both feel let down.

Late miscarriage

This occurs between 13 and 24 weeks, usually because of placental problems or a weakened cervix that opens due to the weight of the growing fetus. It can also be the result of infection. You have a mini-labor to expel the fetus with whatever pain relief you choose.

Stillbirth

Losing your baby at or close to full term is very hard to bear. Holding and naming your baby and having a funeral can help you come to terms with what's happened.

Dealing with your loss

Your distress needs careful handling: it's a bereavement that may be complicated by feelings of guilt and blame. Talk about your feelings to each other and to your obstetrician; ask her to explain the reasons for your loss, but accept that no one may know exactly why your baby died. Above all, look forward to the future; most couples who have lost a baby go on to become proud parents of healthy babies.

Taking care of yourself

Pregnancy is natural and women's bodies are designed to accommodate it. However, your body does have to work hard, so it's important to eat well and keep active to help it cope.

Balancing your diet

Try to follow these tips:

✳ Eat complex carbohydrates, such as pasta, potatoes, and legumes (beans and lentils), for energy.

✳ Eat fish, poultry, dairy, whole-grain cereals, seeds, and legumes for protein. Avoid eating shark and marlin, and limit tuna to once a week to avoid mercury.

✳ Don't cut out fats altogether, but don't eat too much either.

✳ Get vitamin C daily from raw fruits and vegetables, and B vitamins from whole grains, nuts, legumes, greens, dairy, eggs, oily fish, and meat.

✳ Eat lean red meat, fish, egg yolks, apricots, and cereals for iron.

Food safety

Take extra care with food hygiene:

✳ Listeria is a rare bacterium found in foods made with unpasteurized milk (especially some soft cheeses), liver, undercooked meat, and some pre-cooked meals; avoid these as infection may result in miscarriage or stillbirth.

✳ Salmonella is found in eggs and chicken. Infection causes fever, severe diarrhea, and abdominal pain. Cook food well to destroy it.

✳ Toxoplasmosis is caused by a parasite found in cat and dog feces, and in raw meat. It can cause birth defects. Cook meat thoroughly, wash hands after handling raw meat or pets, and wear gloves when gardening.

Weight and diet

Your body uses up a lot of energy during pregnancy, and you need to eat well to fuel your requirements and those of your growing baby. You could reasonably increase your intake of food by 200–300 calories a day and expect to put on 20–30 lbs (9–15 kg) in weight, much of which is accounted for by the baby, uterus, and amniotic fluid. Pregnancy is not a time to go on a diet, but you should also forget the myth about "eating for two"; the rule is to eat to satisfy your hunger, and no more. Later in pregnancy you may find you simply can't take in much food at any one time, so eat little and often. Keep healthy snacks, such as dried fruit, rice cakes, and hard fruits, in your bag, car, or office.

Body maintenance

Pregnancy hormones have profound effects on teeth, hair, nails, and skin, so don't be surprised by some temporary changes.

Teeth Progesterone makes the gums soft so they may bleed more easily. Take care of your teeth and gums, and visit your dentist at the start of your pregnancy. Make sure you tell him you are pregnant in case he wants to take X-rays, as these may be dangerous to the developing embryo.

Hair and nails Straight hair can become curly, and vice versa. Hair grows and falls in phases—pregnancy often prolongs the growth phase, making thin hair thick and glossy, whereas thick hair may become dry and unmanageable. The downside is that you'll experience hair loss after the birth, although it'll grow back eventually. Although they grow faster, nails also become brittle. Keep them short and use creams to keep them moist.

Skin Estrogen gives your skin the legendary bloom of pregnancy, but dry skin may become drier and oily skin more oily. Patches of brown pigment (chloasma) may appear on your face and neck but will eventually fade. All skins deepen in color, with browning of the nipples and a line down the abdomen. Tiny dilated capillaries (spider nevi) on the face are common but disappear later. Stretch marks on the breasts, thighs, and abdomen are very common; they're related to the breakdown of protein in the skin by the high levels of pregnancy hormones. Most marks will fade after the birth.

Dealing with fatigue

Fatigue is a periodic problem during pregnancy, especially during the first three months and the last six to eight weeks. Its extent may take you by surprise, especially during the first few weeks—it's the kind of tiredness when you feel you don't even have the energy to blink. You're sleepy in the early stages of pregnancy because you're sedated by the high levels of progesterone. Your metabolism speeds up to deal with the demands of your baby and the extra work all your organs are called on to do. Later on in pregnancy you're tired because your whole body is working in high gear 24 hours a day, and you're having to carry extra weight that puts a strain on your heart, lungs, and muscles.

Ways of coping

* Never stand when you can sit, never sit when you can lie down.
* If possible, put your feet up whenever you sit—if you're in the office, invert a wastebasket or box under the desk.
* Sleep anywhere: Put your head down on your desk during your lunch break; close your eyes on the bus or train home after work.
* When you're at home, plan specific rest times and let nothing interfere with them; some people like to lie down after lunch, others find they need to rest in the late afternoon or early evening.
* Sleep in every weekend.
* Go to bed early at least three times a week.
* Find ways to help you doze off, such as watching TV or reading.
* Lie down and listen to music—not too loud, since your baby can hear it.
* Find different comfortable resting positions for instant relief of tiredness. Try lying on the floor on pillows with your feet on a bed, sofa, or chair and your knees at right angles, or take up the first-aid recovery position with cushions under your knees and upper body (see below).

Relaxation Use whatever technique you can to relax—you're going to need at least 30 minutes a day from now on and it will be so refreshing if you teach yourself to let go in seconds. Close your eyes and aim to clear your mind of any stressful thoughts and worries. Breathe in and out slowly and regularly and think about your breathing. As you do so, let only pleasant, relaxing thoughts flow through your head. You'll probably be taught some more relaxation techniques at your prenatal classes (see p. 26), and there are plenty of books and CDs to guide you.

On your own

Some women decide to have a baby on their own, without the baby's father. However, most women on their own didn't make that choice. If being on your own wasn't your choice, you need to allow yourself to work through your feelings of disappointment and even anger.

Coping with your feelings

At a time when women naturally expect support, comfort, and the shared pleasure of contemplating parenthood, you are experiencing the very opposite. Ideally, explore your feelings with a friend or, even better, a professional counselor who will help you to isolate each issue and deal with it.

Being positive

Avoid those people who may not take a positive view of either you or your condition. Since you don't have the most obvious form of support—a partner—the last thing you need is negativity from others.

Taking care of yourself

When you're on your own, it's only too easy to skip meals or opt for easy snacks. Make sure you go to all your prenatal checkups. The health professionals are there to help you, and if you need extra support, they will help you find it.

▼ **POSITION FOR RELAXATION** This position takes the weight off your back and allows free blood circulation, increasing oxygen supply to your baby. Support your head with pillows and put pillows between your legs to support the upper knee.

Pelvic floor exercises

The pelvic floor consists of muscles and fibrous tissue suspended like a funnel from the pelvic bones. The layers of muscle are thickest at the perineum, where there are openings for the urethra, vagina, and anus, which the pelvic floor muscles also support. To locate your pelvic floor muscles, stop your urine flow in midstream—the muscles you use for this are pelvic floor muscles.

Exercising your pelvic floor

The pelvic floor is put under strain by pregnancy, when the presence of hormones causes it to soften and relax. Keep it toned by doing the following exercises five times a day. Restart them after your baby is born to minimize the risk of prolapse.

✳ Pull in your pelvic floor muscles, then let them go quickly; do this five times.

✳ Pull the muscles in and hold for a count of five, then let them go slowly; repeat this five times.

✳ Finally, do the first, quick exercise five more times.

Precautions

Do gentle stretches to warm up before exercising and to cool down afterward. Keep your back straight, breathe evenly, and flex your feet. Since your ligaments are softer than usual, take it easy and don't twist suddenly. Stop immediately if you become breathless, overheated, dizzy, or feel pain. Avoid dehydration by drinking lots of water.

Exercise in pregnancy

Both you and your baby benefit from exercise: Your blood starts circulating freely; there's a blast of oxygen to your baby's brain; exercise hormones, such as endorphins, give you both a wonderful high; and your baby loves the swaying motion. Exercise increases your strength, suppleness, and stamina, which will make pregnancy easier and equip you for the rigors of labor. Exercise also helps you to understand your body and to believe in its power, and it gives you a key to relaxation so that you can cope with fatigue and prepare yourself for the actual birth.

Whole-body exercise

Try to do some form of exercise every day, beginning gradually, at a pace that is comfortable. Always stop immediately if you get out of breath or feel any pain. Whole-body exercise is best as it tones your heart and lungs, so walking and swimming are excellent. Dancing is good too, as long as it's not too energetic. Yoga is ideal because it stretches tight muscles and joints and helps relieve tension. Yoga methods will help later on with labor and pain relief. Find a prenatal yoga class, or tell the instructor you are pregnant.

Exercise to avoid

Pregnancy is not a time to start learning an energetic contact sport; however, you can continue sports activities for a while if you're already fit and play often. Don't engage in sports like skiing, cycling, or horseback riding in the third trimester as your balance will be thrown because of the extra weight in front. Take it easy on very energetic sports such as tennis or squash and don't do heavy workouts at the gym.

Preparing for labor and birth

Help yourself prepare for labor and birth by introducing your body to some exercises and postures that will help when the baby is coming. You'll be taught different techniques at your prenatal classes (see p. 26), but it's a great help if both of you can learn the exercises so that your partner can help and encourage you to practice at home. Be especially careful with your posture during pregnancy to protect your back. The hormones of pregnancy soften your ligaments in preparation for the birth; the problem is that this also makes them more susceptible to strain during pregnancy, and your back is the most vulnerable.

Tailor sitting Sit up with your back straight (lean against a wall if you like), with the soles of your feet together. This opens up the hip joints.

Squatting Squat down on your haunches as low as possible, supporting your back against a wall or sofa—or lean against your partner while he is sitting in a chair. Squatting stretches and relaxes the birth canal, and when it comes to the delivery you may well find that this is the position that you adopt naturally, since it will help you to bear down (see p. 46).

All fours Getting down onto all fours is very helpful during pregnancy when you have a bad back, especially if you combine it with a few gentle pelvic floor exercises (see above left). Put a pile of pillows in front of you so you can rest on them with your head on your arms, and ask your partner to massage your back. Many women also find this a comfortable position for backache during labor, and for the actual delivery (see p. 46).

Standing and sitting correctly

As pregnancy progresses, good posture becomes increasingly important. You may have a tendency to bend your spine to balance the bump in front, which leads to an arched back and slumped shoulders. Try to avoid this by keeping a straight back, tucking your buttocks under, and tilting your pelvis forward. Try to drop your shoulders to avoid tension in your neck.

Sitting badly can be as bad for your back as poor posture when standing. If you have to sit for a long time, make sure you use a firm, straight-backed chair and sit well back with your feet raised slightly on a footstool or flat on the floor. Sitting badly, slumped in your chair, forces your baby up against your diaphragm and stomach, constricts your lungs, and causes breathlessness and indigestion.

Carrying and lifting

Avoid carrying a heavy bag for long periods; this can put a strain on your shoulders and neck. If you need to lift something from floor level, always bend your knees and keep a straight back, lifting the object high against your chest, and hold it close. Never bend down or twist from the waist; you could damage your lower back.

Getting up without strain

1 **TURN ONTO YOUR SIDE** when you first get up from lying down, for example after exercise. Keeping your back straight, push yourself up into a sitting position with your hands.

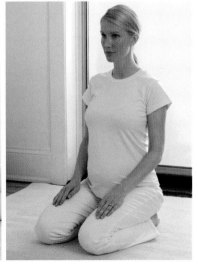

2 **GET INTO A KNEELING POSITION** before you stand up from the floor (or swing your legs over the edge of the bed). Still keeping your back straight, use your thigh muscles to push yourself up.

JUST FOR DAD

Looking after your partner's well-being during pregnancy is good for your unborn baby, good for your relationship, and essential to your partner's long-term physical and emotional health. Try the suggestions below to help her, but don't treat her like an invalid:

How you can help

✳ Your partner's hair and skin will look marvelous, especially during the middle trimester, from four to seven months. Tell her how good she looks to boost her self-esteem. Toward the end of the pregnancy she may begin to get very bored and feel uncomfortable and unattractive; encourage her to go out and treat herself at this time.

✳ Encourage your partner to eat and drink well. Get involved in the shopping and cooking, if you haven't done so before. You can both follow the basic advice on diet (see p. 36)— you'll both benefit.

✳ Give your partner opportunities to rest: Bring her breakfast in bed on weekends; make sure visitors aren't invited when she normally likes to rest, whether it's after lunch or early evening. Put a television in the bedroom, if there isn't one there already, so she can watch in bed.

✳ Do the heavy lifting so that your partner doesn't strain her back or other muscles softened by pregnancy hormones (see left). If she does lift something, make sure she bends her legs, rather than bending from the waist. Carry the groceries and other heavy items for her.

Your new baby, your new life

The birth of your first baby is one of the most amazing moments of your whole life. It's the sort of event that parents remember in minute detail years later, even when other memories have faded. Although no birth experience is exactly like another, your first is special simply because you have never done it before. But just because you can't predict exactly what it will feel like either physically or emotionally, it doesn't mean that you can't be prepared for most eventualities. Knowing how a normal labor progresses, what your pain relief options are, and what can be done if things don't go according to plan, means that together you can approach labor and birth positively. The importance of how you experience the birth and the first few precious moments you spend together with your baby cannot be overestimated. At this time, the bonds of interdependence and love begin to form and tie you together as a family. Don't be perturbed if it doesn't happen immediately. Rest assured the bonds will strengthen gradually as your body recovers and your confidence builds during the first few days after the birth.

Countdown to birth

Beginning at 36 weeks, labor can start any time, so be prepared. Keep a list of telephone numbers of your partner, obstetrician or midwife, and hospital delivery ward nearby. Have your bag (see below) or everything for a home delivery ready (see p. 46). (Some of these items may be provided by the hospital.)

What you need for the hospital:

✳ Your hospital notes.

✳ A large T-shirt or short, loose nightgown for labor.

✳ You may want to take a hot-water bottle for backache, a bottle of water and a natural sponge to suck, a spray bottle of water to cool you, and even a hand mirror so that you can see your baby's head as it appears.

✳ Socks in case you're chilly during or after delivery.

✳ Two front-opening nightdresses or pajamas, a robe, and slippers.

✳ Maxipads and several pairs of cotton underwear. Disposable underwear can also be very useful in the early days of heavy blood loss.

✳ Properly fitted nursing bras and disposable nursing pads.

✳ Toiletries, washcloth or sponge, and a couple of bath towels.

✳ For your baby you'll need onesies or undershirts (see p. 96), diapers and wipes (see pp. 86–88), a blanket and a "going-home" outfit.

As your due date approaches, the days may seem to drag by and you probably feel uncomfortably large. The expectant father may be waiting for the telephone to ring with the call he's been waiting for.

Getting ready

Although pregnancy is said to last 40 weeks, this is only a convenient method of calculation—it's normal for a baby to be born anywhere between 36 and 42 weeks. If your baby hasn't been born by the official due date, don't worry. Most doctors aren't in a hurry to induce a baby if the mother is healthy and there are no obvious problems, such as raised blood pressure. Stay active and arrange some outings and visits. It's better for you—and the baby—to get out instead of hanging around the house feeling apprehensive.

Packing your hospital bag

It's a good idea to have everything ready for your baby's arrival and your bag packed for the hospital three to four weeks before the due date, so that you are prepared for any eventuality. Your obstetrician will give you a list of what you need to take with you in the way of toiletries and other items, such as sanitary pads, diapers, and clothes for your baby (see left). Your tour of the labor ward (see p. 26) will help you decide whether you want to being bulkier items, as well, such as extra pillows.

Getting close to labor

In the few days before labor begins, you may notice some signs that indicate you don't have much longer to wait.

Feeling pre-menstrual You may experience similar feelings to those before your period, such as a low, nagging backache.

Braxton Hicks You may become more aware of these painless tightenings of the uterine wall. Braxton Hicks contractions can begin at around six months, and occur on and off during the last few weeks of pregnancy.

Mild diarrhea You may have looser bowel movements as your system is affected by the increasing uterine activity.

Abdominal lightening There may be an easing of discomfort under your ribs—a feeling of lightening—as your baby's head engages in your pelvis. This may happen a week or two before the birth with a first baby, but just as often it doesn't happen until labor.

Burst of energy Many women experience a sudden burst of energy even if they have been very tired and sluggish for several weeks previously. You may find you want to rush around making sure everything is ready for your baby's homecoming; this is known as the "nesting instinct."

Irritability Understandably, you may become short-tempered and impatient, with a definite sense that it's time for pregnancy to end!

The stages of labor

Labor has three distinct stages. The first stage is when the uterine contractions pull the cervix open; the second stage, from full dilatation to when the baby is born; and the third stage, until the placenta is delivered.

The first stage This is the stage when contractions are established, gradually becoming stronger and longer; this can last up to 12 hours, or longer with a first baby. There are three phases: the latent phase, which lasts around eight hours when the cervix thins; the active phase, when the cervix is opened up wide; and the transitional phase, when it reaches full dilatation. You're most likely to need pain relief during the active phase, and you're likely to feel a burst of energy towards the end.

The second stage During the second stage of labor, your baby leaves the uterus and is pushed through the birth canal. This can take anything from a few minutes to two hours with a first baby, and can be exhausting.

The third stage The delivery of the placenta is the final stage of labor; it is almost painless, although you may feel some cramping like a severe period pain. It happens within half an hour of your baby's birth, sooner if helped by an injection of pitocin (see p. 48).

Thinking about pain relief

Consider options for pain relief before labor starts; discuss what options are available with your doctor or midwife. Many women like the idea of a birth without the need for drugs, but it's good to be prepared, since you can't predict how your labor will progress or how you'll react to it.

Narcotic pain relievers

Pain relievers such as fentanyl, demerol, and stadol, are given by injection. They are quite strong and can make you feel sick or woozy. They can affect a baby's breathing at delivery (though this can be treated), and make him drowsy, so they aren't given late in labor.

Epidural anesthetic

Anesthetic is injected into the spinal canal to numb the body from the top of the abdomen down to the toes, but you remain awake and alert. A hollow needle is inserted into the spinal canal and a catheter (tube) is passed through it. Once the tube is in place, the needle is removed, and the tube remains, taped to your back. If you want to have an epidural, it's best to discuss it with your doctor in advance.

Spinal block

A spinal block is similar to an epidural but is given with a thinner needle and starts working faster. It does not last as long as an epidural, and is often used for cesarian delivery.

Birthing tubs

Buoyancy helps reduce the pressure on the abdomen, making your contractions more efficient, and being in water enables you to change positions easily. Some hospitals now have tubs for use during labor. Check early in your pregnancy to make sure that one will be available at your hospital.

Sudden birth— the father's role

Occasionally labor comes on with such speed that your partner could be overwhelmed by the desire to push before you can get professional help, let alone reach the hospital! The second stage of labor can take a couple of hours, but it may not; babies have been known to be born after a couple of pushes. If this happens, don't panic—babies who come quickly are almost always strong and vigorous, and most births are perfectly straightforward.

What to do

✳ Do not leave your partner alone for more than a minute or two. Help her into a comfortable position.

✳ Call the doctor or midwife. If you can't reach them, call 911.

✳ Wash your hands well and have some clean towels ready. Put one aside for the baby. If you have time, find some old sheets or plastic sheeting to cover the floor.

✳ When you see the top of the baby's head at the vaginal opening, ask your partner to stop pushing and just pant. This lets the vagina stretch fully without tearing.

✳ Once the head has been born, feel around the neck to see if the cord is looped around it. If it is, hook your finger under the cord and draw it over the baby's head.

✳ Hold your baby firmly as he emerges—he'll be slippery. Give him to his mother to hold. Wrap him in the towel so that he doesn't get cold.

✳ Don't touch the cord. If the placenta is delivered before help arrives, put it in a bowl so it can be checked by the doctor or midwife.

What happens in labor

How labor starts

The "show"
A brownish/pink discharge indicates that the mucus plug that has sealed the cervix during pregnancy has now come away in readiness for labor.

Your water breaks
Sometimes the amniotic sac ruptures before labor starts, causing fluid to leak slowly or in a gush from your vagina. This is painless. If your water breaks, put on a clean maxipad and call your doctor or midwife for advice. Most doctors want labor to begins within 24 hours because of the risk of infection.

Contractions start
The muscular tightenings of the uterus—contractions—gradually pull open the cervix. At first they are sharp, cramping pains in the lower abdomen or back that last a few seconds. If they're coming regularly, every 10–15 minutes, you're in labor.

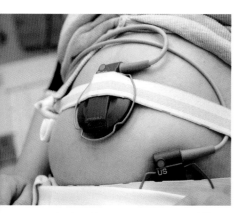

▲ **ELECTRONIC FETAL MONITORING** When you first arrive at the hospital, your baby's heartbeat may be measured during contractions through electrodes attached to your abdomen.

When you go into labor for the first time, it's natural to feel both excited and apprehensive. In spite of all the preparations you've made over the last months, for first-time parents labor is a journey into the unknown.

Keeping active
When you realize you're in labor, your first reaction may be to rush off to the hospital. Try to resist this; the most important thing for a mother in early labor is to keep active. Moving around is a great help in getting and keeping labor established, and most people find it easier to cope with contractions if they're upright. If your partner isn't with you, call him so he can join you as soon as possible. The best thing is to stay at home for as long as possible, trying to behave normally; if you have a contraction, just stop and breathe through it. You might want to have a shower or bath to relax you. However, it's best to avoid having a bath if your water has broken (see left), unless your doctor or midwife advises it. Try to eat and drink often in small quantities. Have high-energy snacks and warm drinks to keep your strength up.

When to go to the hospital
There's usually no reason to rush to the hospital. The first stage usually lasts at least eight hours for a first baby and you'll be more comfortable at home. Call your doctor when you think labor is established, but unless the hospital is far away, stay at home until contractions are coming every five to ten minutes and lasting for about a minute. However, bear in mind that you've got a journey ahead of you, so don't wait until the idea of getting into a car is beginning to sound like agony. If your partner can't get home in time, don't try to drive yourself; call an ambulance or a taxi.

At the hospital
It's now accepted that childbirth is not an illness, and most delivery rooms are designed to be as homelike as possible. You'll be assigned a nurse when you arrive, and she'll check how far the cervix has dilated and listen to your baby's heart, repeating these checks throughout your labor. You'll only need to be near the equipment while your baby's heart rate is being monitored; otherwise, you can move around. Some medical interventions require constant monitoring, however, so you'll have to stay on the bed.

Managing contractions
There are several ways of managing labor pains. Discuss the options with your doctor or midwife, including deciding when and if you want to use any pain relief (see p. 43). She'll try to accommodate your wishes and support you both in finding ways of coping with contractions.

Positions for labor

Staying upright as much as possible helps labor progress, since the contractions are able to work with, not against, gravity. Standing or squatting supported by your partner allows you to control the pain and provides warmth and loving reassurance.

Coping without pain relief

If you want to use natural pain relief, make sure you know as much as possible about the methods you prefer and practice them with your birth partner beforehand. If you need any special equipment, check that it will be available at home or in the hospital.

✳ Relax as much as possible, especially between contractions—concentrate on the out-breath as you exhale, and drop your shoulders. You'll learn breathing and relaxation techniques at your childbirth classes, but make sure you practice them before the big day.

✳ Keep moving around between contractions, then get into the position that feels right for you. This may be a supported squat, leaning against your partner, on all fours, or kneeling down and leaning forward on a pillow placed on a chair.

✳ Try counting backwards from 100 through a contraction—the concentration needed to do this takes your mind off the pain. Keep your eyes open to externalize the pain; focus on something in the room.

✳ Take sips of still water from a sponge if your mouth is dry and ask your partner to massage or knead your back during a contraction.

✳ Don't be afraid to say—or shout—anything you want to; no one's going to hold it against you afterward.

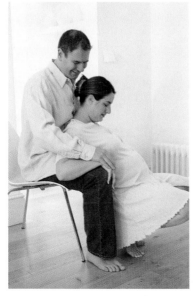

▲ **SQUATTING SUPPORTED** Squat between your partner's knees while he sits on a chair, taking your weight on his legs.

▲ **STANDING UPRIGHT** Stand with knees bent, if necessary, letting your partner take your weight.

✳ JUST FOR DAD

Just being with your partner is a huge comfort for her. Trust your intuition as to what's needed, but ask her what she needs too.

How you can help

✳ Be loving and intimate: slow and gentle, quiet and reassuring.

✳ Be there for her when she wants you, but give her some space when she doesn't.

✳ Be positive and never criticize; she needs lots of praise, encouragement, and sympathy.

✳ Offer practical help, such as a hot-water bottle if she has a backache, sprays of water if she's too hot, water to sip if her mouth is dry.

✳ If your partner doesn't want pain relief, encourage her while it seems reasonable, but if she asks for it, don't discourage her.

✳ Talk to the midwife or doctor if you don't understand what's happening, or if you're worried. They are there to help you both—though their first priorities are your partner's and baby's health and safety. At the same time, don't let the hospital staff and their machines become your focus.

✳ If your partner shouts or swears at you or seems to get angry or overwrought, take it in stride. It's her way of coping with a very stressful situation. This is particularly likely to happen at the transitional phase of the first stage of labor (see p. 43), so stay positive—it's a sign that the second stage isn't far off.

The birth of your baby

Who's who at the birth

For a normal vaginal delivery, you'll probably have your doctor or midwife and an assistant. Sometimes, though, the delivery room may seem crowded with people. They may include:

✳ Your doctor or midwife

✳ An assistant or nurse

✳ A pediatrician if there is a potential problem

✳ A pediatric nurse if your baby is premature

The early stages of your journey to parenthood are now complete. Ahead of you is a shorter, but not necessarily easier, stage: pushing the baby out. At last, you'll meet your new baby.

Coping with second stage

As your baby is gradually pushed down your birth canal, you should try to use gravity as much as possible to help, so keep as upright as you can. Get into whatever position feels most comfortable—it may be sitting up on the bed, squatting on a mat with the support of your partner, leaning against a chair, being on all fours, or using a birthing stool—your partner and doctor or midwife can follow your lead. Between contractions use your breathing techniques; in particular, let your pelvic floor, rectum, and anus relax.

Crowning

Your doctor or midwife will tell you when your baby's head appears at the vaginal opening—this is called crowning. Listen to your doctor or midwife; she'll tell you when to push and when to relax. If you take your time and let your vagina stretch slowly, you may avoid a tear. Once the baby's head crowns, your partner can show you by holding a mirror—this is a great encouragement because you know that your baby will soon be born.

Episiotomy

An episiotomy is a surgical cut in the perineum that helps to allow the baby's head to pass through. Given time, you may not need one, but if it's felt you should have one, the midwife or doctor will ask your permission to do this procedure as your baby's head crowns (see above). It's more common to have an episiotomy with a first baby because the vaginal opening may be less elastic and you are more likely to tear. Episiotomies are also performed if your baby is very large, is in the breech position, or you need assistance with forceps or vacuum extraction (see p. 51). If you haven't had an epidural, the pelvic floor muscles will be numbed first with an injection of local

◀ **THE MOMENT OF BIRTH**
You'll never forget the experience of holding your baby for the first time, immediately after he's emerged. It's so emotional that you may well find yourselves weeping with joy and relief.

Birth at home

Some women deliver at home, though hospital birth remains the norm.

Practical preparations

About a month before your due date, your doctor or midwife will let you know what equipment you need readily available, such as buckets, rubber gloves, and plastic sheeting to cover furniture and carpets. She'll provide all the medical equipment. Decide where in your home you want to have your baby and try to work out your expectations so you can discuss them with your doctor or midwife beforehand.

When you're in labor

✳ Call the doctor or midwife, who will come as soon as possible. She'll probably have an assistant.

✳ For pain relief, most women delivering at home rely on drug-free methods (see p. 45). (You'll probably be better able to cope at home, anyway.)

Talk to your doctor or midwife about other pain relief options, such as birthing tubs..

✳ You're far more likely to feel in control of events on your own turf, and that's an important psychological difference for everyone.

If there's a problem

Talk to your doctor or midwife in advance about when and why she'd recommend a move to the hospital. If that were to happen, you would go in an ambulance. In most cases, the same people who tended to you at home would do so in the hospital.

After the birth

A nurse or midwife will stay for a couple of hours to make sure that you and the baby are comfortable and healthy, and will return later. You, your partner, and your baby can spend your first hours as a family at home.

✳ JUST FOR DAD

Helping your partner and watching your baby being born is an overwhelming experience. The second stage is hard work for mothers—it's a real effort, but there are ways you can help and be involved.

How you can help

✳ Help your partner into the position she feels is best for her, and support her there.

✳ Talk to and encourage her all the time. Keep in physical contact so she knows you're with her.

✳ If you can see your baby's head as it crowns, describe it to your partner or hold a mirror for her to see—this will be a huge encouragement. However, don't get in the way of the doctor or midwife,who needs to monitor the baby's progress second by second and check the birth of the head.

✳ Announce that you have a son or daughter, not just a boy or girl. The words "son" and "daughter" express family feelings.

✳ If the midwife agrees, clamp and cut your baby's cord; he's now become an individual being.

✳ If you feel like weeping, don't hold back. It's one of the most emotional moments of your life.

✳ When the baby is born, share the first minutes of your child's life with your partner.

✳ Photograph or video your partner and baby if you like, but don't do this to the exclusion of helping them. They are more important than anything else.

anesthetic. Then the vaginal tissues, plus underlying muscle, are cut at the height of a contraction to extend the opening. The incision is stitched after the placenta has been delivered (see p. 48).

The delivery

The head is the widest part of your baby—it will slowly emerge, and the midwife will check that the cord isn't around the neck. The doctor or midwife will ask you to pant, not push, at this stage, then with the next contractions she will gently turn the baby so that the shoulders can be born one at a time and the rest of your baby's body will slide out; the pushing contractions stop immediately and you'll feel a wonderful sense of release. Your baby may or may not cry out.

Meeting your baby

This is the moment that will make everything you've just gone through worthwhile. Your midwife will probably lay your baby on your belly or give him to you to hold while the cord is clamped and cut; let your baby feel your skin, hold him close to your face, and let him look up into yours. This is when you can claim your new status as parents. Share this moment—you're both his parents—and savor it.

After the birth

Bonding

Most newborn animals have an instinct to bond—research has shown that human babies are similarly programmed.

What happens at birth

Your baby can recognize your voice at birth and can focus on your face at 8–10 inches (20–25 cm) away. You will be hypersensitive to your baby in the minutes after birth. You can bond for life almost instantly if you are left alone together without interference—if private time isn't offered, ask for it. But don't worry if you don't bond at once—you might be completely exhausted after the delivery. Falling in love will have to wait.

The first hour or so after your baby's birth is a very precious time for all three of you. Although there will be various medical and administrative procedures that need to be carried out, you'll still have time to enjoy your baby. You and your family might like to be left in peace to cuddle up together and start getting to know one another.

Your baby after delivery

The doctor or midwife will check your baby's condition immediately after the birth by assessing her "Apgar score" (see opposite). Providing she is breathing without difficulty from the start, your baby will probably remain in your arms for the first minutes after birth. If she needs help to start breathing, she'll be put on the delivery room resuscitation table, which has an oxygen mask and a heater to keep the baby warm. Usually she'll soon be pink enough to be handed back to you, but in a few cases she may need to be taken to the nursery for a while (see p. 62). Some time in the first couple of hours your baby will be weighed and measured and every part of her thoroughly examined by a pediatrician.

Delivery of the placenta

The placenta is usually delivered with the help of an injection pitocin given as the baby's body emerges. The cord is cut and the doctor or midwife will then press gently on your abdomen and pull the cord slowly to draw out the placenta. Once the placenta is delivered, the doctor or midwife will check to make sure that none has remained inside you. If you'd like the placenta to be delivered naturally, without pitocin, it will take about half an hour, and putting your baby to the breast will help the process.

How you will feel

Immediately after the birth, your body temperature drops a few degrees and you may shiver and shake quite violently as your thermostat resets. You'll need to be wrapped in a blanket, and may need to put on a pair of warm socks. The shivering usually passes in about half an hour, by which time your body temperature will be back up to normal. If you are famished after labor, ask for a small, easily digestible snack—crackers or bread, perhaps—and drink plenty of water if you want to.

If you need stitches

The doctor or midwife will examine your perineum and assess whether or not you need stitches. Research shows that minor tears heal better on their own, so it's not necessarily true that any tear will inevitably mean stitches; however, an episiotomy (see p. 46) must be stitched. Depending on the

▲ **GETTING TO KNOW YOUR BABY** Your relationship with your baby begins the second he is born. As you both learn to care for him, your love will deepen and grow.

The Apgar score

This a standard method of making sure your newborn baby is healthy and well, and to determine whether she needs special attention. At one minute, five minutes, and ten minutes after the birth, your midwife or doctor does five checks on your baby's heartbeat, breathing, muscle tone, reflexes, and skin color, and gives them a score of 0, 1, or 2, with a possible total of 10. A score of 7 or more is normal, and a low first score improving to a normal second or third score is also fine. This may happen if you had a long second stage, or your baby has been affected by medication given during labor (see p. 43). The assessment is named after Dr. Virginia Apgar, who devised it.

How the score works

✻ Heart rate over 100 scores 2; below 100 is 1; no heartbeat is 0.

✻ Regular breathing or crying scores 2; slow or irregular breathing scores 1; absence of breathing scores 0.

✻ If your baby is active (good muscle tone), the score is 2; if hands and feet only are moving, the score is 1; if the baby is limp, the score is 0.

✻ Strong reflexes score 2; weak reflexes score 1; no reflexes score 0.

✻ Pink coloring scores 2; body pink but extremities blue scores 1; blue or pale coloring scores 0. Skin color shows how well a baby's lungs are working.

JUST FOR DAD

You may feel as emotionally exhausted as your partner after the birth, but it's important not to underestimate the physical impact of labor and birth on a woman.

How you can help

✻ You'll probably experience a wave of euphoria now that your baby is born, but if labor has been long and hard, your partner may be too exhausted to experience this same "buzz" immediately. It doesn't mean that she isn't as delighted as you are, but after labor, it's not surprising if she finds it difficult to express immediate enthusiasm. Just hold her close and let her know how proud you are of her and of your new son or daughter. Stay with them both for as long as possible after the birth, including settling them into the postnatal ward.

✻ Congratulate your partner on her achievement, and let her know how much you appreciate her. Don't belittle your own contribution. You may think you haven't really been much help—this is common for fathers who have seen their partners in labor. However, most mothers will say how beneficial it was to have their partners' emotional support and encouragement.

✻ Hold your baby while your partner is being stitched or checked. Go into a quiet corner of the room and get to know your baby. Let her look into your eyes—if you hold her close so that she's just 8–10 inches (20–25 cm) away from your face, she can see you and smell you, and she'll learn to recognize you (see p. 156).

length of the cut or tear, stitching will be done by your midwife or doctor, and you may be given a local anesthetic. You may be able to cuddle your baby while you're being stitched if you want to, but this is also a good chance for your partner to have time with his baby so that you both get a chance to bond individually.

The first breastfeed

Putting your baby to the breast within an hour of the delivery increases your chances of breastfeeding successfully; many women feel able to put their babies to the breast immediately after the birth, although not all babies want to suck then. Ask your doctor or midwife to help you get your baby to latch on, but don't worry if she doesn't want to suck immediately. It doesn't mean she isn't able to breastfeed, just that at this point she doesn't feel like sucking, or she may be tired. She may also be affected by painkillers used during labor, such as demerol, which leave her rather drowsy and may take a few hours to wear off (see p. 43).

The importance of colostrum

You won't produce milk for three or four days after the birth (see p. 65), but it is very beneficial for your baby to have the high-protein "pre-milk" called colostrum that is produced in your breasts at this time. As well as water, protein, sugar, vitamins, and minerals, colostrum contains important antibodies from your body that protect a newborn baby from infections, plus a substance called lactoferrin, which acts like a natural antibiotic. Putting your baby to the breast also helps the uterus to contract.

Special labors

It's okay to feel disheartened if something happens that means you need an assisted delivery, or even an emergency cesarean section (see p. 52). Being prepared for the fact that intervention may be needed can help to avoid too much heart-searching after the birth.

Coping with a special labor

✳ The medical staff will always tell you why a particular course of action is recommended, whether it's before or during labor. Ask questions or for repeat explanations if you need to.

✳ If you're in labor, it may be difficult to concentrate; ask your partner to make sure that all the reasons for certain procedures are clarified so that he can relay the information to you. Remember, unless you're actually unconscious, staff must ask your permission to proceed; they won't accept your partner's opinion.

✳ At the end of the day, the most important thing will be that your baby has been born safely. But that doesn't mean your feelings don't matter, and many women can't shake off the idea—however illogical—that they were in some way to blame because things didn't go according to plan. If you find yourself in this position, talk to your partner or your midwife or doctor. Having a baby can unleash deep emotions and you may need to work through them before you can enjoy new motherhood fully.

There are many different procedures if labor proves difficult. If a particular procedure is suggested, ask the midwife or doctor to explain why it's necessary, what the risks are, and what would happen if you waited a while before it was started.

When labor is induced

Sometimes labor may need to be induced, which means it is started artificially. If you haven't gone into labor spontaneously by 42–43 weeks, or if there are worries about your own or your baby's health in the last few weeks of pregnancy, induction may be suggested. Similar procedures will be needed if your labor is not proceeding as it should. Don't worry if you have to be induced. Induction is fine if it's done strictly for medical reasons and for your well-being or the baby's—although contractions will be stronger.

How labor may be induced

Induction is often introduced gradually, first with a prostaglandin gel inserted vaginally; then, if necessary, ARM; finally, a pitocin drip if things are going too slowly.

✳ You may be given vaginal pessaries containing prostaglandin, a hormone that should trigger labor.

✳ Your membranes may be ruptured artificially (ARM), which can either start or strengthen contractions.

✳ You may be given an artificial hormone (pitocin) into a vein to induce contractions. Pitocin is started at a low rate and increased gradually so that contractions build up slowly. It may also used to speed up labor.

If you're having twins

Twins or higher multiples are exciting for everyone, although you're bound to be apprehensive. Twin deliveries are much safer than they used to be because the exact position and condition of the second baby can be determined by ultrasound and fetal monitors. Medical interest in the birth is likely to be greater if you're expecting more than one baby, and intervention is more likely to be recommended. Often this becomes necessary, but there's no need to think it's inevitable; many twins, and even triplets, are born vaginally after a normal labor. But continuous electronic fetal monitoring is much more common, and, as with breech birth, you'll probably be offered an epidural because of the likelihood of intervention being needed. This means it's in place in case there are problems with the delivery of the second twin and you have to have assistance with forceps or even a cesarean. If the first twin is known to be breech, your doctors will probably advise you to have both babies delivered by elective cesarean.

Breech birth

Instead of being born head first, a breech baby is born buttocks first, usually followed by the legs and lastly the head. Breech babies often need to be delivered with the help of forceps or by cesarean section for the baby's safety, although a natural breech delivery is occasionally possible with the help of an experienced midwife or obstetrician. A breech baby is almost always delivered in the hospital; because of the likelihood of intervention, you'll probably be offered an epidural, so that you're already anesthetized if your doctor needs to apply forceps or do a cesarean (see p. 52). You're more likely to have an episiotomy (see p. 46), because your baby's buttocks may not stretch the vagina enough to let the head out safely, or to allow forceps to be inserted to help lift the head out.

Assistance with vacuum or forceps

Even if you have a normal vaginal delivery, there may be times when you need help, particularly in pushing the baby out during the second stage. Depending on the circumstances, your hospital will provide assistance with forceps or vacuum extraction. You'll need to have an episiotomy for either of these procedures.

Vacuum extraction This is a more gentle procedure than using forceps and is used in similar circumstances. Your cervix has to be fully dilated and the baby's head must be in the birth canal. The vacuum plate leaves a bruise on your baby's head where the suction was applied, but this will fade within the first two to three weeks.

Forceps The two blades of forceps cradle your baby's head and pull it safely through the birth canal without too much compression. Forceps can normally only be used once the baby's head is engaged in the pelvic bones.

✳ JUST FOR DAD

A labor that doesn't go according to plan can be very scary for you as well as for your partner. Be prepared for any unexpected interventions.

How you can help

✴ Well before your baby is due, talk to your partner and make sure you know her views and preferences for any eventuality. Bear in mind, though, that she may change her mind when the time comes.

✴ Unless it's an absolute emergency, make sure that any interventions suggested are talked through thoroughly with your partner, and either or both of you ask questions if anything isn't clear. Remember that the medical team must have your partner's consent for any intervention.

✴ If something is suggested that you know your partner wants to avoid, try to buy time. For instance, if labor has slowed, suggest a change of position before procedures to accelerate labor are introduced.

✴ If the medical team decide the labor needs monitoring with high-tech equipment, try not to be distracted by it. Concentrate on your partner, not the technology.

✴ Remember that if something unexpected happens and intervention is needed, it's never your partner's fault. Everyone will be working in the very best interests of your partner and the baby.

✴ Whatever happens, talk about it afterward, especially with your partner, but also with friends and, if necessary, health professionals.

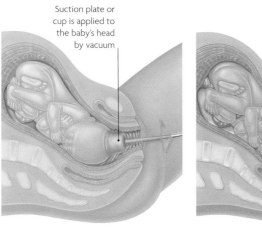

Suction plate or cup is applied to the baby's head by vacuum

▲ **VACUUM EXTRACTION** With vacuum assistance, a small suction plate or cup is applied by vacuum to the lowest part of your baby's head. The doctor will gradually help your baby to be born by applying gentle traction.

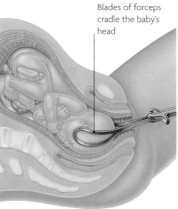

Blades of forceps cradle the baby's head

▲ **FORCEPS DELIVERY** Forceps are instruments that look like the two halves of very large sugar tongs. The blades are inserted one at a time and the baby is drawn out with a few gentle pulls during contractions.

Why you might need a cesarean

There are several reasons for a cesarean delivery:

✳ Baby's head is too large for your pelvis (disproportion).

✳ Baby is breech (bottom first).

✳ Baby takes up a crosswise position (persistent horizontal lie).

✳ You have a medical condition, such as pre-eclampsia or diabetes.

✳ Any problems with the placenta.

✳ Your labor is progressing too slowly or has stopped, which might cause fetal distress.

✳ If there is fetal distress, even if labor hasn't slowed or stopped.

Cesarean section

In many countries, cesarean sections are currently on the increase, partly because this procedure in expert hands may be safer than, say, a difficult forceps delivery. Sometimes, however, interventions earlier in labor, such as induction or epidural anesthetic, may lead to a situation in which a cesarean becomes more likely. If a cesarean is recommended, your doctor is obliged to give you clear reasons why, even in an emergency. If it is something you wanted to avoid, ask whether you could wait, or if there is anything else you could try first.

Elective cesarean

If a cesarean operation is planned in advance it is known as "elective". This means the reason for it became apparent before labor started—for example, your blood pressure may have shot up, or your pelvis is so small that delivery is likely to be difficult, or your baby is breech (see p. 50). Your obstetrician will discuss this with you two to three weeks before your due date, and a date will be booked for you to go into the hospital, so you'll know well in advance exactly when your baby is going to be born.

Emergency cesarean

An emergency (unplanned) cesarean happens when events during labor make it preferable to a vaginal delivery. For example, your baby may show distress (measured by heart rate and movements); the labor may not progress despite the use of drugs to speed things up; or your own condition may deteriorate. If you haven't had an epidural anesthetic, the cesarean will take place under general or spinal anesthetic.

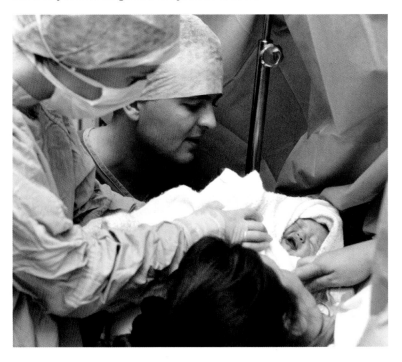

▶ **DELIVERY OF YOUR BABY** If you have a cesarean under epidural anesthesia, you'll both be able to share your baby's first moments after delivery.

What happens during the operation

Before a cesarean, some of your pubic hair may be shaved and a catheter inserted into your bladder. You'll probably be given a saline drip.

The anesthetic Most elective, and some emergency, cesareans are performed under epidural or spinal anesthesia, because women recover more quickly afterward. You'll be awake during the operation, but you won't feel anything, and your partner can be with you throughout if he wants to. You won't be able to see anything because the operating team will be masked by a surgical sheet draped across your chest. Spinal anesthesia takes effect in five to ten minutes and so it can be used in some emergency situations. If, however, you have a general anesthetic, your partner won't usually be allowed into the operating room, but will be able to hold the baby afterward while you recover.

The operation Your abdomen is opened through a small horizontal incision along the line of the top of your pubic hair, and your baby delivered through a similar cut in the uterus. The amniotic fluid is drained off by suction before the baby is gently lifted out. You may feel some tugs as the operation proceeds. Your surgeon will tell you when the moment approaches when she will lift your baby from your uterus.

After the birth It takes about ten minutes to deliver the baby. You or your partner can then hold your baby while the placenta is removed and you are stitched. A baby born by cesarean is likely to need help in starting to breathe, but a pediatrician will be on hand to help. Closing the wound can take as long as 45 minutes. You'll be encouraged to get up and walk around a few hours afterward to stimulate your circulation.

The birth partner's role

Even an elective cesarean can be worrying, because it's a major operation. If it's an emergency, your partner may be feeling distressed, but there's much you can do to help her.

✳ If an emergency cesarean is recommended, and your partner is finding it difficult to talk to the doctors, make sure you ask why it is suggested. Even though she has to give her permission, your partner may still not be quite clear afterward why it was necessary, and it's important that you're able to help her understand.

✳ Unless your partner really wants a general anesthetic or the operation is too urgent, see if it can be done under epidural or spinal anesthesia. This means you can share the experience and meet your new baby together.

✳ During the operation, sit by your partner's head and reassure her that all is well.

✳ You don't have to watch, but if you do and you find it distressing or you feel faint—and many people do—leave the room quickly. Don't hang on; you may cause further difficulties for the medical staff.

✳ If the cesarean is being done under general anesthetic, your partner may not regain consciousness for an hour or more, and you'll probably be given your baby to hold. Cherish this time. Father–child bonding can be at its best after a cesarean, because this early time together is so precious.

✳ JUST FOR MOM

You're bound to feel apprehensive about having a cesarean, and you may feel disappointed if you have an emergency cesarean after going into labor naturally.

Concerns about cesareans

✳ You may worry about being able to deliver a subsequent baby vaginally, but about 75 percent of women who have a cesarean can deliver normally the next time.

✳ If you have a general anesthetic, you'll need longer to recover, so it may be a little while before you feel close to your baby. Don't worry, you will bond with your baby in time, especially when you start breastfeeding (see pp. 48–49).

✳ You'll be left with a scar on your "bikini line," but it will fade.

The first day

You have both been looking forward to this moment for the better part of a year; your baby is safely delivered and you've experienced a heady brew of strong emotions: relief, pride, elation, excitement, and triumph. Now your baby is lying quietly in her crib by your bed and you both have a chance to take stock.

Hospital routine

Some aspects of the hospital routine can be tiresome, though you may enjoy talking to other mothers.

Keeping your baby close
Almost all hospitals expect babies to remain in bassinets or cribs beside their mothers' beds most of the time.

Food and drink
Food may be bland; ask your partner to bring fresh fruit to prevent constipation. Drink plenty of water.

Visits from staff
Your doctor or midwife will check your stitches, lochia, and uterus (see p. 64), and give advice on cleaning your baby's umbilical cord and breastfeeding. At some point, an obstetrician will check you and a pediatrician will check your baby. Your baby will also be taken to the nursery daily to be weighed.

Your reactions to the birth

Unlikely as it may seem, this could be an awkward moment for you both. It could be passing through either or both of your minds that there is something missing. Where is the rush of love for your baby? It isn't a subject that gets much attention, but it is, nevertheless, a fact that large numbers of parents, quite possibly the majority, don't feel an overpowering attachment to their baby right after the birth. Most highs, because of their intensity, are followed, not necessarily by a low, but by a diminution of emotion that leaves you feeling somewhat flat in comparison. Having a baby is no exception. It may have been a momentous event for you both, but the hospital routine has to proceed as normal and, anyway, a hospital ward isn't conducive to the kind of closeness that you would like to feel for each other on this shared birthday, especially if you're both exhausted.

Looking forward

When you go to the postpartum floor—and this may be two or three hours after the birth—the father often goes back to an empty home and the mother is left wondering what her first night as the mother of a baby is going to be like. If it isn't quite what either of you envisioned, don't worry. In a very real sense, life with your baby will actually begin on the day you take her home.

After a cesarean

A cesarean section involves major abdominal surgery, and you're likely to feel quite sore once the anesthetic wears off. As well as asking for pain relief, there are other ways of coping:
❋ Holding and feeding your baby may be difficult, since pressure on your scar may be painful. Try laying her next to you on the bed (see p. 79) or supporting her on pillows in the "football position" (see bottom left).
❋ Mobility helps you recover, so you'll be encouraged to get up and move around as soon as possible after the birth. Support your wound as you walk around. Be very careful how you move, especially when you're getting up from sitting or lying down. Be careful not to strain your abdominal muscles.
❋ Your dressing will be taken off after a couple of days. Keep the wound dry. Most stitches are absorbable; if not, they'll be removed after about a week.

▲ **COMFORTABLE FEEDING** Put your baby on a pillow and tuck her body under your arm.

Handling your new baby

It's natural to be nervous about holding and handling your baby for the first time; although she may seem vulnerable, remember that she is really very robust. The main problem is that she has no neck control so her head is very floppy, and her joints are very soft so you need to be gentle when putting on her clothes (see p. 96). Support your baby's head at all times and pick her up as shown here.

◀ **LIFTING YOUR BABY** Slide one hand under her rump and cradle her head with the other. Lift her gently but firmly toward you, using a smooth upward movement so that she isn't startled. Then hold her close to you. Talk to her all the time and make eye contact with her as you chat.

▲ **HOLD HER ALONG YOUR FOREARM** Some babies like to be held face down on your arms so they can see out. Hold her so that her cheek rests on your forearm and she can feel your skin against her face.

First discomforts

You'll feel a little shaky in the first 24 hours, and there may be some specific discomforts, although these will pass quickly:

✱ Your perineum will feel bruised and tender, especially if you had stitches. Don't stay in the bath too long as water can harm scar tissue and soften stitches.

✱ You may find it difficult or even painful to pass urine. Take a jug of tepid water to the toilet to pour over your vulva as you pass urine.

✱ A sore perineum plus stitches may deter you from opening your bowels. Support your vulva with a pad of tissues as you bear down.

✱ Sitting upright can be awkward when your abdominal muscles are weak and your vulva and perineum are sore. Prop yourself up with plenty of pillows and half sit and half lie on your side to reduce pressure.

◀ **CRADLE HER IN YOUR ARMS** You baby will feel safe and secure cradled in your arms, or on the crook of your elbow. Remember she can see you clearly if you hold her so that she is about 8–10 inches (20–25 cm) from your face. Support her head throughout.

Preparing to go home

New fathers

If you leave your partner and baby in the hospital, you are likely to feel a bit lonely when you go home. Use the time to call everyone—you'll probably have a strong urge to talk through everything that's happened.

Fathers need sleep too

Although you may feel too excited at first, make sure you catch up on sleep. You've had an exhausting time during the labor and you can't support your partner when she comes home if you're worn out.

Prepare for the home coming

Use your time at home alone to do the washing and cleaning and stock up on groceries and other household items. Figure out how to work the carseat, if you haven't already done this, so that everything is ready for your new baby to come home.

When the family comes home

Most hospitals discharge new mothers and babies two days after delivery for vaginal births, and three to four days after a cesarian. Remember, though, that going home doesn't mean everything is back to normal. Childbirth leaves a mother exhausted, so try to keep the first day or two virtually visitor-free.

▶ **RESPONDING TO YOUR BABY** A newborn has only three states he can be in: awake and quiet, awake and crying, or asleep. Crying is his way of communication. He may be hungry, uncomfortable, tired, or just cry for no apparent reason.

Your baby's first day

There's a lot to learn on your baby's first day, and you may feel awkward and anxious about looking after him. On top of trying to get him to nurse, you'll have to get used to changing a diaper, "topping and tailing" (see p. 90), and dressing your baby. (Most hospitals and midwives leave the first bath for three or four days.) Don't worry though, no-one expects you to be an instant expert. The nurses on the postpartum floor will show you both what to do; if you're uncertain about anything, don't be afraid to ask.

Reluctance to nurse

You may be concerned if your baby is reluctant to nurse for the whole of the first day, but this is no cause for worry. Express colostrum (see p. 83) if your breasts feel uncomfortable, so you'll find it easier to feed him as soon as he is ready. Once your baby feels the need to nurse, you may find you are putting him to the breast as often as every two hours.

Your sleepy baby

Your baby will probably have been wide awake and alert for the first hour or two after the birth, but then he may well sleep on and off for much of the first day. Take turns just holding and looking at him rather than simply leaving him in his crib.

Your baby's cries

Unless he is very sleepy, you'll probably experience your baby crying several times during this first day and you may be astonished by its force. Just as amazing is the fact that you'll recognize it immediately. Neither of these things is accidental. Newborn babies are programmed to signal their needs vociferously and adults are programmed to respond to these needs with a feeling of urgency. Pick your baby up right away when he cries; sit and cuddle him in bed with you unless you want to sleep. Over the next few weeks, you will gradually learn exactly what his cries mean.

ENJOY YOUR NEW BABY Take turns holding your new baby and talking to him, or just letting him sleep in your arms. You can't spoil a baby by giving him lots of attention in the precious early days.

Adjusting to parenthood

JUST FOR MOM

Even though you're longing to be home, use your time in the hospital to regain your strength and lean on the professional staff for advice. If you're back home within a couple of days of the birth, accept offers of help from friends and relations.

How you can adjust

✳ When your partner visits you both in the hospital, share anything you've learned about your baby's care with him. If you learn how to care for your baby together, you'll start out on an equal footing and he'll be more likely to take initiative once you're home.

✳ Use these first few days to build on the network of support systems that you will hopefully have set up through prenatal classes before the baby was born. Prepare for time on your own when your partner has gone back to work and friends and family aren't around as much.

✳ At some point during the first few days, you may experience tearful moments—it often happens just as your milk comes in, three or four days after the birth. The so-called "baby blues" (see p. 132) are a normal reaction to the sudden withdrawal of pregnancy hormones and to the enormity of your new situation. They usually subside in a week to ten days. You'll probably be very tired too, especially if you had a fairly long labor. Be open and share your feelings with your partner.

The first few days of parenthood can be bewildering as you seesaw between intense periods of close attention from health professionals and moments of isolation, when you just have to get on with things by yourselves. You may feel that caring for your new baby leaves little room for your own relationship as a couple, but it will help if you concentrate initially on sharing the simple practicalities of your baby's care and acknowledge rather than hide your natural nervousness and apprehension.

Taking care of each other

When a baby comes to first-time parents, three new relationships begin: mother–baby, father–baby, mother–father. The last is the most complex. Of course a relationship has existed between the parents that predates the baby, but you will not have related to each other before in the roles of mother and father. You have to start thinking of each other in an entirely new way. You have to "redesign" your relationship in the light of your new roles—being more understanding, more patient, more flexible, more long-suffering than you were before. Most of all, you have to be more generous and less self-centered. This can put a strain on your relationship, so you need to be ready to respond to each other (see p. 128).

Help and advice

Use your time in the hospital, or when you are in the daily care of a midwife or doctor, to get the advice you need. Don't feel shy about asking, even if it seems trivial; most health professionals recognize that it's vital to provide reassurance. However, in a hospital setting they may not have enough time to advise you exactly when you need it, particularly with breastfeeding problems, so it may be helpful to contact a lactation consultant when you get home. Most lactation consultants are themselves mothers who have been trained to provide support in a non-medical way and will continue their support for some months. This helps to alleviate the nervousness many mothers feel when they are finally discharged by the obstetrician or midwife, ending a close relationship that's grown over months.

Advice from family and friends

In the early days of parenthood, your friends and relations may be keen to offer advice. Although it can be irritating if delivered in an overbearing way, the advice that other parents give you reflects their own experience and can be very reassuring. However, if the advice goes against your own beliefs, simply ignore it and do things the way you know is best. If you're confused about what to do for the best, try talking things through with your pediatrician, who'll be able to help clear up any worries.

Feeling isolated

After the intense activity of labor and birth, when you were fully involved and couldn't think about anything else, you may both feel quite isolated, disoriented, and lonely for a few days; this could affect how you relate to each other when you do have time together. The new mother may feel bewildered in the hospital. Even though she's surrounded by other people, she suddenly finds herself in sole charge of the needs of her tiny new dependent when she's feeling exhausted and possibly in pain. The new father, too, may feel very odd and detached from his new situation when he has to come and go from an empty home.

Talk to each other

When you're together, try hard to talk about how you feel and make sure you tell each other what you have been doing while you're apart. Most hospitals now have unrestricted day and evening visiting for new fathers, or even provide a place for them to stay overnight, so it should be possible to spend quite a lot of time together supporting each other after delivery. It may be difficult to find time alone to articulate your feelings, but it is important for all of you that you do.

JUST FOR DAD

As a new father you may feel rather cut off from your partner, particularly while she's in the hospital. At the same time, you may feel an intense elation that you want to share with your partner, but she may seem a bit distant as her body recovers from the birth and she tries to establish breastfeeding.

What you can do to help

✳ Take the initiative—learn how to do all the practical things your baby needs while your partner is still in the hospital.

✳ Get to know your baby. Use these early days to establish a close relationship. Even if your partner is in the hospital, change your baby, learn to handle her, talk to her, hold her close so that she can focus on your face if she's awake, or simply hold her if she's asleep. Bring her to your partner when she needs to be fed, carry her around, try to be there for her first bath.

✳ Be ready for your partner's mood swings. At some point during the first week your partner will probably experience the so-called "baby blues" that come as a reaction to the sudden withdrawal of the pregnancy hormones as well as to new responsibilities. She may also be very tired if the labor was prolonged. The "baby blues" subside after a week to ten days. Your partner may try to hide her feelings from you so as not to worry you or because she fears that you won't take her seriously. Be sensitive to her needs and talk to her about them (see p. 128).

▲ **FAMILY TOGETHERNESS** A period of peace and relaxation in the days following the birth of your baby is vital. It gives you both a chance to celebrate the birth, welcome and bond with your new baby, and get used to being a family.

Your newborn baby

A newborn's reflexes

A newborn has a set of built-in reflexes that help him survive. They disappear within a few weeks as he develops (see p. 156).

Grasp

He grasps anything put into his fist; the reflex is so strong that he can take his own weight. The reflex is lost in a couple of weeks.

Step

If his feet touch a firm surface, he will take a step—this has nothing to do with real walking.

"Moro" response

If startled, your baby throws out his arms and legs in a star shape to stop himself from falling.

Rooting

If you stroke his cheek, he will automatically turn his head ("root") to find the nipple.

Few newborn babies are conventionally pretty, but even though everything is perfectly normal, your baby's appearance may make you slightly apprehensive, so you'll find it hard to resist going over him with a fine-tooth comb, just to make sure.

What your baby looks like

The size of a newborn baby varies enormously—a perfectly normal birth weight could be anything from 5½ to 10 lbs (2.5 to 4.5 kg). But even a 9–11-lb (4–5-kg) baby will seem tiny and vulnerable when newborn. Your baby may look slightly battered and bruised after the birth, and his head may be rather elongated because of squeezing in the birth canal, but it will return to a normal rounded shape in a week or so. There may be the odd bruise here and there on his head, especially if your birth was assisted (see p. 50), or there may be a small scar if a fetal monitor was attached to his scalp. Until he has his first bath, his hair may be a bit matted with dried blood and fluid from the birth.

Hands Your baby's hands will be curled into fists most of the time. Nails may be long and sometimes stained with meconium (see opposite).

Legs His legs may be so tightly flexed that you can't easily straighten them, but don't apply force. His feet may be rounded and toes curled.

Genitals These will look large because of the action of pregnancy hormones. For the same reason, both girls and boys may have pronounced breasts, which will shrink, and girls may also have a slight vaginal discharge for a day or two.

Umbilical cord The stump usually dries and shrivels within a few days, and your healthcare provider will remove the clamp. The rest drops off.

▶ **YOUR BABY'S HEAD** Your baby's head may look quite large compared to the rest of him. There may also be a bump on one side where the cranial bones have been squeezed during birth—the cranial bones are soft and can override one another to protect the brain. They don't fuse completely for a few months, leaving a diamond-shaped soft spot on the top of the head, called the fontanelle, covered by a tough membrane. You may notice a pulse beating there.

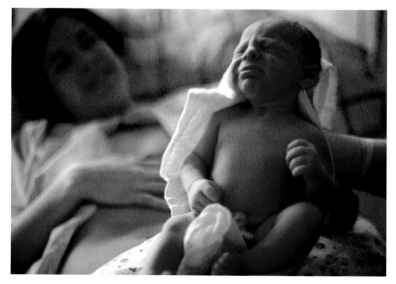

What your newborn baby can do

Sight Babies like looking at faces more than anything else. He can see you clearly if your face is 8–10 inches (20–25 cm) from his. He's wired to respond—his heart rate rises when he focuses on your face—so talk and smile. He'll react with body jerks and fish-feeding movements of his mouth—that's his first attempt at a conversation.

Hearing His hearing is acute—he knows both your voices from having heard them in the womb and he'll respond instantly to pleasure in your voice. Start talking and singing from the moment of birth and never stop.

Movement He loves physical movement—after all, he's been jogging and swaying in the womb for nine months—so carry him around as much as possible. Slings allow you to carry your baby close while keeping both hands free. Move his limbs gently while changing him, clap his hands gently, do gentle knee bends. But avoid sudden movements that startle him.

✳ Concerns about your newborn baby

Your concerns	What it is and how it is treated
Birthmarks	Many babies have birthmarks, most of which fade within a few months. Some, such as the strawberry mark, which is raised, may take much longer and usually become bigger and redder before fading. The Mongolian blue spot, a bluish birthmark on the lower back of babies with dark skin tones, is sometimes mistaken for bruising.
Milia	Tiny white spots on the bridge of the nose. These disappear after a few weeks.
Erythema Toxicum	A blotchy rash, a bit like hives; there may also be small yellow spots. It only lasts a couple of days.
Meconium	At birth your baby's bowels contain dark green or almost black meconium, a sticky substance that is usually passed into the diaper during the first two to three days.
Jaundice	Neonatal jaundice is quite common due to a baby's immature liver. It makes the skin yellowish and the urine dark. Your baby may be sleepy, so he'll need to be wakened for feeds to ensure he has enough fluid. Persistent cases may be treated with ultraviolet light.
Breathing	Babies snuffle and sneeze a lot, and get hiccups. They may even stop breathing for a second or two, but breathing soon becomes strong and regular.
Lip blisters	Some babies develop a white sucking blister on the lips. It doesn't cause discomfort and will fade in a few days.
Scalp swelling	Some babies develop a swelling on the scalp due to bleeding under the skin during the birth. This is quite normal, but it does take a few weeks to disperse.

✳ Newborn baby check

Your baby is given a head-to-toe check by a doctor before you leave the hospital.

Vision
The doctor will shine a light into your baby's eyes and will note if they move on hearing her voice. She will also check for cataracts.

Heart and lungs
She'll listen to your baby's heart and check his lungs and breathing.

Ability to suck
She'll put her finger into his mouth to check the palate and that he can suck properly.

Internal organs
She'll gently feel his abdomen and check his anus.

Spine
She'll feel his spine to make sure the vertebrae are in place.

Hip manipulation
She'll remove his diaper and check his legs and hips for any sign of congenital hip dislocation.

The PKU test
On about the second day, a tiny drop of blood will be taken from his heel to test for thyroid function and for phenylketonuria, a rare disorder that may cause mental retardation if undetected. It may also be tested for a number of other conditions, including cystic fibrosis.

Hearing
In addition to the head-to-toe check, all new babies are now also given a special hearing screening test in the days after the birth. It's quick and doesn't hurt. If the response is not clear, your baby may be given a second test.

The special-care baby

How a pre-term baby may look

If your baby is born prematurely, she may look a little different from what you expect:

✳ Her skin will be loose, wrinkled, and red because she hasn't had time to fill out with fat.

✳ She'll be covered in downy hair called lanugo.

✳ Her head will seem very large.

✳ She'll be very thin and bony, especially her ribs and buttocks, with stick-like limbs.

✳ Her breathing may seem labored and uneven.

✳ Her movements may be jerky.

Feeding special-care babies

At first your baby may need to be fed glucose intravenously, or have milk fed through a tube in her nose, but hopefully she will soon be able to try sucking. Breastmilk is especially good for a premature baby, since your body will make milk suited to your her gestation. You can express milk so your baby can be tube-fed.

Introducing breastfeeding

It may take time to get your baby used to breastfeeding. Avoid bottles as much as possible if you want to breastfeed fully, since weaker babies can get used to bottles and may reject your nipple.

If your baby needs specialist care, you'll understandably be anxious. However, it will only be done for the best of reasons: to increase your baby's chances of thriving as a normal, healthy baby.

Why do babies need special care?

Although many people think special care only applies to premature births, in fact about one in ten babies needs some sort of special attention, and by no means are they all born before term. There are several possible reasons.

Prematurity A baby born before 37 weeks is pre-term or premature, and may need close monitoring, as well as help with breathing and nursing.

Low birth weight Any baby who weighs 5½ lbs (2.5 kg) or less at birth is considered to have a low birth weight. Low birth weight babies may be either pre-term or full-term but "small for dates" (see p. 34), and may need to spend a short time in a special care unit.

A health risk A baby who may have had difficulties with breathing during the birth, or have picked up an infection, may need special attention for a while. Alternatively, there may be birth defects, such as a "hole in the heart," that may have been diagnosed before or at the birth.

What special care means

If your baby needs special care, her needs can be catered for in the unit called a neonatal intensive care unit (NICU). In some situations this may mean she has to be moved to a different hospital. If she was premature or of a low birth weight, she could have difficulty with breathing, be prone to infections, be unable to regulate body temperature, or nurse properly. Without support, low blood sugar levels can cause brain damage and she may lack iron and calcium. For these reasons, she may need the protection and constant monitoring of incubator care, with intravenous or tubal feeding (see left), until she catches up on growing and learns to eat and breathe without help.

Getting through it

Having a baby in special care can feel like you've lost a limb. Something is missing; your baby is born, but isn't yet able to be where she should be—in your arms. If she was born early, you may feel cheated on having missed out on the end of your pregnancy. Another common reaction is to feel that your baby isn't really yours—while she's in the NICU, it may seem as though she belongs to the medical staff. Try to remind yourself that this is your child, and that soon she will be home with you where she belongs. Be as involved as possible in discussions about her condition and in her care while she's in the hospital, and try to look forward to the day when she'll be truly yours, and you can take her home.

Helping to care for your baby

All special care baby units welcome parents and actively encourage them to help with feeding, washing, and diaper changing. There may be rooms where you can stay overnight from time to time, and many units provide space for parents for a day or two before your baby is discharged so that you can get used to the normal care routine of a small baby—this is particularly important if you had a multiple birth.

Making contact

Just because your baby is in an incubator doesn't mean you can't touch, kiss, and cuddle her. This sort of contact is vitally important because it actually helps your baby to develop and become strong. If it's a closed incubator, you can reach into her through hand-holes to play and caress, and you should talk and sing to her as much as you can so she hears your voice. Open special-care cribs enable you to handle your baby directly. All this will keep her contented and help her to thrive—love is an essential vitamin for premature babies.

If it's practical, give your baby as much skin-to-skin contact as you can. When you hold your baby to your skin, her body temperature rises if she is cold, and then falls once she has warmed up. A successful experiment has also revealed that babies who are born prematurely thrive if they are nursed continuously between their mother's breasts—ask if you can try it. Skin-to-skin contact is essential for your baby, but it's essential for you, too, in fostering the bonding process. It will especially help you if you're nervous; you may feel this way because your baby is so small and you're finding it difficult to relate to her because she's in a special care unit. It's also very important for your partner to have skin-to-skin contact with his baby to help his bonding process.

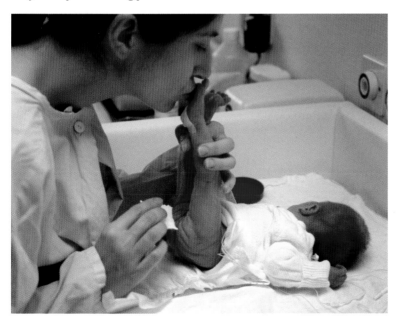

Coping with the technology

Many parents are worried by special-care technology. Share your feelings with the unit's staff and ask them to explain what the equipment does:

✳ An incubator provides a warm, humid environment for the baby.

✳ A ventilator takes over the baby's breathing, getting air into and out of the lungs.

✳ A humidifier ensures air in the ventilator is warm and moist before it goes into the lungs.

✳ The apnea alarm alerts the staff if a baby stops breathing.

✳ The saturation monitor and blood gas analyzer measure levels of oxygen and carbon dioxide in the blood.

✳ The blood pressure gauge measures a baby's blood pressure.

✳ A nasal canula may be used to provide extra oxygen when the baby is breathing on her own.

✳ The glucose monitor records the baby's glucose levels.

✳ The electro-cardiogram (ECG) monitor measures heart rate.

✳ The bilirubinometer measures the risk of jaundice.

✳ A phototherapy lamp treats jaundice with ultraviolet light. A shield protects the baby's eyes.

✳ A heat shield keeps the baby warm in an open crib.

◀ **SPENDING TIME WITH YOUR BABY** It's important to spend as much time as possible in the special care baby unit with your baby. It will help to demystify the technology and allow you to bond with your baby.

You and your body

Postnatal check

Your doctor or midwife will examine you about six weeks after the birth. Your baby will also be checked at about this time (see p. 155). This check will make sure that your body has fully returned to its pre-pregnant state. Your doctor will examine your uterus, heart, and blood pressure, your breasts, and any scarring if you had stitches. This is an ideal time to discuss contraception or anything that concerns you. At the checkup your doctor may:

✳ Test your blood pressure.

✳ Check your heart rate.

✳ Check your weight.

✳ Examine your abdomen to make sure the uterus has contracted down.

✳ Look at your breasts and nipples.

✳ Do an internal examination to assess the size and position of your uterus and the state of your vaginal muscles.

✳ Check on the site of perineal stitches. Tell your doctor if it's still sore, especially during sex.

✳ Carefully check your scar and abdomen if you had a cesarean.

✳ Give you advice about contraception. During the internal examination, an IUD can be inserted or a diaphragm fitted.

It takes a woman's body more than nine months to recover completely from pregnancy and childbirth. For the first week or so, you'll be weak and unable to walk any distance or carry anything heavy. Even if you feel well, try not to overdo it, or you'll prolong your recovery period.

Getting back to normal

The medical term for the immediate period of recovery after the birth of your baby is the puerperium. It's defined as the first four weeks, but most women are physically back to normal well before that, even if their emotional adjustment takes much longer. However, you may well be concerned about what is happening to your body during the first week or two after the birth, when changes are rapid but often accompanied by a certain amount of discomfort. When this is your first experience of childbirth, it's important to realize that vaginal discharge, painfully engorged breasts, and unexpected abdominal cramps are quite normal!

How your body recovers

Cervix and vagina Because both were stretched during delivery, they will take at least seven to ten days to regain their former elasticity and close up. Doing your pelvic floor exercises (see p. 38) will help your vagina to tighten again. Start immediately after the birth.

Placental site (lochis) As the placental site heals, it may bleed for up to six weeks. This discharge (lochia) has three color phases: red (four to five days), pink to brown (six to eight days), yellow to white (seven to ten days). If you over-exert yourself, you may start to bleed, making the lochia red and copious again. If this happens, tell your doctor and rest with your feet up.

Uterus Immediately after the birth, your uterus shrinks down to the size it was at about the fourth month of pregnancy. By about the tenth day it can no longer be felt in your abdomen—your doctor or midwife will check to make sure that it is shrinking normally. It takes about six weeks to revert to its normal pre-pregnant size.

Ovulation If you're not breastfeeding, you may begin to ovulate within six to fourteen weeks of the birth; menstruation will follow between eight and sixteen weeks. Breastfeeding hormones can suppress menstruation, but don't rely on breastfeeding as a contraceptive. Use contraception as soon as you want to start penetrative sex again (see p. 137).

Postnatal sex

You can have non-penetrative sex whenever you both feel like it after the birth, but you'd be wise to abstain from penetrative sex until after the lochia has stopped (see p. 136). However, neither of you will probably feel like it for

Postnatal discomforts

Discomfort	How to relieve it
Stitches	Discomfort from stitches can last up to a couple of weeks. Don't stand for long periods and bathe daily to prevent infection. Dry stitches with a hair dryer rather than a towel. Keep a bottle of witch hazel in the fridge and apply cold on a sterile pad to soothe the stitches. Occasionally stitches may not dissolve and need to be removed by your midwife or doctor.
Stress incontinence	Leaking urine when coughing, sneezing, exercising, or even laughing is a common though embarrassing problem for many women after childbirth. It's the result of stretched and weakened perineal muscles, so once again it's important to concentrate on doing your pelvic floor exercises (see p. 38).
Breast engorgement	Three or four days after birth, lactation begins; your breasts become engorged with milk, making them uncomfortably large, hard, and tender. Relieve this by expressing, nursing as often as your baby wants, and having warm baths or laying hot washcloths on your breasts. Always wear a supportive nursing bra.
Afterpains	As your uterus shrinks, you may continue to experience severe cramps, similar to menstrual pain, especially during breastfeeding. This is due to the action of the hormone oxytocin, which controls the "let down" of milk in your breasts (see p. 78), and also causes the uterine muscles to contract (see p. 49).
Headaches	In a few cases (less than one percent), some women experience a severe headache after an epidural. It's caused by a minute puncture in the membrane of the spinal column, made when the needle was inserted. If you experience this, you'll be advised to lie flat, drink plenty of fluids, and take painkillers such as acetaminophen until the hole has healed and the headache lifts. This usually takes a couple of days.

a while. Nature has seen to it that most men have a low sex drive for some time after the delivery of their baby, especially if they are present at the birth. Not surprisingly, low libido lasts longer in women who have just had babies. No one who has vaginal bruises, painful stitches, and enlarged, tender breasts finds it easy to feel sexy; your need for rest and recuperation is much more important. If you've had stitches, make sure your partner feels your scar when it's healed—he'll be much more understanding and compassionate about sex after he's felt the extent of it (see p. 46). It's best to be open about these things, and discuss them honestly and lovingly. This will help stop them from developing into long-term difficulties.

After a cesarean

If you've had a cesarean delivery, you'll be monitored more closely in the hospital, and your stay will be longer than after a normal delivery. The doctors will want to be sure that you and your baby are progressing well. Even so, your stay in hospital is likely only to be about four days.

Stitches

Stitches are usually dissolvable and do not need to be removed.

Time for recovery

It may only be when you get home that you realize how much the cesarean has affected you. This won't last long, but you won't feel completely back to normal for at least a month.

Help in the home

You need to avoid exertion while the wound is healing, so it's a good idea if your partner can take extra time off work, or if a friend or relation can stay for a while. You won't be able to lift heavy things, and you'll probably be warned not to drive for several weeks.

Your healing scar

At first your scar just needs to be kept dry and well ventilated, and you can bathe once the dressing is removed. If the wound becomes red or inflamed, consult your doctor—there may be a slight infection that can be treated with antibiotics. Your scar will feel less sore gradually, but may itch as the pubic hair grows back. Since the scar is on your "bikini line," it's a good idea to wear underwear that come up to your waistline to avoid irritation.

Resuming sports

Even if you were taking part in regular sports activity before you were pregnant, it's best to avoid strenuous aerobic exercise for at least nine months after the birth. Your body has just completed nine months of extra work ending in the huge effort of labor, and needs time to recover. Avoid anything that puts a strain on your abdominal muscles, and don't resume working out at the gym until your doctor advises it. Ask a qualified fitness trainer or sports instructor to give you a graded program, take it very easy, but don't expect to be back to your previous level of fitness or stamina for at least a year.

▲ **GET OUT AND ABOUT** Simply taking your baby for a walk is a good way to get some exercise. Your baby will also enjoy the fresh air and change of scene.

Taking care of your body

Pregnancy and childbirth aren't illnesses, and your body is designed to recover naturally. However, this doesn't mean it couldn't do with a little help along the way.

Gone are the days when women were literally "confined" for several weeks But you do need to conserve your energy during the first few weeks after the birth to help the healing process and to enable you to get breastfeeding successfully established (see p. 78). The fat that is laid down in your body during pregnancy specifically to provide the calories for breastfeeding will take a few weeks to be used up, but many women are surprised to see how quickly they regain their pre-pregnancy shape and weight when they breastfeed.

Postpartum exercises

Losing weight isn't the same as regaining muscle tone; you'll need to exercise the muscles in your abdomen and perineum to bring them back to normal. But finding the time and energy to do postpartum exercises may seem like an impossible dream immediately after the birth.

Your abdominal muscles will have stretched and parted to accommodate your growing baby; this muscle tone can be regained if you find ten minutes a day to do the simple exercises suggested here and on pp. 68–69. And you can even do things like simple stretches and forward bends while your baby lies kicking on his play mat. Make sure you warm up properly first (see below).

Getting started

Start gently—your muscles and ligaments are still soft from the action of progesterone—and don't forget your pelvic floor muscles (see p. 38); just because you can't see them doesn't mean they aren't important.

Before you exercise

You can start the gentle program of exercises outlined here at any time after the birth, but avoid vigorous exercise until the lochia has stopped (see p. 64). And if you've had a tear or an episiotomy, don't do any stretching exercises until you've healed.

Warming up Athletes and dancers always warm up before exercise or performing, since they know the damage they could do to their bodies without it. It's equally important for you when doing postpartum exercises. Warming up helps relieve tension and warms up muscles and joints so that they don't overstretch when you begin more demanding exercises. It also helps to avoid cramps and stiffness afterwards.

If you've had a cesarean You can start doing pelvic floor exercises right away, but don't attempt any other exercises until you've had your postpartum appointment.

Taking care Don't exercise if you feel exhausted or unwell, and be careful if you've had back trouble. Avoid sit-ups or straight leg lifts and always stop doing an exercise if it hurts.

How to exercise

Little and often is best; start with one or two repetitions of each, every day, then progress to ten. Remember to exhale on the effort, and inhale as you relax. Always stop if any exercise hurts.

Cat arching

1 **KNEEL ON ALL FOURS** with knees and hands slightly apart. Make sure your back, head, and neck are straight.

2 **TIGHTEN YOUR BUTTOCKS** and slowly arch your back upward. Keep your arms straight, but don't lock your elbows. This exercise is wonderful for relieving lower backache.

Stomach toner

1 **LIE ON THE FLOOR**, with knees bent and arms straight by your sides. Pull in your stomach muscles and press the small of your back down. Hold the position for four seconds, then relax.

2 **KEEPING YOUR FEET FLAT**, tilt your pelvis up and lift your head off the pillow as far as you can. Don't try to sit up, it's enough just to lift your head and perhaps your shoulders.

Curl-ups (after two weeks)

1 **TRY THIS MORE ADVANCED** abdominal exercise at least two weeks after the birth. Lie down with your legs bent as before. Try to reach your knees by sliding your hands up your thighs.

2 **WITH YOUR HANDS** as close to your knees as possible, as you exhale, pull in your stomach muscles and lift your head for a count of four, then relax.

Leg lifts

1 **STRENGTHEN YOUR THIGHS AND ABDOMINAL** muscles with these simple lifts. Lie on your side comfortably, supporting your head with one hand, and balancing your body by resting the other hand in front of you. Make sure your legs are in line with your hip and shoulder.

2 **KEEPING YOUR KNEE AND FOOT** facing to the front, lift your whole leg straight upward to shoulder height, hold for a count of two, then lower. Do this a few times, then turn over and repeat with the other leg.

Side bends

STAND WITH YOUR FEET APART and arms by your sides. Slowly bend sideways at the waist, stretching your leg outward at the same time. Return to upright, and repeat on the other side.

Caring for your baby

The excitement of the birth is over, and now you're back home. But as new parents the chances are you'll feel daunted by the sheer work involved in the day-to-day care of your baby. There are practical details to think about, such as making sure you've got all the equipment and clothes you need, which diapers to use, and how to keep your baby clean. And then there are the more serious questions like how to get breastfeeding established, how to pacify your crying baby, and how to cope with broken nights. As time passes, you'll get to know your baby and her needs will become easier to predict and cater to. It will still be hard work, but if you share the joys and burdens equally, you'll find the pleasure of watching your baby grow and develop makes it all worthwhile.

The first weeks

Your baby's first few months of life would be tiring for you even if you hadn't been through the rigors of labor and birth. Spoil yourself and look after your own needs.

How to be kind to yourself

✳ Rest with your baby. Use the time when your baby is asleep to catch up on your own sleep. If he has his longest unbroken sleep in the morning, take advantage of it, or rest in the afternoon when he does.

✳ Share with your partner. If stress is piling up, he needs to know, for your sake and for your baby's. Encourage him to take care of the baby when he's at home; don't be overprotective and try to do everything yourself.

✳ Ask for help. If you're feeling isolated, don't soldier on alone. Early offers of help may tail off because friends and family don't want to impose, but often they are glad to be asked.

✳ Get out (see p. 134). Being tied to the house can make you depressed, so try to take outings as much as possible. It's helpful if you have friends locally who are also at home with young babies. You'll probably have met like-minded parents at prenatal classes. Having other new parents around you means you can share the good times as well as the worries. In addition, as your baby grows, he'll have a ready-made circle of friends to play with.

After all the months of preparation and the excitement of the birth, you're back home and at last you're a family. Now you can get down to the serious business of learning how to care for your child as he grows and develops from a small, vulnerable baby to a social, communicative one-year-old. It's immensely rewarding, but there's a lot to do and it's a full-time commitment from the start.

Finding a pattern

When you become a new parent, perhaps the most difficult thing to adjust to is the fluidity and unpredictability of your new lifestyle. Most people's lives have very distinct patterns, based on doing roughly the same things at roughly the same times, and they feel discomforted if this structure dissolves. Alternatively, you might be used to doing what you want exactly when you want to do it. But trying to impose this sort of orderliness on a young baby is the equivalent of spitting into the wind. If you can both relax and follow your baby's lead, you'll find that a pattern of some sort will eventually emerge.

Following your baby's lead

Ignore anyone who tells you that you shouldn't pick up your crying baby because "he's only exercising his lungs" or "he'll cry himself back to sleep in a minute"—very young babies shouldn't have to wait. If a baby learns that he has to scream for ten minutes to receive attention, he is laying down a pattern of behavior that you will not appreciate in the future. So-called "good" babies are either those who are contented because all their needs are met promptly, or those who have been taught by experience that their needs won't be met at once and have become apathetic. You cannot "spoil" a young baby except by imposing a regime that is governed by the clock—and by placing your needs before his. This is what will lead to him becoming discontented and hard to pacify. Helping him to separate his needs from others' needs will come much later on in his development.

Changing your priorities

If you're both following your baby's lead, you'll have to learn to be as relaxed as possible about things like meal times and housework, even if you normally have a set routine and an organized home. It's much more important for both of you to concentrate on becoming skilled and confident in the practical care of your baby. Initially, there may seem to be a lot to learn, and you'll feel clumsy and nervous (everybody does), but you'll soon find that it becomes second nature, and you'll gradually develop a routine that allows you time to fit in household chores at some point in your day.

If you feel low

If either or both of you feels disillusioned or dissatisfied with what you imagined you would be experiencing at this time, you're not necessarily depressed, you're probably just out of sorts. This is natural—you're both tired. If the baby is fractious, a mother may feel that somehow it is her fault and she may also be suffering from the "baby blues" (see p. 132), while a new father may feel inadequate if he's unable to help as much as he'd like, because he's at work. Don't worry, you'll both soon begin to adjust to the new situation, but if negative feelings persist, talk to your doctor or health visitor. They'll help you to see that lots of people feel the same way, but will also be able to tell if you're suffering from the signs of actual postpartum depression, which is easy to treat if recognized early (see p. 133).

Reassure each other

If you both start out in the knowledge that these first few months can seem like hard work, you'll be able to reassure each other that you're coping well. If you accept the validity of each other's feelings, and hold on to the fact that any difficulties are temporary, you'll discover that parenthood really is as pleasurable as you expected.

JUST FOR DAD

The first few weeks with your baby are important in helping you get used to your new role as a father.

How you can help

✳ Support your partner. At first, she will be very tired as a result of going through labor and birth, and then from the physical and emotional responsibility of breastfeeding. Provide her with the time and space to meet your baby's nutritional needs, and reassure her constantly that she's doing a difficult job well. Your support can make all the difference.

✳ Find time to help. If you're back at work, relish the opportunity to do as much as you can for your partner and your baby when you're at home.

✳ Give your baby love. Babies need as much love as they can get, and there's no difference between the love of a father and a mother. If your baby is being breastfed, then obviously he'll need his mother when he's hungry, but at all other times he'll benefit just as much from your closeness and attention. This closeness from you will mean that your baby learns to be secure with both of you, which will help him to settle down and take the pressure off your partner.

✳ Build a relationship with your baby from the start. Your own feelings as a parent will be strengthened if you spend as much time as possible with him. Being an equal partner in your baby's care will be rewarding and beneficial to you and to your family.

✳ Coping with the night shift

What to do	How it helps
Prepare yourselves for broken nights	Many babies continue to wake once or twice during the night well beyond 12 months of age. If you're both prepared for this, you'll find it much easier to adjust.
Share the burden	Taking turns to get up is important. You may have followed the traditional pattern of father going to work, while mother stays at home, but remember, looking after a baby is also a full-time job.
Change your sleep pattern	Broken nights are not necessarily sleepless nights. By developing a new sleep pattern, you'll find that you're able to wake, attend to your baby, and then go back to sleep immediately.
Keep your baby close	If your baby's crib is by the side of your bed, you don't have to disturb yourselves too much when he wakes to nurse. Put him back in his crib when you're ready to go back to sleep (see p. 102).
Stay together	Sleeping separately could undermine your relationship as a couple. Only sleep in separate rooms as a last resort—for example, because of illness or extreme fatigue.
Avoid sleep deprivation	Long-term sleep deprivation can have serious consequences, so it's better that you both lose some sleep than for one parent alone to take all the burden and become completely exhausted.

Equipment

Safety measures

Before your baby becomes mobile, be sure you have the following safety devices to keep him safe:

✳ Covers for all electrical sockets.

✳ Corner protectors for furniture.

✳ Locks and catches for video and DVD players, doors, cupboards, and drawers (especially in the kitchen), and the refrigerator.

✳ A stove guard.

✳ Retractable cords for electrical goods, such as the coffee maker, iron, and toaster.

✳ A gate at the bottom of stairs and across the kitchen door.

Providing for your new baby is exciting and rewarding, and you naturally want the best. However, as you set out to plan the nursery, bear in mind that at first your new arrival will need very little in the way of essentials.

The basics

Manufacturers of nursery "hardware" have recognized that couples expecting their first child are among the biggest spenders around, but you don't need to break the bank to provide for your newborn baby if you stick to the basics shown here.

▶ **HIGH CHAIR** Choose a high chair that allows your baby to sit at the table with the rest of the family. Some high chairs have adjustable seats and footrests so that they can be used when your child is older..

▲ **BABY BATH** For use in the first three to four months, a flat-based bath comes with a stand or can be rested on a firm surface; others fit over the big bath.

▲ **CHANGING MAT** A comfortable and practical changing mat helps avoid mess when changing diapers and at bath time.

BABY CHAIR A rigid or bouncing baby chair with back support is useful for young babies before they can sit. Always place the chair on the floor.

▲ **FULL-SIZE CRIB** When your baby outgrows her bassinet, you'll need a crib. Choose one with two mattress positions and a drop-side to protect your back when lifting her.

◀ **BASSINET** A bassinet is as useful for a newborn as it is portable. You can make linings and trimmings yourself. You can use a sleep sack instead of bedding, but make sure it's the right size.

BABY CARRIERS There are several types of carriers suitable for young babies; try them on to see which is most comfortable. A backpack may be more comfortable once your baby can sit up.

Out and about

Your baby may not walk until he's at least a year old, and even then he'll need to be transporting in a stroller or car seat for safety. Still, it's worth looking ahead to future needs when you're thinking about buying any of these larger, more expensive items.

▲ **INFANT CAR SEAT** All babies under 22 lbs (10 kg) should be put in a rear-facing safety seat in the car. The seat must be fixed in position. Your baby is always safest in the rear seat. Rear-facing seats provide better protection for a young baby's head, neck, and spine.

◄ **STROLLER** A stroller with a bassinet attachment is ideal. Check ease of folding, and that the height of the handle doesn't make you stoop. The bassinet is used until your baby can sit up by himself (around six months). The seat attachment makes the stroller suitable for older babies.

Buying secondhand

If there's a secondhand shop in your area, it's well worth a visit. You can also try shopping at charity shops, yard sales, and internet sites. Check all equipment carefully, and avoid certain items (see below).

Good secondhand buys

✳ Clothes, especially newborn baby clothes and outerwear.

✳ Bedsheets (except comforters), but always wash before use.

✳ Bassinet, but you may want to buy a new mattress.

✳ Plastic or wooden toys, but check carefully for cracks or splinters. Avoid anything that has metal or moving parts; even soft toys or dolls may contain hidden metal parts.

✳ Large plastic items, such as sterilizing equipment.

Possible secondhand buys

✳ Stroller, but check brakes, folding mechanism, and all accessories.

✳ Crib, but check drop-side mechanism is safe, and you may also want to buy a new mattress.

✳ Travel crib, though always check the folding mechanism and carrying case. Buy a new mattress if necessary.

✳ High chair, but make sure that all screws are really secure and check crevices for food remains.

✳ Safety items, such as baby monitors or gates, but check that they work properly.

Bad secondhand buy

✳ Never buy a secondhand car seat, as the seat may have been weakened in an accident.

Breastfeeding

Breastmilk is the most suitable food for your baby, providing all her nutritional needs during her first six months. As a father, you can be involved by supporting your partner.

Advantages of breastfeeding

Here are some of the many advantages of breastfeeding.

✳ Baby and mother bond closely.

✳ Helps burn off fat laid down in a mother's body during pregnancy.

✳ Milk is readily available, sterile, and is the correct temperature.

✳ Milk is easy for a baby to digest.

✳ Milk has a perfect balance of protein, carbohydrate, fat, salt, and other minerals, vitamins, and iron.

✳ Milk protects against infection.

✳ Milk may protect against allergies.

✳ Breastfed babies have fewer diaper rashes, and their stools are softer and sweet-smelling.

Getting started

You don't need any special equipment, but you will need two or three nursing bras and some nursing pads. Some people have no difficulty with breastfeeding; but for many others it doesn't go smoothly at first. Don't give up: Follow my step-by-step guide (see p. 80) and discuss any problems with your obstetrician, pediatrician, midwife, or lactation consultant, who will be happy to give advice. Remember, your baby is learning too, so you have to be patient.

Ensuring a good milk supply

When your baby nurses, the milk she drinks first—the foremilk—is thin, watery, and thirst-quenching; the hindmilk that follows is richer in fat and protein, so your baby gets all her nutritional needs at one feeding. To ensure that you provide a good milk supply, make sure you are eating a good diet and drinking lots of fluids, especially in hot weather when your baby will be thirsty too. Feed on demand, when your baby is hungry; your body will automatically produce enough. If your baby nurses slowly in the

▶ **SITTING IN A CHAIR** Sit with both feet firmly on the ground. Support your back and arms with pillows and place an extra pillow on your lap to raise and support your baby if necessary.

first few days, you may have to express milk (see p. 83) in order for more to be produced. If she nurses often, you will keep pace, no matter how small your breasts are; breast size is irrelevant to the amount of milk you make. However, it is important to rest between feedings so your metabolism can catch up. Many women find nursing in the mid-evening most difficult; milk supply is often lower because they are tired, and so the baby may be fretful at this time of day. Try to rest in the afternoon, prepare an evening meal earlier in the day, or better still, leave the cooking to your partner.

Frequency of feedings

Be prepared to nurse often—your baby could eat 10 or 11 times in 24 hours for the first few weeks. Nursing will take over your life in the beginning, but you'll find that your baby is contented, goes to sleep easily, and by the time she's six to eight weeks, she'll be nursing more efficiently and less often. Don't try to impose a rigid routine—your baby will get upset and the stress will affect your ability to nurse. During the first few weeks, use alternate breasts each time you nurse. This helps to balance the milk supply and prevent soreness in either breast. Many babies find one side easier than the other; if this happens with your baby, put her to the less favored breast first.

Breastfeeding positions

It's important to be in a comfortable position before you start feeding, since you're likely to be there for some time. Make sure you have a glass of water with you, too. Whatever your position, make sure your baby's whole body is angled toward you; she'll be more likely to latch on well the first time. Lying down is ideal for night feedings; when your baby is very small you may need to lay her on a pillow so she can reach your nipple. You may also find the lying-down position the most suitable if you've had an episiotomy and sitting is uncomfortable. If you've had a cesarean section and your stomach is still tender, try tucking your baby's feet under your arm.

The "let-down" reflex

When your baby suckles at your breast, she needs to latch on properly with her gums firmly gripping the areola and the nipple so far into her mouth that the milk can be squeezed right into her throat for her to swallow. As she sucks, nerves in the areola stimulate the hypothalamus in your brain, which in turn stimulates the pituitary gland to secrete oxytocin. This causes the breast to release (or "let down") milk.

▼ **NURSING WHILE LYING DOWN** This is a good position when you're tired or if you need to keep your baby's weight off a cesarean wound. Lie down on your side and lay your baby next to you so she can reach your lower breast.

Latching on

1 **SUPPORT YOUR BABY** along the length of his back with your arm. Support the back of his neck and bring him up to your breast. Line up your nipple with your baby's nose. As soon as he smells your milk, he'll open his mouth. While your baby is very young, you can gently stroke the cheek nearest the breast; when you do this, he'll turn towards your breast as a reflex action.

2 **YOUR BABY SHOULD** "latch on" to your nipple at once. If not, support your breast with your hand and guide him on to it so that he has a mouthful of nipple. Your breasts are stimulated to produce milk by your baby's sucking, so the more eagerly he feeds, the more milk your breasts will produce. You supply what your baby needs and you won't run out.

3 **RELEASING**—a breastfeeding baby creates a strong vacuum on the breast, so when he is finished, you may need to release his grip on the nipple by gently easing your little finger into the corner of his mouth. Never pull your nipple away from your baby; this is a sure way to make it sore, and sore nipples (see opposite) may deter you from breastfeeding.

Latching on

The key is getting your baby's mouth correctly fixed or latched on to your breast, with your nipple well inside his mouth. Your baby stimulates milk flow by pressing the tip of his tongue against your areola. Then he presses the back of his tongue up towards his palate to squeeze milk from your nipple into his throat.

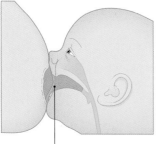

Baby's gums should encircle the areola.

Being determined

Few women breastfeed without encountering problems at least once, and sometimes several times. So while you shouldn't necessarily expect to find it difficult, neither should you be surprised if you seem to have a run of problems. The important thing to bear in mind is that most breastfeeding difficulties can be put right—provided you have support and the commitment and confidence to continue.

Taking care of your breasts

Your breasts need special care when you start breastfeeding. Buy at least two maternity bras—the best you can afford. A good bra will minimize discomfort if your breasts become sore. A few weeks before the birth, get advice from an in-store expert who will help you try some on. Look for a bra with front fastenings and wide straps that won't cut into your shoulders. Drop-front or zip-fastening bras are easy to undo with one hand while you hold your baby. Wear your bra all the time, even at night, as you'll need lots of support.

Take great care of your breasts and nipples. Bathe them every day with water—don't use soap because it dehydrates the skin and encourages sore or cracked nipples—and gently pat them dry. Dry them gently after nursing, too. If you can, leave your nipples open to the air for a while after nursing. Nursing pads and shields help you keep your nipples clean and dry, although not everyone finds them essential.

Concerns about breastfeeding

Your concern	What you can do
How long on each breast	Your baby takes 80 percent of the milk he will drink in the first five minutes; five minutes more and he's sucked out the creamy hindmilk. So as a rough guide, expect him to spend about 10 minutes at each breast. Breastfed babies are rarely underfed, although they may only nurse for a short time. Do not restrict breastfeeding. If your baby is feeding happily, allow him to take his time.
Slow feeding	Many babies take a few days to get the hang of latching on and may be slow to nurse. If this becomes a problem, seek advice. A baby who sucks for a long time isn't necessarily nursing the whole time. He may just love sucking. If your baby tends to fall asleep at the breast, let him take all he wants from one side, then offer the other breast first next time.
Baby's weight gain	Don't weigh your baby before and after feeding. Weight gain in breastfed babies should always be calculated over a two-to-three-week period, as weight is often gained unevenly. The very rare instances of underfeeding usually occur because the baby isn't properly latched on.
If you're ill	Common infections such as colds don't need to interrupt breastfeeding. Stay in bed and let your partner bring your baby to you just to nurse. You could also express milk so your partner can feed your baby instead. If you need medication of any sort, make sure your doctor knows you are breastfeeding, since some medicines are not recommended for breastfeeding mothers. If you go to the hospital, breastfeeding is usually still possible if you take your baby in with you.
Breastfeeding in public	Breastfeeding is the most convenient way to feed your baby, and you should be able to breastfeed any time, anywhere. It's possible to nurse discreetly if you use a nursing bra that undoes easily in front with one hand, and a big shawl or cardigan to screen yourself. A baggy T-shirt or sweatshirt also works—you can tuck your baby up underneath it.

Sore nipples

Painful nipples are the most common reason women give up breastfeeding. However, there are ways to avoid them. Make sure your baby is correctly positioned and properly latched on and never pull your baby off the nipple (see opposite). Keep your nipples dry with disposable or cotton washable nursing pads or clean cotton pads. Don't use tissues as they will fall apart. Let the nipples dry naturally after nursing whenever possible. If they become cracked, ointment such as a lanolin cream may be helpful. If your nipples become very sore, feed your baby before he is desperate as he will be calmer and treat you more gently. Try to get the milk flowing before nursing begins by expressing a little first.

Blocked ducts and mastitis

Tight clothing or engorgement can cause a blocked milk duct, resulting in a hard red patch on the outside of the breast where the duct lies. You can prevent this by nursing often and encouraging your baby to empty your breasts, and by making sure that your bra fits properly. A blocked duct can lead to an acute infection known as mastitis. The breast will be inflamed, and a red patch will appear on the outside, as with a blocked duct. Continue to breastfeed, because you need to empty the breast. Your doctor may prescribe antibiotics to clear up the infection.

▲ **NURSING AWAY FROM HOME** One of the advantages of breastfeeding is that it's possible to feed your baby at any time and anywhere.

JUST FOR DAD

Your support is essential.

What you can do to help

❋ Be gently encouraging.

❋ Don't leave your partner to feed the baby alone unless she asks you to—she could feel isolated, and you may feel neglected.

❋ Your partner may like to express milk that you can give in a bottle at night. Undo your shirt and hold your baby against your skin to mimic breastfeeding.

❋ Be aware that your partner's breasts may be tense, sore, and very sensitive to touch for the first few weeks of breastfeeding.

What if it's twins?

Don't be put off by people who say you can't breastfeed twins. Lots of mothers prove otherwise and, like all babies, twins benefit enormously from breastmilk. All the usual advantages of breastfeeding apply, but especially the protection against infection—it's important to twins because prematurity is more common with them than with single babies. It may be slightly more difficult to establish breastfeeding for twins, but once it's established you can feed them at the same time (though it's not as easy to feed both babies together when you're away from home).

Get advice Confidence is a crucial factor in breastfeeding twins. Try to talk to other mothers who've done it successfully—there are support groups to help you (see p. 187).

One at a time to start with Concentrate on latching on with one baby at a time at first. Feeding singly may be easier in the early days, and it gives you a chance to get to know each baby individually—each of them has the

▶ **FEEDING YOUR TWINS** Once breastfeeding is established, you can try feeding your babies together.

same need to bond with her parents. However, feeding one at a time does take much longer than feeding them together.

Feeding together To feed your babies at the same time, lay them on their backs, one under each arm, with their heads forward, supported on pillows.

There's plenty of milk Human breasts are quite capable of nourishing two babies. Breastfeeding is always controlled by demand, so your breasts will produce as much milk as your babies need. If one feeds more readily than the other, put the slower baby to the breast first; the stronger baby will stimulate more milk.

Look after yourself Eat heartily, drink a lot of fluids, and rest when you can. Although twins' practical needs are the same, there are two of them to care for, and you'll tire more easily. Accept any offers of help you get.

Expressing milk

When you're breastfeeding, you can express milk so that your partner can feed your baby; it also helps to relieve overfull breasts in the first days. If your baby is in a special care unit (see p. 62), you can express milk for her. Few women find expressing milk easy, so don't be disheartened—it's a knack. If you "leak" milk while feeding, place a breast shell against the other breast, and keep the milk in a sterile container.

Using a breast pump

You can express milk more quickly using a pump, which applies a rhythmical suction to the breast. A funnel is fitted over your areola, you then operate the lever or plunger to express the milk (see right). Electric pumps are more expensive than hand pumps, but they imitate the baby's sucking cycle more closely. An electric pump is best if you need to express often—for example, if you're going back to work before weaning. You can get pumps that allow you to express from both breasts at the same time.

▲ **USING A MANUAL PUMP** Start by fitting the funnel of the pump over your areola carefully to form an airtight seal. You then operate the lever or plunger of the pump to express your milk.

Expressing milk by hand

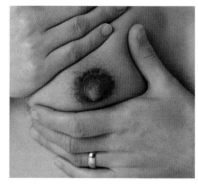

1 MASSAGE YOUR BREAST with flat hands, beginning at your ribs and working toward your areola, gradually going over the whole breast.

2 THEN ROLL YOUR fingers and thumb together below and above your areola so that you press on the wider milk ducts behind the nipple.

3 COLLECT THE MILK in a sterile bowl, transfer it to a sterile container, and keep it in the refrigerator for up to a day or two. Freeze it for longer storage.

Bottle-feeding

I'm not going to pretend that bottle-feeding is as good for your baby as breastfeeding, but I don't want you to feel guilty, either. If you're undecided, look back to the sections on breastfeeding so that you're aware of its positive advantages. Bottle-feeding does, however, mean that both of you can share all of your baby's care equally.

Sterilizing and preparing bottles

Hygiene and making up bottles correctly are important if you are bottle-feeding to avoid health problems with your baby. To ensure your baby thrives and to avoid infection:

✳ Buy equipment well in advance and practice cleaning and sterilizing bottles and nipples.

✳ Wash your hands thoroughly before handling bottles or feeding your baby.

✳ Always follow the manufacturer's instructions carefully when you are sterilizing bottles.

✳ If using a chemical sterilizer, bottles and nipples should be fully immersed in sterilizing fluid and left for at least two hours, or according to the manufacturer's instructions.

✳ With six or seven bottles to make in 24 hours for the first few weeks, change the sterilizing fluid twice a day. Later you can do this once a day.

✳ Make bottles one at a time; don't make them in advance and store them in the refrigerator.

✳ Never add extra scoops of formula, sugar, or baby cereal to a bottle.

✳ When a feed is over, pour out leftover milk, clean and rinse the bottle, cover it and place to one side until you are ready to sterilize it.

✳ Never give a baby leftover milk from an earlier bottle—it may be contaminated with bacteria.

✳ Keep a couple of cartons of ready-made formula for emergencies.

Feeding your baby

Either of you can bottle-feed your baby, but bottle-feeding really allows a father to come into his own. When you are giving your baby a bottle, you can mimic the closeness of breastfeeding by cradling him close in the crook of your arm. Hold him so his face is 8–10 inches (20–25 cm) away from yours, in a position where he can make eye contact with you (see p. 61). If possible, open your shirt and hold him against your bare skin.

Giving your baby a bottle

Before you start, check that the flow from the nipple is neither too fast nor too slow—before giving the bottle, invert it to make sure the nipple produces a flow of several drops per second. Your baby may break naturally for a burp halfway through the bottle, but it isn't necessary to force him to burp by rubbing his back; if he's still hungry, he'll just get upset. If he seems comfortable, let him keep going without a break until he's had enough.

BOTTLE-FEEDING YOUR BABY
Cradle your baby close enough to have eye contact throughout, and talk to her while you feed. She'll soon learn to associate the pleasure of feeding with the sight of your face.

Making up a bottle

✳ You will need

✱ Steam or chemical sterilizing unit

✱ Freshly boiled water

✱ Powdered formula
with measuring scoop

✱ Straight-backed knife
for leveling powdered formula

✱ Bottles, nipples, and covers

1 **FILL A BOTTLE** with freshly boiled water. Using the scoop provided, level the powder with the back of a knife.

2 **ADD THE SCOOPS OF FORMULA** to the boiled water. Add it one scoop at a time; never add extra.

✳ Keeping bottles clean

Scrupulous hygiene is essential when bottle-feeding. Milk can be a rich breeding ground for the bacteria that cause diseases such as gastroenteritis, so sterilize bottles, nipples, and all other equipment used for feeding until your baby is six months old. Clean bottles and nipples thoroughly as described below before sterilizing. Once your baby is over 12 months you can wash bottles in a dishwasher.

3 **MAKE SURE THAT YOU'VE ADDED** the right amount of formula. Put the nipple on the bottle.

4 **SHAKE THE BOTTLE** to make sure the formula mixes thoroughly. Cool the bottle in a bowl of cold water.

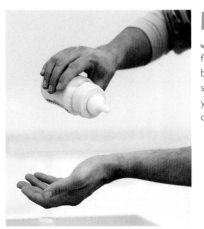

5 **CHECK THE TEMPERATURE** before offering your baby a bottle to be sure that the milk is not too hot. Shake a few drops on to your wrist. The milk should be blood temperature, which means it should feel neither hot nor cold against your skin. If necessary, put it back into the cold water to cool it down.

✱ Scrub bottles and nipples with a bottle brush and hot, soapy water to remove all traces of milk, then rinse well in cold water.

✱ Wash nipples thoroughly, making sure that the inside rim and holes are clear. Then rinse in cold water.

Your baby's diapers

Diaper rash

Diaper rash is preventable if you always change your baby's diaper promptly, particularly after she's had a bowel movement; bacteria in feces breaks down the urine to release ammonia, which can irritate and ulcerate the skin. Always keep your baby's skin clean and well aired. Use barrier cream as a preventive measure. If your baby develops a rash, leave her diaper off whenever possible and let her kick on her changing mat. Apply diaper cream at every change. Check with your doctor if the rash persists for more than two to three days.

You'll have to use diapers for at least two and a half years, until your baby gains full bladder and bowel control, so it's worth familiarizing yourself with the most efficient way to change your baby. Give some thought, too, to which type of diaper best suits your circumstances—there's certainly plenty of choice nowadays.

Which diapers to use

Your first choice in diapers will be between cloth and disposable types. Many parents prefer disposables, although an increasing debate on environmental issues has led more parents to consider cloth diapers. Yet the issue is not clear cut: the detergents required to clean cloth diapers can be viewed as pollutants to the water supply, and the energy required to wash them might also be regarded as wasteful. You need to consider the increased electricity bills for frequent washing and the cost in your time, although there are diaper-laundering services in many areas. Another option is to use "green" disposable diapers, which are produced with fewer chemicals, biodegrade, and have less of an impact on the environment.

Diapers, liners, and fasteners

Here is a selection of diapers. Provided your baby is changed as often as necessary, she will be happy in whatever style you choose.

Disposable diapers

Plastic covers

Shaped cloth diaper

Cloth diaper with Velcro fastener

Cloth liner

Liners and safety pins

Cloth diapers

Traditional cloth diapers are bulky, and can be uncomfortable for your baby when she's mobile. Modern types are usually shaped, and many have strong Velcro fastenings or snaps, or you could use pinless fasteners, so you don't have to worry about using safety pins. If you're using these diapers, it's a good idea to also use disposable or reusable liners (see box left) to avoid heavy soiling with feces.

Diapers for boys or girls

Some manufacturers of disposables have taken the differences between the sexes into account: boys tend to wet the front of their diapers, so boys' disposables have extra padding in the front. Girls tend to wet the back of diapers more, and this is also accounted for in the design of girls' disposables.

Cleaning your baby

Change your baby's diaper whenever you notice that it is soiled or wet. The number of times the diaper needs to be changed will vary from baby to baby and from day to day.

Cleaning girls

Always clean your baby's vulva and anus from front to back to avoid spreading bacteria from the anus to your baby's vagina. Don't clean inside the labia; just rinse away feces gently with a damp cotton ball.

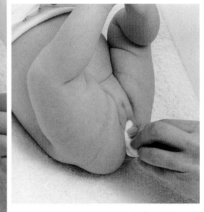

1 **LIFT YOUR BABY'S LEGS** by holding her feet or ankles. Use a cotton ball or baby wipes to clean the labia on the outside only.

2 **USE A CLEAN** cotton ball or baby wipe to clean the vulva, wiping from front to back.

Cleaning boys

Cover a boy's penis with a tissue as you take off his diaper in case he passes urine. Clean around the penis and scrotum with a damp cotton ball. Don't try to pull back the foreskin, since it remains fixed until your son is much older.

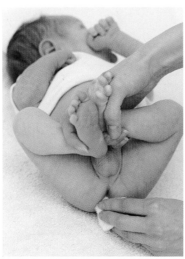

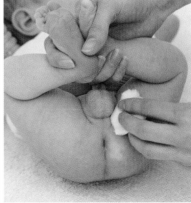

1 **LIFT HIS LEGS** by holding both ankles as shown. Clean around genital area with water, making sure you use a new cotton ball each time you wipe.

2 **MAKE SURE ALL** soiling is removed. Work from the leg creases in toward the penis.

Changing your baby's diaper

Always change your baby on a firm, flat surface, covered with a changing mat or towel. Protect your back by using a changing table of the correct height, or kneel beside the bed. Never leave your baby alone on the changing mat if it's on a surface above floor level. Even a newborn baby can wriggle off a mat, particularly if he's upset or angry. Collect all the equipment you need before you start. Dispose of feces in the toilet if possible; but don't flush disposable diapers or cloth-diaper liners down the toilet. Put dirty diapers in diaper sacks (and preferably in a covered trash can) or in a diaper pail.

You will need

* Changing mat
* Tissues
* Clean diaper
* Bowl of warm water
* Cotton balls or baby wipes
* Barrier cream
* Diaper sacks or a diaper pail

1 **REMOVE THE SOILED DIAPER** and clean carefully as shown on p. 87. Make sure all creases are clean and dry if you used water to clean. Slide the clean diaper under your baby, lifting her buttocks gently into position.

2 **USING BOTH HANDS**, bring the front of the diaper up between your baby's legs, as high as it will go. Tuck in the corners securely around her waist, ready for fastening.

3 **HOLDING THE DIAPER** in place with one hand, fix the adhesive tabs firmly onto the front flap.

Changing a cloth diaper

The technique for changing cloth diapers is the same as for disposables, but there are a few more layers to deal with. You need to soak dirty diapers in a bucket of water containing diaper solution before you wash them.

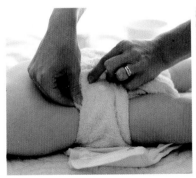

1 **CLEAN YOUR BABY CAREFULLY** as decribed on p. 87. Put a clean liner inside the main diaper. Slide the prepared diaper and the waterproof outer wrap under your baby's bottom. Bring the front of the diaper up as far as it will go and secure it using the fastenings.

2 **PULL THE OUTER WRAP** up over the main diaper and secure it with the snaps. Make sure it is comfortable and that the outer wrap fits snuggly over the diaper to prevent leaks.

▶ **FREE TO MOVE** Shaped cloth diapers are far less bulky than traditional cloth diapers. Your baby will be just as comfortable when she is crawling and learning to to walk as she would be in disposable diapers.

Keeping your baby clean

Bathing tips

To bathe your baby as quickly and as safely as possible:

* **Wash or bathe her** in a room that is warm and draft-free; it doesn't have to be the bathroom. Use a bucket or bowl to carry the water and to fill and empty the bath.

* **If you use a sponge** and washcloth, make sure they are reserved strictly for your baby's use and wash them frequently.

* **Never poke around** inside your baby's ears with a cotton swab—you could easily damage her delicate eardrum. Only remove ear wax that is visible at the opening.

Very young babies don't get dirty, so they don't need frequent bathing—but bath time provides an opportunity for cuddling and playing that infants come to relish. It also gives fathers a chance to spend time with their babies. Later, bath time will become part of your baby's bedtime routine, a signal that it's time to wind down.

While your baby is young

Many parents are understandably nervous about bathing their newborn baby while she's still tiny and seems so vulnerable. It is, however, worth remembering that a baby is quite resilient provided she's handled gently but firmly, so try to be as confident as possible. You'll be shown the safest and easiest methods for bathing your baby in the days after delivery by a nurse or midwife at the hospital. As with all aspects of caring for your baby, bathing her will soon become second nature once you've given yourselves time to get used to it. The first few times, your baby may get distressed when she's being bathed, so don't feel you have to bathe her every day. Thorough cleansing using the "topping and tailing" method outlined below and opposite will be sufficient.

Topping and tailing

"Topping and tailing" means cleaning your baby thoroughly by washing her face, hands, and diaper area, without undressing her completely. You can do this most days as part of your baby's diaper-changing and dressing routine, and then just give her a bath every two or three days. This will save you time and is less distressing for your baby.

1 UNDRESS YOUR BABY on a changing mat or towel. Leave her undershirt on, or wrap her in a towel. Gently wipe her face, ears, and neck folds with cotton balls moistened with warm water. Pat her dry, making sure that you have dried thoroughly between her neck folds.

2 **TAKE TWO MORE CLEAN** cotton balls and moisten them with water. Using separate cotton balls for each stroke, to avoid the risk of cross infection, carefully wipe your baby's eyes from the inner corners outward.

3 **USE ANOTHER COTTON BALL** moistened with water to clean her hands and feet. Dry them with a towel.

You will need

✻ **Cotton balls** for face, eyes, and diaper area

✻ **Clean water** for washing the eyes

✻ **Bowl of warm water** for washing face and body

✻ **Soft towel** for wrapping and drying

✻ **Diaper-changing equipment** (see p. 88)

✻ **Clean clothes**

4 **TAKE OFF HER DIAPER** and clean the diaper area (see p. 86), then wipe with cotton balls moistened with warm water, especially around the folds in your baby's thighs. Wash the genital area front to back. Pat dry and put on a fresh diaper, then dress her in clean clothes.

Bathing your baby

Choose a bath time that suits you and your baby; it doesn't always have to be in the evening, especially if your baby tends to be fretful at that time of day. However, if you're working parents, bathing your baby in the evening is often a good way for you to spend time with him; you can even have a bath with him when he's older (see p. 95) to make it more fun! Make sure you've got all of the items you need within easy reach before you start.

1 **UNDRESS YOUR BABY** down to his undershirt and wash his face and neck. Remove his undershirt and wrap him firmly in a towel. Holding him under your arm and supporting his head over the bath, gently wash and rinse his hair with bathwater. Pat his hair dry with a towel.

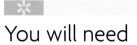

You will need

* Baby wash

* Two towels

* Cotton balls for face, eyes, and diaper area

* Clean water

* Diaper-changing equipment (see p. 88)

* Clean clothes

2 **LEAVE A DRY TOWEL** ready for after the bath. Unwrap the first towel, remove the diaper, and lift your baby into the bath, supporting his head and shoulders firmly with one hand, and his bottom and legs with your other hand.

3 **SUPPORTING YOUR BABY'S HEAD** and upper body with one arm, gently wash his body with your free hand, and encourage him to kick and splash.

4 **TO LIFT YOUR BABY** out of the bath, support his head and shoulders with one hand, and slide your free hand under his bottom. Lift him out of the bath and on to the dry towel. Wrap him up immediately so he doesn't get cold. Pat him dry all over, paying particular attention to the folds of his neck, bottom, thighs, and underarms, then put on his diaper and dress him.

Bathing an older baby

Once your baby is three to four months old and has good head control, you could start using the big bath. Once she has gotten used to it, she will appreciate the extra room to play in the water. The same principles apply—keep your baby warm before and after the bath, don't overfill the bath, and check that the water isn't too hot before you put her in.

Safety first

When you use the big bath, bear in mind that your baby could drown in just an inch of water (see p. 123). Take the following precautions to avoid accidents:

✻ Put all equipment on the floor beside the bath and change your baby there. It's safer than carrying a wet slippery baby to a changing table.

✻ Put a non-slip mat in the bath.

✻ Kneel on the floor to support your baby, and to prevent straining your back.

✻ Never leave your baby alone in the bath, even if she can sit up.

You will need

✻ Non-slip bath mat

✻ Sponge or washcloth

✻ Baby wash and shampoo

✻ Towel

✻ Diaper and clean clothes

✻ Face shield can also be useful to protect her eyes from shampoo

Using the big bath

Making the transition from the baby bath to the big bath can cause some babies distress, while others love it. It's a good idea to begin by putting the baby bath into the big bath the first few times so that the change is gradual and less frightening. Once your baby has gotten used to it and can sit up in the bath by herself, she'll begin to look forward to it as part of her routine, and enjoy bath-time games and play (see opposite). You'll find bath time can become a riotous affair with lots of shouts and splashing, but the problems may come when you want to get her out! It's advisable to make bath time a part of your baby's overall bedtime routine (see p. 103) so that it acts as a clear signal to her that the day is over.

Having fun at bath time

Older babies really enjoy bath time, and it's an excellent time to catch up on your baby's developing personality and skills if you aren't able to be with her during the day. Bath time is a wonderful opportunity for creative play, and you can use it to help stimulate her development in a variety of ways. Babies love the freedom to sit in the warm water and you'll find that your baby will be endlessly fascinated by filling things, pouring, and splashing

BATH-TIME SAFETY Give your baby toys that float to play with in her bath. But, however much she is enjoying playing, watch her all the time; don't leave her on her own, even for a second.

Giving your baby a towel bath

Cleaning your baby by towel bathing her is midway between topping and tailing (see p. 90) and a real bath. It's useful if your baby isn't feeling well or if she doesn't like having a bath. As it's much quicker, so it's useful for those times when she needs a bath, but you're short on time.

1 **TOP HALF** Collect the same equipment as for topping and tailing (see p. 90). Undress her to her diaper and wrap her lower half in a towel. Wash her face, neck, and upper body and pat dry.

2 **LOWER HALF** Put a clean undershirt on your baby. Remove the diaper. Wash her legs and feet, followed by her diaper area. Dry her thoroughly, then put on a clean diaper and clothes.

water. This really is learning through play—your baby is finding out about the properties of water and other liquids. Help your baby to do this by:
* Using household items like plastic cups, spoons, and sieves to show her what holds water and what doesn't, and how it can be poured and stirred.
* Introducing floating toys such as boats or traditional bath ducks that your baby will enjoy handling.
* Having fun with your baby by taking her into the bath with you; have a skin-to-skin soak together. Keep the water at an even temperature with a slow trickle from the tap.

Hair-washing

Even though your baby may love her bath, hair-washing can be difficult if she hates having water poured onto her head or over her face, especially if it goes in her eyes. Don't worry; this is very common. Take your time to get your baby used to water on her head and face; make it into a game by dripping tiny amounts over her head from time to time. Until she's more confident, you can just sponge her hair clean or wipe it with a washcloth.

Some babies love having water on their faces and don't even mind it in their eyes. If your baby likes water, use a shower attachment or a cup to rinse her hair and have fun with it. But even mild baby shampoo will sting your baby's eyes a little. Use a face shield to keep the soap and water out of her eyes until she's old enough to keep them shut or to hold her head back for you. Towel-dry her hair and brush it with a soft brush.

✳ JUST FOR DAD

Your baby will grow to love bath time, particularly if it is her special time with you. Encourage this bonding by handling her with confidence; the more often you do it, the less nervous she (and you) will be. Giving a bath is a positive way of contributing to your baby's care, and it helps her to see that you're an equal partner in her life with her mother.

Make the most of bath time

✳ When you take a bath with your baby, lay her on your chest half in and half out of the water. Smile and talk to her as you wash her.

✳ Splash water gently over her body, carefully avoiding her face. This way your baby will learn to enjoy, and be unafraid of, water.

✳ Allow plenty of time; a bath is not much fun for either of you if you have to rush. Remember, sharing a bath with your baby is also a good and enjoyable way for you to wind down after a stressful day at work.

Dressing your baby

Choosing clothes

Look for clothes that are simple to put on and take off, and quick to wash and dry:

✳ Choose roomy garments, with loose elastic at the cuffs.

✳ Snaps are better than buttons. Avoid ribbons as they may be difficult to undo.

✳ Avoid pure wool, which may irritate skin. Choose non-irritating fabrics, such as cotton.

✳ Only get machine-washable, color-fast clothing.

✳ Always look for labels that indicate clothes are non-flammable.

✳ Clothes can safely be bought secondhand, but check for inflammability, shrinkage, and the condition of snaps and buttons.

✳ Nightgowns are quick to put on and allow easy access to the diaper.

✳ Buy adequate protective clothing to avoid sun damage (see p. 118).

Babies grow out of clothes very quickly in the early months so don't spend a lot of money on newborn-size babywear. Many of the presents you will be given for your baby will be tiny outfits that will only fit your child for the first few weeks, so you should concentrate on buying a few practical, simple items for the first four months.

How to dress and undress your baby

Many parents are nervous about dressing their very young baby, particularly when it involves handling his "wobbly" head with its soft fontanelle (see p. 55). Lay him down on his back on a changing mat or towel to dress and undress him; it's safer and you'll both feel more secure. Although your baby doesn't know day from night, nightgowns may be easier to use when he's tiny.

Putting on your baby's undershirt

Undershirts may be the most awkward items of clothing to put on a tiny baby because they have to be put on over his head, which is the biggest yet least manageable part of his body. Most undershirts are now designed with wide, "envelope" necks or shoulder snaps to make them easier to slide over his head. By the time your baby is three or four months old, he will have developed some head control, and you can safely dress and undress him on your lap, if you haven't had the confidence to do so previously.

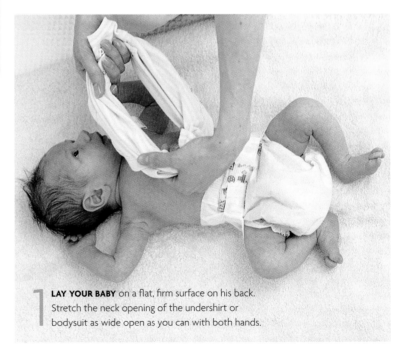

1 **LAY YOUR BABY** on a flat, firm surface on his back. Stretch the neck opening of the undershirt or bodysuit as wide open as you can with both hands.

2 **SLIDE THE UNDERSHIRT** over your baby's head, gently lifting his head up to bring it over to the back of his neck.

3 **WIDEN EACH SLEEVE** or armhole with your fingers and bring your baby's arms through, fist first, one at a time. Draw the shirt down over his body.

You will need

Basics for a new baby
* 6–8 undershirts or bodysuits

* 6–8 stretchsuits

* 2–3 sweaters or cardigans

* 2–3 pairs of socks

* Blanket or shawl

Useful extras
* 2 pairs of scratch mittens

* 2 nightdresses

* All-in-one outer suit for a winter baby or protective clothing and a sunhat for a summer baby

Practical clothes for older babies

Once your baby is sitting up, and especially when she becomes mobile, clothes have to be robust and comfortable, as well as machine-washable. Look for:

✻ Bigger sizes, especially with outdoor clothes, so movement isn't restricted and she doesn't grow out of them too quickly.

✻ Clothes that have easy access to the diaper area, such as overalls or one-piece suits with snaps, or tights.

✻ Lightweight clothing to protect your baby's skin from the sun. Use a wide-brimmed sunhat and shirts with sleeves and collars.

✻ Soft boots or socks with non-slip soles for when she starts to pull herself up to stand.

Putting on a stretchsuit

Stretchsuits and one-piece pajamas are very practical and economical items of clothing for you to buy for your baby. They're particularly useful at first because they allow freedom of movement, easy access to the diaper area, keep your baby warm, but not too hot, and they are simple to put on even the tiniest baby. They are ideal for all-day use for the first three to four months and can also be used as sleepwear when your baby is older. To put on a stretchsuit, follow the steps illustrated here; to take it off, reverse all the steps, beginning by undoing all the snaps.

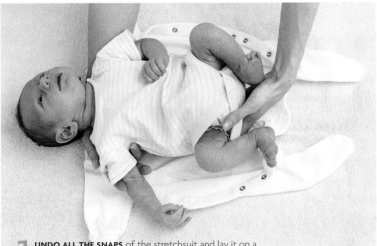

1 **UNDO ALL THE SNAPS** of the stretchsuit and lay it on a flat surface. Then, lay your baby on top of the suit so that her neck lines up with the neck of the suit.

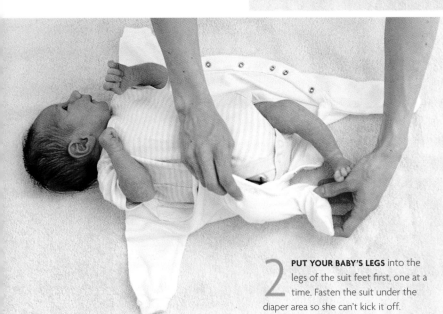

2 **PUT YOUR BABY'S LEGS** into the legs of the suit feet first, one at a time. Fasten the suit under the diaper area so she can't kick it off.

3 **TO PUT HER ARMS** in, roll back one arm of the stretchsuit, holding it open with one hand. Then guide your baby's arm, fist first, into the arm of the suit and roll the sleeve down into place. Repeat with the other arm and fasten the rest of the snaps.

DRESSING OLDER BABIES Once your baby can sit up, you'll find she's a lot easier to dress. But she may also wriggle and protest when you want to put on her clothes, so hold her firmly while you dress her. You could make a game of it to keep her occupied.

When your baby sleeps

✳ JUST FOR MOM

If you're always struggling to get your baby to sleep, ask yourself why.

Does your baby need to sleep?
Trying to get your baby to sleep when he doesn't need to is pointless. If he's longing for your company, talk and play with him instead, or put him in a baby seat so he can watch you. Research has shown that even young babies are receptive to interaction with their parents, and with increased stimulation, your baby is more likely to sleep more soundly and for longer.

You need rest too
You may become overwrought from lack of sleep. Being over-tired builds resentment and makes you irritable and liable to lose perspective. If you're exhausted, express milk (see p. 83) so your partner can handle nighttime feeds for a couple of days.

✳ You will need

For the first three months:

✳ 4 small crib blankets
cotton is better than wool

✳ 6 flat cotton top sheets

✳ 6 fitted cotton mattress sheets

✳ Spare mattress (optional)

✳ Portable bassinet, cradle, or carrier (see p. 75)

Young babies spend up to 14 hours of any 24-hour period asleep. Unfortunately, this doesn't often coincide with their parents' sleeping pattern, because it takes a few months for babies to learn the difference between night and day.

How babies sleep

The way babies fall asleep differs from adults; adults can crash suddenly, whereas babies sleep lightly for about 20 minutes, then go through a transitional stage before reaching deep sleep. Nothing will wake them until they've had enough sleep. This means that babies who are simply "put down" will not necessarily go to sleep peacefully. You may need to nurse your baby to sleep for quite a while, so try to be patient, particularly at night, when you're longing to go back to bed yourself.

Where should a baby sleep?

Where a baby sleeps isn't important to him at the beginning. He won't automatically fall asleep when put into a darkened bedroom; light doesn't bother him at all. He's much more likely to be disturbed by being too hot or too cold. Your baby will be happiest going to sleep hearing your voices and the household noises that he is used to in the background, so let him sleep in a bassinet or carrier in whichever room you happen to be.

Using a baby monitor

If you leave your baby in another room, set up a baby monitor so that you can hear him as soon as he wakes. He may feel disturbed by the silence when you leave the room, and this could make him more fretful; leave the door open so he can hear you moving around—unless you have a cat that may climb into the crib. Avoid going back into the room once your baby is asleep; your smell could wake him, so resist the temptation to check on him too frequently.

Encouraging longer sleeps at night

A young baby needs food at regular intervals, so he'll wake to nurse when his body tells him to. The way to encourage your baby to sleep for a stretch (four, then rising to five or six, hours) during the night is to make sure he's taken in sufficient calories to last that long. This means feeding him whenever he shows he's hungry during the day. As he steadily gains weight, he can go longer between feedings and by about six weeks he could be sleeping for at least one period of about six hours—hopefully during the night. When he wakes for a night feeding, make as little fuss as possible— feed him in bed; if he needs changing, do it quickly in a dim light. Don't make this a time for chatting and games and he'll learn that waking at night doesn't bring any special privileges.

▲ **USE A BASSINET** While your baby is very young, put him to bed in a bassinet or carrier. You can then put the basket in the room with you while he sleeps.

Rescue package for a sleepless baby

Night after night of broken sleep is wearing for parents, and a young baby who perhaps only "catnaps" during the day makes it hard to catch up. Use this checklist of strategies to reduce unnecessary fatigue.

Be aware of background noise Don't shield your baby from the sounds of your home. They won't disturb his sleep; in fact some babies are soothed by the rhythmic noise of household appliances!

Keep him close to you At night, put your baby's bassinet next to your bed so you can take him into your bed to nurse him. Then put him back in his bassinet afterward with minimum disturbance.

Play music Babies respond well to soothing music (classical is best). Keep certain pieces for when your baby shows signs of tiredness.

Carry him in a sling Rhythmic movement can hasten sleep, but your baby may wake up when you stop moving. Carry him around in a sling when you're in the house, whenever possible. As well as being relaxed by the constant movement, your baby will be comforted by your body and your smell when he is close to you.

Rock him in his stroller Take him for a walk in his stroller, or simply rock him back and forth gently over a slightly uneven floor to get him to sleep—again, he may wake when you stop.

Give him plenty of fresh air Fresh air is said to tire babies out. In fact, it's probably the stimulation they receive from the sounds and sights outside, or simply the movement of trees or branches, that makes them sleepy.

❋ **JUST FOR DAD**

Understanding the way your baby's sleep patterns work will help you to tune into his and your partner's needs.

Being realistic

Your new baby will probably sleep less than you think. He spends 50–80 percent of the time in light sleep, when he wakes very easily. His sleep cycle—light, deep, light—is shorter than an adult's sleep cycle, so he's vulnerable to waking each time he passes from one sleep state to another. He's programmed to wake up for all kinds of reasons—when he's wet, hot, cold, unwell—because his survival depends on it. It's good to know that light sleep is likely to make your baby more intelligent because the brain remains active and it enhances brain development.

Having a sleep routine

Your baby has to be deeply asleep before he'll settle, so try a tranquilizing sleep routine—gentle rocking, quiet songs, and talking. Or lay him down and gently pat his shoulder at about 60 beats a minute for a few minutes. He's deeply asleep when his eyelids don't twitch and his limbs feel limp.

Getting home late

If your baby is asleep when you get home from work, ask your partner if your baby can nap in the afternoon so that he's awake later. Be patient if this isn't possible. Try getting up earlier and spending time with your baby before work.

Safe sleeping

The way babies are put to bed can affect the likelihood of sudden infant death syndrome (SIDS). The number of babies dying has halved due to better awareness:

✱ Quit smoking—and NEVER let anyone smoke in the same room as your baby or in your home at all.

✱ Always lay your baby on her back to sleep so that her breathing is unimpeded and she can lose heat from her front, face, and head.

✱ Don't let your baby get too hot, as she isn't very efficient at controlling her temperature. If the air temperature is hot to you, it's very hot for her.

✱ Never over-wrap your baby. Cover her with a cotton sheet and cellular blankets according to the room temperature (see right). Don't increase the bedding when your baby is unwell.

✱ Lay your baby in the "feet-to-foot" position at the end of the crib so she can't wriggle down under the blankets and get too hot (see below), or put her in a sleep sack.

▲ **FEET TO FOOT** Lay your baby with her feet touching the foot of the crib, even if it means her head is halfway down the mattress.

Wakeful babies

Most babies develop a napping routine of sleeping for perhaps two hours in the morning and again in the afternoon, but there are always exceptions. While wakeful babies can be trying, they reward you in the end as they're usually very bright and affectionate—so don't be downhearted. Your baby is wakeful because she loves you and craves your friendship; she doesn't mean to starve you of sleep, she just wants to learn and be sociable. Every minute spent awake with you, she'll be forging new links with the world and developing many skills. Think about this, too, when she's awake during the day; if she isn't tired, why should she sleep? From her point of view, it's much better for her to stay with you, so don't be surprised if she cries when you leave her in her crib.

What you can try

✱ Keep her temperature even; touch her skin to check that she isn't too cold or hot, add or remove blankets if necessary (see below). Check the room temperature; temperature of about 65°F (18°C) is comfortable for her.
✱ Change her diaper if it's wet or soiled and soothe the diaper area with a bland diaper cream (zinc oxide), if necessary.
✱ Use a rocking cradle or push her rhythmically in her stroller.
✱ Play her a tape of the human heartbeat, the sound she heard in the womb.
✱ Play her music you listened to during pregnancy; an old-fashioned music box with a simple repetitive melody can also be very effective.
✱ Play her a tape of you and your partner quietly talking.
✱ Put the crib on alternate sides of the bed each night so that you can take turns caring for her when she wakes. Talk to her and rock her back to sleep; you don't need to actually pick her up.
✱ If she's obviously reluctant to sleep, get her up, and put her in her baby chair where she can see you.
✱ Hang a mobile over her crib so she has something interesting to watch when she wakes up. A mobile that plays music is ideal.
✱ Suspend a "baby gym," with different noises and textures, across her crib or attach it to the bars so she can reach for it when she's bored. Remove it when she can sit up, since she could use it to climb out of her crib.

✱ Which bedding to use

Temperature	What to use
57°F (14°C)	A sheet and four blankets or more
60°F (16°C)	A sheet and three blankets
65°F (18°C)	A sheet and two blankets
68°F (20°C)	A sheet and one blanket
75°F (24°C)	A sheet only

Blankets and bedding

Use enough bedding to keep her comfortably warm (see opposite). When your baby is under 12 months, don't give her a pillow, and don't use quilts, comforters, or baby nests because they prevent loss of heat.

Sleep and your older baby

As your baby grows, her sleep pattern will gradually change; she'll begin to stay awake and alert for longer periods during the day, even after nursing. When she's being stimulated with play and talk from you, she'll start needing longer periods of sleep. The trick is persuading her that these longer sleep periods should be at night, to align with your own.

Establishing a bedtime routine

Your baby may get upset at bedtime—she could be anxious about being separated from you (see p. 162), or she may simply want to continue playing, so establishing a bedtime routine is essential to build her confidence and to help her learn that there is a time when playtime has to stop. Set up your own routine at a time that suits all of you—for example, if you're working you may want it to be a little later—but try not to vary the routine, whatever time you do it. A suggested routine might be as follows:
* Give her the day's final meal—though not her main meal (see p. 113).
* Give her a calming bath, and change her into her nightclothes.
* Spend some quiet time in your baby's room; sing gentle songs or read a story (depending on her age and stage of development).
* Give her the last breastfeed (unless your baby still wakes at night).
* Lay her in her crib, with any security object she is attached to, turn the dimmer switch down low, then sit quietly with her for a few minutes.
* Go out of the room quietly, saying good night, but leave the door open.

▲ **THE BEDTIME ROUTINE** Allow your baby to play quietly. Put books and toys in her crib or hang a mobile above it. Remove hard objects from the crib when you lay her down.

You will need

For 3–12 months:

* 4 crib blankets

* 6 flat cotton top sheets

* 6 fitted cotton bottom sheets

* Full-size crib (see p.75)

Nursery extras:

* Dimmer switch for the nursery light

* Baby monitor

* Crib toys (see below)

* CD or tape of soothing music

Daytime naps for your older baby

As babies grow older they sleep less, but up to 12 months your baby will still nap in the day. Many children still nap up to the age of three:

* To help your baby relax and drop off, put her in her favorite place, which may not be her room. Make sure she has any special comforter with her. Play calming music, let her have toys and books, and keep her within earshot so she can hear you. If she calls out to you, it's probably only for reassurance, so calmly call back.

* If she doesn't want to sleep, that's okay; just make it a quiet time when she can sit in her crib and play. But never let her cry for more than a few minutes without going to her.

* If your baby falls asleep in the car or her stroller, don't wake her suddenly; she needs time to adjust. Never leave her asleep alone in the car or her stroller outside a store.

When your baby cries

Why you should respond promptly

✳ Your baby is longing to communicate with you, but his repertoire is limited. Crying is the only way he can convey his feelings, so don't just ignore him.

✳ Your baby will develop good communication skills and outgoing, friendly behavior.

✳ It will make him feel secure and self-confident.

✳ It will not "spoil" your baby or teach him "bad habits"; you can't spoil a baby this way, only love him.

What happens if you don't respond

✳ Not responding to your baby's cries is a form of rejection, and your baby will soon sense this.

✳ If you don't respond, he will cry for longer, continuing until he gets the attention he needs.

✳ He will be driven to create a pattern of frequent crying.

All young babies cry at some time during the day. Whether it's a subdued grumble or a full-throated roar, a baby's cries are his only means of communicating his needs. Having said that, there is no doubt that a persistently fretful baby can be a strain for parents, so it's worth thinking about the underlying causes. Look upon crying as conversation rather than an irritant designed to upset you.

What makes a newborn cry

The circumstances of your baby's birth may affect the amount that he cries. It helps if you understand the possible underlying causes of a fretful baby's behavior. Try not to become impatient with him, since it is out of his control. He'll begin to settle down as he gets older. Your baby may cry more:

✳ If you had a general anesthetic.

✳ If you had a forceps delivery.

✳ If he was born after a long labor, after which babies tend to sleep in short bursts.

✳ If he is a boy. Boys may cry more than girls in new situations. Try not to make the mistake of some parents of boys who have been known to attend to them less, in the mistaken belief that it will "toughen them up."

Responding to your baby's cries

Research shows that babies do better if you respond promptly when they cry. It's a mistake to think of a baby as "good" if he doesn't cry much and

▶ **GIVING YOUR BABY ATTENTION** All babies thrive on the company of their parents, and will cry because they miss the comfort of your presence. Try to give your baby as much contact as you can.

one who does as "bad," because a baby's cries have nothing to do with good or bad behavior. Responding to your baby's cries is a crucial part of bonding—your attitude to your baby in the first few weeks forms the blueprint for your future relationship with him, and for all his future relationships. He'll learn kindness and sympathy from you, which is why you should always answer his cry, whatever anyone else tells you.

A loved baby will be secure and when the time comes he will be able to take separations in stride if he's learned that you will answer his needs. A baby who's left to cry is more likely to grow up clingy and attention-seeking because he's learned that he has to work harder to make you respond to him.

Persistent crying

Some young babies have prolonged bouts of crying, which typically occur in the late afternoon and evening, and can last anywhere from two to four hours. Babies often begin this pattern of persistent crying at about three weeks of age, and will usually have grown out of it by about three months. This pattern of crying has become known as "colic," because as the baby becomes increasingly upset and difficult to soothe, he may often pull his legs up and arch his back as if experiencing abdominal pain. In fact, it's probably misleading to give it any special name, because there doesn't seem to be any known cause for this pattern. A treatable condition known as acid reflux often presents as colic, especially in a small baby who vomits a lot. Talk to your doctor if your baby fits this description.

▲ **SOOTHING "COLIC"** If your baby cries persistently, you may find that laying him across your lap makes him more comfortable. Support his head and then gently massage his back and legs.

✳ What to do when your baby cries

Problem	Description	What you should do
Hunger	If your baby has been asleep for two or three hours and begins to cry insistently, he is probably ready to eat.	Nurse him. If he cries afterward, he may not have had enough so offer more. If it's very hot, offer him a drink of water.
Discomfort	A cold, wet, or soiled diaper could be uncomfortable enough to cause your baby to cry. Your baby may also be too hot or too cold.	Check and if necessary change his diaper. Treat diaper rash (see p. 86). Check bedding and air temperature (see p. 102).
Insecurity	A jerky movement, bright light, or sudden noise can startle a young baby. Many babies are also upset by being undressed and bathed.	Cuddle your baby to promote security. Handle your baby as gently and firmly as possible when dressing or bathing.
Fatigue	Your baby will cry when he is tired, and may become quite upset when over-tired, which can make it doubly difficult to soothe him.	Create a soothing bedtime ritual (see p. 103) of rocking or rubbing him when you lay him in his crib, or push him in his stroller.
Boredom	As your baby grows, he is more aware of people and cries because he wants company.	Cuddle him; at four to six weeks, sit him in a baby chair where he can see and hear you.
Pain	Your baby may have earache, abdominal pain, or persistent diaper rash.	Contact your doctor if he's hard to soothe, nursing poorly, or appears unwell (see p. 120).

Soothing your crying baby

A baby who is persistently fretful may cry readily at other times, not just in the evening (see p. 105). However, the evening pattern of crying can be a particular strain for parents, especially if one or both of you has been away at work during the day. It may be that your baby senses and reacts to your tiredness at this time. Although the crying pattern may only last three months, this period can seem never-ending to new parents who have to deal with their baby's distress day after day. Trying some of the suggestions for soothing your baby given below and on p. 105 should help you through this difficult time.

▶ **USE A PACIFIER** Encourage your baby to find his thumb or give him a pacifier. There is no stigma attached to a baby sucking a pacifier, but make sure it is sterilized and never sweeten it with honey or juice. However, it may only be a temporary relief so it's probably better to look for the underlying cause of the crying, keeping the pacifier as a last resort.

▼ **LAY YOUR BABY ON YOUR CHEST** Lie on the bed or sofa, well supported by pillows. Lay your baby on your chest and gently rub her back. It will relax both of you, but never fall asleep with your baby like this because it increases the risk of SIDS.

CARRY YOUR BABY IN A SLING Put your baby in a sling and carry him around with you. Your baby will love being close to you and will enjoy the movement as you walk around.

▲ **COMFORT WITH MOVEMENT** Most babies are soothed by regular movement: It was what they were used to in the womb. Put your baby in a rocking cradle (make sure it conforms to safety standards) or in her stroller and gently rock her backwards and forwards while you sit and watch television or eat a meal.

▲ **HOLD UPRIGHT** Bring your baby up against your shoulder and gently rub her back. (Put a burp cloth on your shoulder to protect your clothes from any regurgitated milk.) Walk around, gently singing or talking to your baby.

HELPFUL GRANDPARENTS
Grandparents know you need a break and enjoy developing their relationship with their grandchild.

Accepting help from others

Sometimes a crying baby can make parents who are already tired from broken nights feel desperate: This is the time to seek help. Don't ever feel that you are failing as parents if you accept assistance; countless other parents have felt as frustrated and exhausted as you when their babies cried a lot and were difficult to soothe. Jump at the chance if your baby's grandparents or other friends or relations offer to look after your baby for a while so you can get out on your own for a couple of hours' break, or enjoy some unbroken sleep. If they don't offer help, don't be afraid to ask them. There's no need to feel guilty—they'll be glad to have the chance to relieve you, they can get to know your baby, and it will help you to get things back into perspective. It's a great help, too, to talk to healthcare or baby-care professionals, who are there to support you. You are not the first parents to experience this; it happens all the time.

Comforting your older baby

As your baby grows and becomes more aware of her surroundings, her pattern of crying will change because it's not the only way she can communicate with you now. Her reasons for crying will also be easier for you to both predict and interpret. You'll learn to distinguish between frustration, hunger, pain, or loneliness. Even when your baby is beginning to become more mobile and independent, the best way to comfort her if she's unhappy is with your company, hugs, and cuddles.

Security objects

Toward their first birthday, many babies will have become attached to a particular security object—a favorite soft toy, a cloth, or blanket—that probably helps them sleep and that may be grabbed when they're feeling insecure and upset. Other babies become attached to a pacifier or suck their thumbs (see p. 106). This is perfectly normal and there's no point in distressing your baby by removing a security object on the grounds that it is a "bad habit"; it isn't. As your baby's confidence and independence develop after her first birthday, she'll gradually become less dependent on her security object, although it may take a year or so. It's also a good idea to have some spares on hand in case the main one needs a wash or gets lost.

Teething and crying

Your baby's teeth will normally start to come in around the age of six months (see p. 154), although it can be later or even earlier than this. When this happens, you will notice that she drools a lot and her gums will occasionally be sore. Your baby may become rather grumpy when she's teething and it's usually pretty obvious if she's uncomfortable; she'll want to chew a lot and may have a hot, red area on her cheek. She may also become more wakeful than usual.

However, it isn't a good idea to blame persistent crying on "teething" too readily. It may in fact be that your baby is bored (see right), or even ill (see p. 120); teething does not cause a fever, for example.

Troubleshooting

There are lots of reasons why an older baby may cry.

She's bored

Your baby may cry from boredom if left alone, unable to hear your voice and with nothing to look at or play with. You are her favorite playmate, so keep her where she can see you and you can talk to her, and don't leave her alone in her crib for long periods if she's crying. Some babies do play happily in their cribs for a while after waking, so leave toys and books within reach.

She's frustrated

As your baby grows, her desire to do things outstrips her ability to do them and so she gets frustrated and often starts to cry as a result. She may also cry if you don't let her have something she wants. Try to change her toys frequently—her attention span is still short. Find time to sit down and play with her (see p. 174).

She's frightened

At about six months old, your baby will cry when she's separated from you and she'll be nervous of other people, even when she knows them well. Right from the start, get her used to seeing you leave the room and come back in again. She'll gradually learn that she can trust you'll always to return to her. Make sure she meets lots of other people before she reaches this stage and learns that even if you leave her with someone else for a while, you always come back.

She's ill or has hurt herself

If your baby hurts herself, you'll know at once from her cry, but it may be more difficult to tell when she's ill. See pp. 120–123 for what you should do if your baby is ill or has an accident.

Touch and massage

Massage tips

Babies love massage as much as you do, and it's a good way to calm an unsettled baby. It's also an expression of love and your baby knows it. Always prepare carefully for massage:

✳ Make sure the room is warm. Lay your baby on a soft blanket or towel.

✳ Play his favorite music or a recording of a heartbeat. Talk in a low, gentle voice or sing a song quietly.

✳ Although massaging your baby's skin directly is best, many younger babies don't like being undressed. If your baby is one of these, dress him in a simple cotton shirt, through which you can easily feel his body.

✳ Work around his body, massaging both sides with slow even strokes. Keep your face close to your baby's and look into his eyes as you massage him.

Being touched is an essential part of the bonding process that helps young creatures to thrive. Premature babies are known to gain more weight on lamb's-wool blankets than cotton ones because it feels as if they're being stroked when they move and they feel contented.

The importance of touch

Your baby is born sociable and he craves physical affection. This is best communicated through touch, cuddles, being gently held, kissed, and nuzzled. It's important, therefore, that you're both completely free with your physical affection from the start. Your baby longs to be close to you and to be carried, and he will cry less and be more easily comforted if you carry him. Remember also that being carried in a sling close to your body feels like being cuddled to a baby (see p. 106), and allows you to do other things at the same time. Small babies are much stronger than you think so be firm, but avoid sudden jerky movements—your baby may think he's falling and he'll be startled rather than comforted.

As your baby gets older you can be more robust with him; he'll enjoy tickling and rolling about on the floor with you, but don't overdo it if he becomes at all distressed, and don't blame him if he pulls your hair or scratches you—under a year old he won't know that it hurts. And as children grow up, they need the reassuring and loving embrace of caring parents more, not less as some parents may think.

Giving your baby a massage

1 NECK AND SHOULDERS Lay your baby on her back. Gently massage her neck from her ears to her shoulders and from her chin to her chest. Then stroke her shoulders from her neck outward.

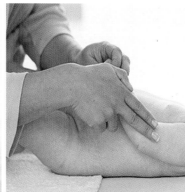

2 ARMS Stroke down each arm using your fingertips, first from wrist to elbow, then from elbow to shoulder. Gently squeeze all along her arm, starting from the top.

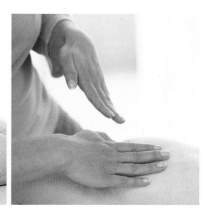

3 CHEST AND ABDOMEN Gently stroke down your baby's chest following the line of her ribs. Massage her abdomen in a circular motion with one hand, working outward from the navel.

Physical affection

Children should be encouraged to express their emotions—boys just as much as girls. Indeed, a child's ability to achieve some kind of emotional stability is more or less determined before the age of 12 months—a sobering thought, but true.

Emotional feedback

A child learns to master his emotions by getting sympathetic feedback from adults that mirrors the emotions he's feeling. If your baby holds out a hurt hand, what helps most—as any parent knows—is lots of sympathy, "kissing better," and hugs. Physical affection is necessary for emotional growth. If you deprive a child of physical affection, you deprive him of an essential "growth vitamin."

Your baby needs you both

This applies equally to both parents, and continues through babyhood, childhood, and, in some cases, into adolescence. Nothing should be allowed to discourage loving parents—mothers and fathers—from doing what their child needs.

4 **HEAD** Using both hands, lightly massage the crown of your baby's head using a circular motion, then stroke down the sides of her face. With your fingertips, massage her forehead and cheeks, working from the center outward. This is particularly calming for a fretful baby.

5 **FEET AND TOES** Rub your baby's ankles and feet, stroking from heel to toe, and then concentrate on each toe individually. Your baby may kick her legs and curl her toes while you're doing this. If she's less than four months old, show her her toes—it will help her to realize they're part of herself (see p. 159).

6 **LEGS** Massage your baby's legs one at a time. Work from her thigh down to her knee. Stroke down her shin, and move around to her calf and ankle. Place your free hand on her tummy, then gently squeeze her leg from the thigh down to the ankle. Then work on the other leg.

7 **BACK** Once you've massaged your baby on her front, gently turn her over on to her tummy and massage her back. Using both hands, run your palms down her back from under her arms to her buttocks, pressing gently against her spine with your thumbs. Talk to her all the time, since she can't see your face.

Weaning your baby

Weaning may seem like a huge step. There are so many questions—when to start, what food to give first, how much to give—but it doesn't need to be daunting or difficult. Try to think positively and see this as encouraging your baby's independence rather than as an obstacle.

Trouble-free weaning

Knowing what food to give and when to give it will help you to introduce it with confidence.

What age to start
Don't start weaning until six months; you can give cereals at four months if your baby is drinking only formula.

What to offer
Offer a simple, semi-liquid food once a day. Give her one new taste at a time. Start with non-wheat cereal mixed with her normal milk—it's closest to what she's used to. Offer puréed fruit or vegetables gradually. Introduce food at a second meal when she happily takes the first. Milk is still her main food. Try new foods 10–12 times; don't assume she doesn't like it after only a couple of tries.

How much to give
Start with a teaspoonful a day for a week, since her digestive system needs time to adapt, then go on to two spoons. Use the weaning schedule (see opposite) as a guide.

You will need

To start weaning:
* 2–3 plastic-backed fabric bibs
* 2–3 feeding spoons and a cup

For the older baby:
* 2–3 molded plastic bibs
* 2 spill-proof plastic bowls
* Two-handled training cup

Introducing solids
Weaning is rarely a problem from the baby's point of view, but some babies take longer than others to get used to having solid food as well as their normal milk. It really doesn't matter—until six months, milk is enough for many babies' complete nutritional needs. However, after that time they will need the extra calories, vitamins, and minerals in solid food, since there won't be enough for them in milk alone. (Look at the weaning chart opposite for a suggested pattern of feeding.)

▲ **FIRST FEEDS** Choose a time when your baby will be relaxed. Hold her firmly on your lap as you offer the spoon. She may take a while to get used to taking food from a spoon, and may push out more than she takes in at first.

Weaning schedule from six months

Feeds	Week 1–2	Week 3–5	Week 6
1st feed	Milk	Milk	Milk
2nd feed	Half milk 1 tsp cereal Finish milk	Half milk 1–2 tsps cereal Finish milk	3–4 tsps cereal Milk
3rd feed	Milk	Half milk 1–2 tsps puréed fruit or veggies Finish milk	2–3 tsps chicken- and-veggie purée 2–3 tsps puréed fruit Water
4th feed	Milk	Milk	2–3 tsps puréed fruit or veggies Milk
5th feed	Milk	Milk	Milk

When you introduce her first solids, choose a meal time when you know she's usually alert and awake—for instance, at midday, halfway through nursing. Sit her on your lap or in a baby seat and offer her tiny amounts on the tip of a sterilized plastic spoon. Don't force it into her mouth; brush her upper lip with the spoon and let her suck it off. She might splutter and dribble the first few times, but keep trying. When she has had a few tastes, finish nursing her. She will gradually take more solids before wanting the rest of her milk. Once she is used to solids she'll want it before the milk.

Extra fluid

Remember milk is a food, it isn't a drink, and so from the moment mixed feeding is introduced, your baby will also need another fluid to drink. Cooled, boiled water is best. Start by giving your baby ½ fl oz (15 ml) of fluids between feedings, increasing it gradually according to her needs. It's a good idea to take this opportunity to introduce a training cup, or if she prefers it, give the water in a bottle.

Trouble-free meal times

Just as it was important not to get hung up about how much your baby drank when you were establishing breastfeeding, try not to worry now about how much she is eating, or about how much is going on the floor! It will be messy—until the age of five or six all children are messy eaters—so just put newspaper under the high chair and clean up afterward. As long as meal times are happy and relaxed, don't worry. It's important that you don't allow them to become battlefields. You can't win—your baby will simply refuse to eat (you can't force her). She'll learn that food is a weapon she can use to manipulate you, so don't join in the struggle.

Starting self-feeding

Self-feeding is an important step toward your baby's independence, so be patient with her:

✳ Use shaped plastic bibs that catch spilled food, and put a plastic sheet under the high chair.

✳ Give your baby her own spoon and offer food that is of a stiff consistency, such as mashed potato or other puréed vegetables, in a spill-proof bowl. Don't worry if she gets very little at first, she'll have a lot of fun. Have a spare spoon handy so that you can feed her, if need be.

✳ Even if she finds a spoon difficult, she'll love feeding herself with finger foods (see p. 117). Finger foods can keep her busy if the meal isn't ready.

✳ Above all be flexible; if one food doesn't work, try another—no single food is essential.

✳ Introduce a training cup for drinks as soon as your baby can manage it. Some breastfed babies never accept a bottle and go straight to a cup for water; others like a bottle.

▲ **RELAXED SELF-FEEDING** While your baby feeds herself, have your own spoon to feed her at the same time.

Best food for your baby

Do's and don'ts

Foods to give
Vary your baby's diet so that he learns to like different tastes and textures. Make sure you include:

* Fruits and vegetables: wash them thoroughly in cold running water, and peel potatoes, carrots, apples, and peaches to avoid the risk of pesticide residues. Aim to give some vitamin C at each meal, whether as fruit, vegetables, or juice, since it helps your baby's body to absorb iron.

* Milk: from seven months use full-fat cow's milk in cooking. From one year, give it as a drink.

* Meat and fish: try to offer at least one serving every day of lean meat or boneless fish.

* Protein in the form of low-fiber foods such as cheese or tofu, if your baby has a vegetarian diet.

Foods to avoid
Take some sensible precautions:

* Don't give foods containing wheat flour or gluten before your baby is seven months old.

* Don't add sugar or salt—sugar encourages bad habits and bad teeth; salt is too much for your young baby's kidneys to cope with.

* Avoid giving your baby soft-boiled eggs until he is about one year old.

* Very high-fiber breakfast cereals have little place in your baby's diet— they are too difficult to digest.

* Avoid unpasteurized cheese until your baby is at least two years old.

* Avoid peanuts and peanut butter until age two to reduce allergy risk.

To grow and develop well, babies need as varied a diet as possible; research shows that babies who are offered a wide menu to choose from invariably choose a healthy diet and accept varied tastes. On the other hand, if they're only given fast foods and sweet things, they'll inevitably want French fries and ketchup with everything.

What your baby needs

To provide for your baby's needs for healthy growth and development, you need to give him foods in the right proportions from all the different food groups. He needs most foods from the complex carbohydrates group. These include sugar-free cereals, whole-wheat bread, potatoes (not fried or roasted), rice, and pasta. Secondly, he needs the vitamins and minerals contained in fresh fruit and vegetables—at least five portions a day. He needs protein, which he'll get from lean white meat, fish, and legumes such as beans, and, after he's about seven to nine months, eggs (only the yolk until age one) and cheese. Offer the vegetables first, then follow with proteins, to make sure that he has enough vegetables. Your baby needs some fat, but he should be able to get enough for his nutritional needs

Suggested menus for an older baby

Time	Day 1	Day 2	Day 3
Breakfast	Rice cakes Chopped hard-boiled egg Milk	Mashed banana Whole-wheat toast fingers Milk	Cottage cheese or yogurt Whole-wheat toast Milk
Lunch	Vegetable or chicken casserole Stewed apple Diluted fruit juice	Mashed potatoes and cheese Pear slices Diluted fruit juice	Strained lentils and mixed vegetables Banana and yogurt Diluted fruit juice
Snack	Toast fingers Peeled peach slices Milk	Rice cakes Peeled apple pieces Milk	Graham crackers Peeled seedless grapes Milk
Dinner	Cauliflower with cheese Semolina and fruit purée	Pasta with sauce Yogurt and fruit purée Diluted fruit juice	Tuna, mashed potatoes, zucchini Rice pudding Diluted fruit juice

from the other foods you give him, especially milk. You can use cow's milk in cooking now and he should have full-fat milk until he's two years old. Use very little oil or fat in cooking and don't add salt to foods. Avoid giving him the "empty" calories of sweet foods like cookies and sugary cereal.

Preparing your baby's food

At first your baby's food needs to be puréed, but this stage doesn't last for long. As your baby gets used to solid foods, introduce him to coarser mashed or minced foods so that he learns about different textures. Use a variety of liquids to thin down home-prepared foods: the water used to steam vegetables is ideal as it contains the minerals. You can thicken foods with whole-grain cereals, cottage cheese, yogurt, or mashed potatoes.

Enough to eat?

Even if you think your baby isn't taking enough food, he is. Don't make the mistake of forcing adult standards on him. Think of a balanced diet in terms of what you offer your baby over a period of time, such as a week, and make sure it's varied. Accept that there will be a certain amount of waste and don't force him to finish everything if he does not want to. Don't worry about fads either; he's eating what his body needs.

Food hygiene

Once your baby is taking solids you don't need to sterilize his feeding utensils. But bacterial infections picked up from badly prepared food can be dangerous.

✱ Wash your hands thoroughly before handling any food and after you've handled raw meat.

✱ Store raw meat away from other foods in the refrigerator and keep fish in the coldest part.

✱ Clean the spout holes of your baby's feeding cup regularly.

✱ Throw away leftover baby food; don't reheat it. If you're using ready-made baby food, spoon it into a bowl; don't feed from the container.

✱ To avoid waste, prepare small amounts and freeze it in individual containers.

✱ If you use a microwave, stir the food thoroughly to ensure the heat is evenly distributed.

▼ **HAPPY MEAL TIMES** Once your baby happily takes one or two different solids, it's important to introduce him to a variety of textures and tastes. Never force him to eat more than he wants.

Finger foods

Once your baby is more than seven or eight months old and has been weaned onto solid foods, she'll want to try feeding herself—so give her easy-to-hold finger foods. Try:

✱ Any fresh fruit that's easy to hold, such as a banana or peach: remember to peel and remove pits.

✱ Vegetables, particularly cooked carrots, cut into a shape that's easy to grasp. Don't cut them too small.

✱ Pieces of dry, sugar-free cereal.

✱ Whole-wheat bread or crackers (without grains), toast fingers, bread sticks, or rice cakes.

✱ Cooked pasta shapes.

Make meal times fun

It's frustrating to find that good food is being thrown on the floor or wiped over the high chair, but remember that your baby will eat if she's hungry. If she starts to throw food around, she's probably bored with eating because she's had enough, so she's moving on to experiment with the textures instead. Try tempting your older baby to try new tastes with fun food, and she'll learn to see meal times as enjoyable occasions.

Remember, a baby's stomach can't hold very much, and she'll need to eat more often than an adult. Encourage her to have regular meal times, but don't insist that she finish her meals if she's had enough. Give her healthy snacks between meals if she is hungry.

Joining family meals

As soon as your baby is sitting in her high chair to eat, she'll enjoy joining you at the table for meals too. The sooner you can include your baby in this, the sooner she'll learn by example what is and isn't acceptable behavior at the table.

You may find it easier occasionally to feed your baby before you sit down to a family meal, then give her some finger foods to eat and play with while you eat. That way she can learn about tastes and also join in the "conversation" at the table with the family.

▲ **FUN FOODS** You can encourage your baby to eat by making her meals look interesting and attractive. Try making her vegetables into a friendly face.

▶ **TEETHING FOODS** When your baby is teething she'll like to chew and suck to soothe her gums. Any piece of raw vegetable or fruit that's large enough to hold easily and can be sucked or chewed makes a good teething food.

FINGER FOODS If your baby has difficulty using a spoon, he'll enjoy having finger foods, which are easier to handle; vegetables are ideal for this. Don't give him very small things that he might choke on, and never leave him alone with finger foods.

Out and about

Baby-friendly activities

There are lots of activities available for new parents and their babies:

✳ Coffee mornings and parent-and-toddler groups (see p. 138).

✳ Music groups for babies.

✳ Swimming—ask if your local pool has parent-and-baby sessions.

✳ Baby movement classes or yoga classes.

✳ Baby massage classes.

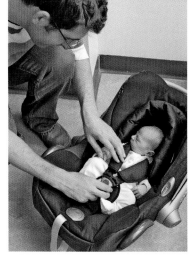

▲ **TRAVEL SAFELY** Your baby must travel in a special car seat. Laws regarding car seats and booster seats vary by state, so check your local regulations for age guidelines.

Try to get out and about with your baby as soon as you feel up to it. It's good for both of you—it helps get him used to travel, new places, and people, while giving you a change of scene and keeping you in touch with the world outside your home.

First outings

The first few outings that involve more than pushing the stroller around the neighborhood may seem daunting, and you'll probably be a little nervous and unsure about how your baby will react. Stay calm and try to relax—your baby will pick up on any anxieties you have. You'll soon become a family of seasoned travelers. The easiest time to be out and about with your baby is while he's small and portable. Make the most of it—when he's toddling and needing constant supervision, the range of outings will become more limited for a while. Don't be too ambitious on your first outings: Go to the park, or for coffee at a friend's house. Make sure you're confident about being away from home with your baby before you go further afield. Travel at off-peak times when there's less congestion, especially if you're traveling by bus or train.

Going shopping

There's no need to leave your baby at home when you go shopping, since most supermarkets and department stores now provide facilities to help parents with babies (see chart opposite) and some even have diaper-changing facilities. Shopping malls can be more difficult if they are on more than one level, but most have elevators as well as escalators. When you are in the supermarket:

✳ Always use a grocery cart that is appropriate to your baby's size and weight and strap him into the seat with a harness. Be aware that he may try to grab items off the shelves.

✳ Shopping tends to make children hungry and therefore fretful. Avoid this by taking a snack and drink with you. These will provide refreshment for your baby and also keep him occupied.

Traveling by car

Rear-facing car seats (see p. 76) make traveling by car with a young baby relatively trouble-free, but the car seat must be correctly installed. An older baby or toddler should sit in a front-facing car seat. Car seats should be put in the back seats of the car. You can only use a child seat in the front passenger seat if there is no airbag or the airbag has been switched off. Keep a few diapers, wipes, and plastic bags in the car for emergencies. Place a detachable shade on your car window to protect your baby from the sun. If you ever have an accident, replace your seat belts, your child's car seat, and car seat anchors, as they may have been strained and damaged.

Shopping with your baby

Facility	What to look for
Parking spaces	Some stores have dedicated parent-and-baby parking spaces close to the entrance.
Wider checkouts	Some supermarkets have at least two wider-than-average checkouts to accommodate prams.
Special discounts	Some stores offer discounts for parents with a baby under 12 months.
Babycare	Supervised childcare rooms are available at some stores, as long as you're nearby to be called if necessary.
Changing and feeding	Many stores have a baby changing area in their restrooms, and some have a room where you can breastfeed—but if you're happy just to sit out of the way to feed your baby, don't feel you have to do it in private.

Vacations

If you're going away with a very young baby, you may feel more comfortable not going abroad in case you need medical help. Having said this, young babies—especially breastfed ones—often travel abroad very well, but it's sensible to take out adequate medical insurance. Whatever the age of your baby, when you're away you should:

* Find out how far you'll be from a doctor's office, clinic, or hospital while you're away.

* Make sure the crib in your hotel conforms with safety standards—the tour operator, travel agent, or Tourist Information Office should be able to reassure you on this. Alternatively, take your own travel crib; modern designs are very compact.

* Always make sure your baby is protected from the sun (see below): use adequate sunscreen, dress your baby in protective clothing, and keep him in the shade.

Sun protection

Babies have very little skin pigment so they have much less protection from the sun's ultraviolet rays than adults. Direct sunlight can cause skin damage and skin cancer later in life. If your baby is under six months, never expose his skin to direct, strong sunlight. Keep him as cool as possible, with light cotton clothing that covers almost all his body. When he's in his stroller, shield him with a sunshade. For older babies and children, use a sunscreen with a protection factor (SPF) of at least 30. Apply the sunscreen 30 minutes before going out in the sun and then every two hours, or after swimming. Keep your child out of the sun between 11am and 3pm when the heat is at its strongest. There are also now special T-shirts and sun suits that filter UVA and UVB rays for additional protection.

Using public transportation

Planning ahead is the secret to trouble-free travel by public transportation:

* If you're traveling alone, make sure you can manage everything yourself.

* Allow plenty of time to reach the station or airport to avoid the extra stress of worrying about missing a train or airplane.

* On an airplane, feed your baby during takeoff and landing—sucking reduces the risk of earache caused by changing air pressure.

* If you're flying overseas, call the airline to reserve a seat with a bassinet for your baby to sleep in.

* A portable car seat is invaluable, though for air travel you may have to pay for an extra seat on busy flights if you want to use one.

▲ **USING A BACKPACK** A backpack is more convenient for an older baby than a stroller if you like to do a lot of walking.

Caring for your sick baby

Medication

The doctor may prescribe medicine such as liquid acetaminophen or an antibiotic for your baby's high temperature or infection. Give the medicine orally using a sterile dropper or spoon. Always give the dosage recommended by the doctor or instructed on the bottle.

Taking your baby's temperature

A raised temperature usually means your baby is fighting off infection. With a digital thermometer, take temperature rectally for infants. For older children, hold it firmly under her bare armpit for three minutes. Bear in mind that the temperature in the armpit is about 1°F (0.6°C) lower than in the body. Temperature strips are less accurate. Don't put a thermometer in a baby's mouth. You can also use an ear thermometer.

▲ **CHECKING THE TEMPERATURE** Place the thermometer under your baby's bare armpit and hold her arm across her chest to keep it in place.

If you suspect that your baby is ill, don't hesitate to get medical advice if you're worried. You're the best judge of when your baby is unwell because you know and understand her moods and personality, so you are the best observer of changes.

Nursing your baby

When babies are sick they are often grumpy and fretful, probably waking more frequently at night and needing constant attention and cuddles. However, a very ill baby will become listless and unresponsive. If your baby has a cold, it might make feeding difficult since she won't be able to breathe well through her nose. Be patient and let her come up for air when feeding. If this becomes a real problem, ask your doctor about using nose drops.

Recognizing a fever

A fever is a temperature over 100.4°F (38°C). The best way to recognize it is to lay your hand on your baby's brow. If her skin is hot, red, and clammy, take her temperature. If the temperature is very high, she may also shiver.

Lowering temperature

If your baby has a very high fever, you should try to lower it to prevent overheating. Remove all her clothing, but don't let her get too cold. If your baby is over three months, you may also give her liquid acetaminophen (see above left).

Preventing dehydration

Dehydration in babies under 12 months can be dangerous, and steps must be taken to replace lost fluids. Signs of dehydration in babies are general listlessness and a sunken fontanelle (the soft area of skin on the top of the skull). Your baby may

▶ **COOLING BABY** Undress your baby if she has a fever, but be sure she's not getting too cold.

also wet her diaper less frequently. When your baby has a temperature, or when the weather is hot, make sure she doesn't become dehydrated by offering the breast more frequently or giving her cooled, boiled water in a bottle or on a sterile spoon.

If your baby suffers from vomiting and diarrhea for more than 24 hours, always consult your doctor. If you are bottle-feeding, try giving an electrolyte solution such as Pedialyte, and encourage your baby to drink water. If your baby has been weaned, stick to a bland diet. Breastfed babies should continue with their normal milk feeds. If you're breastfeeding, give rehydration fluid in a bottle, if possible, before the feed. If your baby is reluctant to take a bottle, you will need to breastfeed her more often to maintain fluid her intake.

Mild diarrhea can sometimes occur when you introduce new types of solid food (see p. 112)—if you suspect this is happening, stop giving your baby that particular food and then try again after a couple of weeks.

Recognizing an illness

Ailment	When to call the doctor
High or low temperature	✴ If your baby's temperature rises above 100°F (38°C) and she's obviously ill, or if it rises above 103°F (39.4°C), even if she doesn't seem ill. ✴ When your baby's temperature goes up and down. ✴ If your baby is unusually quiet and limp and her skin is cold, though her hands and feet are pink (see p. 123).
Breathing difficulties	✴ If your baby's breathing becomes difficult. ✴ The rate of breathing speeds up and you notice her ribs being drawn sharply in with each breath.
Loss of appetite	✴ If your baby is under six months and refuses to eat either at the breast or from a bottle. ✴ If your older baby refuses food and drink.
Vomiting	✴ If your baby is burping up whole feeds or the vomiting is violent, prolonged, or excessive, it can cause rapid dehydration and medical help should be sought immediately. However, all babies regurgitate a little milk from time to time after feeding.
Diarrhea	✴ If the stools are watery, possibly greenish in color, foul smelling, and are abnormally frequent. ✴ If diarrhea is accompanied by a raised temperature, you should always consult a doctor.
Rashes	✴ If you notice an unusual rash it can be a sign of infection, especially if it's accompanied by a raised temperature, or it might be an allergic reaction. Your baby's doctor will want to examine the rash. ✴ One type of rash caused by meningitis is very serious and should be treated as an emergency (see above right).

Meningitis

This is an inflammation of the membranes that cover the brain, resulting from an infection. Viral meningitis is usually relatively mild; bacterial meningitis is life-threatening and requires immediate action. The main symptoms can develop over a matter of hours.

Symptoms
In a baby under 12 months, the main symptoms are irritability, a slightly tense and bulging fontanelle (see p. 60), fever, and a rash of flat, pink, or purple spots that don't disappear when you press them. There may be listlessness, vomiting, loss of appetite, and pain in the eyes from light.

What to do
Press a glass to her skin to see if the rash remains visible through it. If you think she has meningitis, get her to a hospital immediately.

Febrile seizures

These can happen when children have a rapid increase in temperature due to infection. This causes the brain cells to discharge impulses to muscles, which contract jerkily. Although frightening to see, they are fairly common and rarely serious. The risk of epilepsy is very small.

Symptoms
Loss of consciousness and uncontrollable twitching of limbs. There may also be frothing at the mouth and the eyes may roll back.

What to do
Clear a space and remove her clothing to lower her temperature (see opposite). Call an ambulance.

Emergency first aid

Is your baby unconscious?

Gently tap or flick the bottom of your baby's foot. Try calling his name to see if there's any response—never shake your baby.

✳ If there is no reaction, he is unconscious. Tilt his head back gently to open his airway and check to see if he is breathing (right) before you call an ambulance.

✳ If he responds, he is conscious; check him for other injuries. Get medical advice if you are concerned.

The following isn't a substitute for first-aid training, but it's a good idea to familiarize yourself with the information so that you are prepared if there is an emergency. The American Red Cross runs first-aid courses (see p.187).

Unconscious baby

Check whether or not he is breathing. Place one hand on your baby's forehead and one finger on his chin, then tilt his head back gently to open the airway to the lungs. Remove anything obvious from his mouth, but don't put your finger in his mouth to look for anything. Put your ear near his mouth and look along his chest. Look for any movement and listen and feel for breathing for no longer than ten seconds.

If your baby is not breathing

Ask someone to call an ambulance while you begin CPR (cardiopulmonary resuscitation)—a combination of rescue breaths and chest compressions. If you're on your own, give CPR for one minute before you call an ambulance.

If your baby is breathing
KEEPING THE AIRWAY OPEN If your unconscious baby is breathing, cradle him in your arms, with his head lower than his body, and take him to the phone with you while you call an ambulance. If possible, ask someone else to call for you while you stay with the baby.

GIVING RESCUE BREATHS
✳ Tilt the baby's head and lift the chin to make sure that the airway is still open.
✳ Take a breath. Place your mouth over the baby's mouth and nose and blow steadily into his lungs until you see the chest rise. Take your mouth away from the baby's and watch the chest fall. If the chest rises and falls you have given a rescue breath.
✳ Repeat to give him TWO rescue breaths.
✳ If the chest does not rise: adjust the baby's head; re-check his mouth and remove anything that is obviously blocking the airway; check that the seal is airtight.
✳ Make no more than two attempts to give rescue breaths before you start giving chest compressions, see right.
✳ Don't stop to check signs of circulation.

GIVING CHEST COMPRESSIONS
✳ Put the index and middle finger of one hand on the center of the baby's chest.
✳ Press down vertically on the breastbone, depressing it by about one third of its depth. Release the pressure and let the chest come back up again, but leave your fingers on the chest.
✳ Repeat to give 30 compressions at a rate of about 100 per minute.

COMBINE CHEST COMPRESSIONS AND RESCUE BREATHS Alternate 30 compressions followed by TWO rescue breaths for one minute, then call an ambulance if this has not already been done. Continue until help arrives, the baby starts breathing normally, or you are too tired to continue.

First aid for accidents

Injury	What happens	What you should do
Severe bleeding	If your child has an accident that causes severe bleeding, you must act quickly to stop the bleeding before seeking help.	Press firmly on the wound and raise the injured part. Keep it higher than the baby's heart. Cover the wound with a sterile dressing and bandage the dressing in place. Call an ambulance.
Head injury	If a baby bumps his head he may sustain a concussion, causing a brief loss of consciousness, or a more serious injury.	if your baby is unconscious, see opposite. If he is conscious, treat any wound (see above) and take him to hospital, even if he appears to recover.
Electric shock	Your baby may get an electric shock from electrical sockets or cords. This can cause his breathing and heart to stop and cause burns to his body.	If possible, switch off the source of the current. Or stand on dry, insulating material, such as a phone book, and push the source away from the baby with a broom. Call an ambulance.
Drowning	Just 1 in (2.5 cm) of water is enough to drown a baby if he falls forward. Never leave him in a bath alone, even if he can sit unaided.	Hold him with his head lower than his chest to allow water to drain. If he is unconscious, treat as described opposite and call an ambulance.
Bites	Bites can range from minor insect stings to animal bites, and the treatment will differ accordingly.	For insect bites, soothe with a cold pad, then cover with an adhesive bandage. For animal bites, follow the procedure for severe bleeding.
Burns and scalds	If your baby is burned or scalded, you need to act quickly to cool the burn and remove any clothing before the burn begins to swell.	Cool the burn under cold running water for ten minutes. Cover it with plastic wrap or a plastic bag and take him to the hospital.

Choking baby

If your baby is choking, he may turn blue and make strange noises because he is trying to cry, or he is unable to make any sound at all. Don't turn him upside down or shake him. Try to clear any blockage in his throat.

Clearing a blockage

* Lay the baby face down along one forearm and keeping your hand flat, give him up to five sharp slaps between his shoulders (see right).
* Turn him face up along your other forearm and check his mouth. If the blockage has not cleared, supporting his head, place two fingers on the lower part of the breastbone. Press down and forward up to five times (chest thrusts). Check the mouth each time.
* If he is still choking, repeat the back slaps and chest thrusts three times, then call an ambulance. Continue until help arrives or the baby becomes unconscious.
* If the baby becomes unconscious, treat as described opposite.

Hypothermia

Hypothermia occurs when the body temperature falls below 95°F (35°C). The temperature-regulating mechanism in babies is immature, so they can lose body heat rapidly in a cold place.

Symptoms
He will look misleadingly healthy because his skin will have a pink glow, but it will feel cold. He may refuse to eat, and may be limp and quiet.

What to do
Call a doctor. Warm him gradually. Take him into a warm room and wrap him in blankets. Put a hat on him and hold him close to your body.

Your special baby

Early signs

Although the rate of normal development is enormously varied (see p. 147), it may become apparent that your baby's development is delayed. Don't leap to conclusions, but as parents, you're likely to be the first to recognize some of the signs.

Hand awareness

A baby becomes aware of her hands at about eight weeks (see p. 158). At 12–16 weeks this interest wanes, but it may last up to 20 weeks in a baby whose development is delayed.

Grasp reflex

From birth to about six weeks, a baby wraps her fingers tightly around anything placed in her palm, then the reflex fades as she begins to gain control of her hand movements. This reflex may last longer in a developmentally delayed baby.

Exploration with the mouth

At about four months, a baby puts everything in her mouth. Most stop at one, but a developmentally slow child may go on longer.

"Casting"

From 8–16 months, all babies go through the stage of "casting" – dropping things to see where they fall. This may last longer in a baby whose development is delayed.

Drooling

Most babies achieve mouth control at 12 months; delayed babies may drool for much longer.

Chewing

Most babies develop the ability to chew, even without teeth, by about seven months. A developmentally delayed baby may take longer.

Fortunately, few parents ever have to learn that their baby has a problem. This doesn't make it any easier for those parents who have to face the fact that their baby has a condition that is going to affect, and perhaps dominate, her life, and theirs too.

Diagnosis

Your newborn baby will be examined by a pediatrician before you leave the hospital (see p. 61). He or she may find something that requires further investigation at this point. If not, you may be the first to spot that something isn't quite right (see left). If this is the case, talk to your baby's doctor about your concerns and he should refer your baby to a specialist—insist that this happen if you're concerned. Among the first things to exclude are impaired hearing or vision; these should be tested at your baby's developmental check ups (see p. 155).

Coming to terms with the news

Whenever you find out about your baby's disability, you'll need time to adjust to the shock and pain. Every new parent has expectations and hopes for their child, and it's as though all of these are dashed in the space of a few minutes. In many ways, it is like a bereavement; you need to mourn for the baby you thought you were expecting, the perfect, able-bodied child you longed for, and come to terms with the special baby you have. In time, of course, this child will be your perfect child, and you'll feel ashamed that you ever thought her second-best, but in the early days, it's almost impossible not to feel a sense of loss.

Talk to others

Many of the congenital conditions that affect children and babies are extremely rare, but it will help you enormously if you can find other parents to talk to who have a child with exactly the same problem as your own. Your doctor can help put you in touch with specialist organizations. These may have self-help groups that include other parents who are in the same or a similar position to you (see p. 187).

Physical problems that can be corrected

With advances in neonatal pediatric surgery, many of the physical problems babies are born with can be corrected, even in the first months. This is a very worrying time for parents because it's distressing to see your baby having to undergo a series of operations. It can also be a strain emotionally (and financially), particularly if the hospital where your baby is undergoing treatment is far away from your home, but it helps to know that there is every chance that your baby will be able to grow up to be a normal, healthy child.

Recognizing developmental problems

A baby with a developmental problem is going to reach her milestones (see p. 146) at a slower than average rate, and in some cases may not reach them at all. You may notice early on that your baby is behind from various signs, such as unusual quietness, lack of alertness, no interest in her surroundings, floppiness (lack of muscle tone), docility, and sleeping for long periods. Sometimes a baby who's been termed "good" turns out to be a baby with a problem, because this kind of baby cries rarely, makes little noise, and doesn't interact well with her environment.

Later signs

As your baby grows older, at around seven or eight months, you may notice that her attention span is very short and she'll spend time moving quickly from one toy to another instead of examining one slowly and carefully as most babies do. Later still, she may be hyperactive and have difficulty concentrating on a single activity. She may also be reserved and unresponsive to people, even when she knows them very well.

Avoid comparisons

Comparing one baby with another is never a good idea, but if you have a baby with delayed development it's doubly important to see your baby for herself, rather than against the standard of other people's children. With perseverance, the support of specialists, and encouragement from you, your baby will reach some of her milestones (see p. 146) eventually, and the reward of seeing her do so will give you huge satisfaction.

Other people's attitudes

Most people don't have direct experience of a disability, and have little idea of how to react to a disabled person or child. Indeed, this may have been your own position until recently. Almost inevitably there will be those who will say the wrong thing, make a crass comment or remark without thinking. You'll just have to remind yourself that their insensitivity comes from ignorance and embarrassment, and they probably don't mean to be offensive. Try not to let this get you down; be open about your baby's disability so that it doesn't become a taboo subject.

Giving a lead

What you'll find is that many of your family and friends will take their lead from you in learning how to relate to your child. Make it clear that although her disability may be permanent, she is in no way inferior to anyone else and has the same right to love, understanding, and support as any child. You'll need courage, but you'll discover, like many other parents of disabled children, that you've got an inner strength that you never thought you would have. If you can be positive and hopeful about your child, and show by example how much you value her individuality and personality, other people will learn to do the same. It can be helpful and comforting to talk to people in similar situations, so find a support group if you can.

How you can help

If and when your baby is diagnosed with a developmental delay, disability, or learning difficulty, you'll be given advice on how to stimulate her both physically and intellectually. Here are some ideas:

✴ Stimulate your child from birth. Do this visually—make sure she can see your face close up as much as possible and hang a picture of a face on the side of her crib. Stimulate her aurally by playing music or a heartbeat, by talking and singing. Use touch with different textures, such as fleece, cotton, rubber, or plastic.

✴ Talk and sing to your baby in pronounced rhythms and rhymes, such as "Jack and Jill."

✴ Read and talk aloud to her as much as you can.

✴ Make her aware of her body with gentle clapping games and baby massage (see p. 110).

✴ Find toys that are educational and enjoyable and show her how to play with them (see p. 146).

✴ Introduce her to as many people as possible.

✴ Give her lots of love and make her feel secure. Praise her often.

✴ Give her lots of hugs and kisses; make sure others do, too.

✴ Never scold or punish her slowness.

✴ Encourage her to be independent— help her try to do things, even if it's hard.

✴ Be patient when she's frustrated. Life will be more difficult for her, especially when she realizes that she can't do things that other children her age can.

Adapting to parenthood

As well as mastering the practical care of your newborn baby, you need to think about your lifestyle and your relationship so you're able to get the most out of being parents and a family. Your baby will undoubtedly be your main priority, and it's easy to let him soak up all your emotional and physical energy. But to maximize the many joys of parenthood, it's worth ensuring that you have time for each other and time for yourself. You are, after all, still individuals and still in a loving relationship, and it would be wrong to think that your baby could fulfil all your needs. How easily you adjust will depend on your individual circumstances: Having a good and equal relationship with each other already and an adequate support network can make the transition to parenthood that much easier. If you have difficulty in adjusting at first, don't worry—things will get easier. Parenthood is full of ups and downs, but if you work together to get the balance right, hopefully it will turn out to be all that you wanted it to be.

Helping each other

If you're at home with your baby while your partner is at work, you may begin to feel that you know your baby better than he does. Or, you may feel that you don't get enough help from him. Think about how your attitudes may affect your partner.

Supporting your partner
✳ Try to avoid thinking that your partner isn't as "good" as you are at caring for your baby. By encouraging him to get involved with your baby's care and to share the workload, you'll all benefit.

✳ If your partner is tired after work, be patient. Let him unwind, then encourage him to spend time with your baby as a way of relaxing, not as a chore. Bathing the baby is often a good way for him to take care of the baby and to relax (see p. 95).

✳ Tell him about your day. If it's been difficult, don't bottle it up—but try not to convey it accusingly, as if it's his fault.

Building your self-esteem
✳ Be proud of your achievements. As the main caregiver, take pride in the upbringing of your baby.

✳ Keep in touch with work colleagues so you're up to date with career developments and office gossip! That way it will be less of a shock when you return to work.

✳ Try to have some time away from your baby, on your own and with your partner (see p. 134).

New parenthood is a joyful but trying role, when both of you are faced with a new set of priorities and when expectations come up against hard realities. So spare a thought for each other's needs, as well as those of your baby.

The initial impact of the baby

As first-time parents you may have seriously underestimated the amount of work and disruption caring for a baby entails and the extent to which this affects your relationship. Many couples are shocked to find that rather than bringing them closer together, their baby can bring to light differences that drive them apart. This is normal and very much part of your growth into parenthood, when you begin to lay the foundations of your new parental relationship with your baby and with each other.

Different patterns of bonding

While two-thirds of mothers bond with their babies almost immediately or within a few days, many fathers admit that intense paternal feelings take

▲ **SHARING THE CARE** Your child can't have too much attention and love from her parents. Family meal times can be a great time for both of you to feed her and talk to her. She'll enjoy the company, and you'll learn to be parents together.

Defusing areas of conflict

What to do	How it helps
Discuss who does what	You probably both have views about what roles men and women should play; this can be a powerful hidden agenda. Discuss how you feel and be prepared to have your views challenged.
Talk about your expectations	Disappointed expectations may produce disillusionment, so it's best to give and take in those areas where your views diverge, even though you won't escape hard choices.
Listen to each other	Try to talk openly about your feelings and think about how to express them. Do this in a way that avoids accusation, sarcasm, or belittling your partner. Give "I" rather than "you" messages.
Resolve conflict immediately	Resolve conflict by determining the cause and coming to a mutually agreed solution. A common area of conflict is the division of labor (see below).
Put your family first	Self-denial isn't a very popular concept these days, but if you're to turn your trio into a family, you'll each need to forgo some individual pleasures in the interest of building that family.
Learn to cope with stress	Reactions to stress differ from person to person. Try to evolve together a pattern of "stress management" for difficult periods, to minimize any possible damage to your relationship.

JUST FOR DAD

If you're at work and your partner is at home with the baby, try to see her point of view. At work, you'll have the challenges and friendships of working life to stimulate you, while your partner may be missing these if she's stopped work to take care of the baby, and she may well be finding the change difficult.

Supporting your partner

✴ Call her during the day, several times a week. If possible, go home for lunch every now and then.

✴ Let her know what time you're going to be home and stick to it. She'll need a break in the evenings, and this is valuable time for you to spend with your baby.

✴ Share the ups and the downs. If you've had a rotten day at work, talk to her about it, but listen to her and be sympathetic if she's also had a bad day at home.

✴ Make sure she has time out to relax away from the baby and to see her friends (see p. 134).

Becoming more involved

✴ Even if your partner is at home with the baby most of the time, remember that your role in caring for your baby is vital and will be rewarding for you.

✴ Find out what happened during the day and what milestones your baby may have reached—then spend time with your baby so that you can experience them too.

✴ Try to use your weekends and days off to have extended time with your growing baby.

much longer to develop. Many mothers are overwhelmed by the depth of their feelings for their baby. Unfortunately, some fathers view this as an obsession, to which they are not sympathetic, and they resent being excluded from their partner's affection and attention. A man whose partner breastfeeds often feels excused from nurturing as a result, driving a wedge between himself and his baby. Fathers who are involved in their baby's daily care will strengthen their paternal bond in the early weeks and close the gap between how differently fathers and mothers feel about their baby.

Division of labor

By far the biggest bone of contention between new parents is how they should share caring for the baby and the workload that goes with it. Many fathers do their fair share, but others help with the enjoyable tasks, such as bath time and bedtime stories, but are less enthusiastic about changing diapers, washing clothes, and getting up in the middle of the night. This attitude is inappropriate—parenting should be a partnership. Find ways of sharing the drudgery and the delights of caring for your baby. Look positively at her development and how you can stimulate and enjoy it together (see p. 146). You and your partner should think of parenthood as one of the most demanding jobs you can have, and reinforce each other's equal responsibility to succeed in this new role.

Learning to cope

Minimizing stress

Most family arguments happen at stressful times. Early in the morning when you're only half awake, it's easy to feel clumsy and irritable. If you're working, you may bring stress home with you, making it more difficult to cope with the demands at home. It's at times like these that you need to work together to help each other; taking out your stresses on each other or on your baby will probably only make things worse.

✳ Try to find ways of relaxing with each other and by yourselves (see p. 134).

✳ Try to be honest about how you're feeling to help prevent any misunderstandings.

✳ Don't try to do too many things at once—you'll only get frustrated and over-tired.

✳ Try not to bring work home with you—physically or mentally.

Negative feelings

Having negative thoughts toward your baby because he's kept you up all night or because he's crying a lot is normal. There's no point in refusing to accept how you feel; it doesn't make you a bad parent. It's abnormal, however, to use violence as a way of expressing yourself; if your temper is being pushed to the limit, talk to someone or take time out before you do something you'll regret.

Caring for a baby tests all parents. Getting through the difficult times is part of being a parent; you'll learn from every occasion and be a better parent and partner for having come through it.

Why anger is normal

If your baby cries for long periods or sleeps only for brief intervals, you're bound to feel concerned and worried. If this worry is then compounded by a feeling of impotence, it often expresses itself as anger. You may sometimes be seized by acute feelings of helplessness, guilt, and inadequacy when nothing you do seems to pacify your baby. At such times it's difficult not to feel victimized, and the worry can often quickly escalate to resentment and then anger. You may also feel angry that nothing you do seems to work, and resentful that you're left with little time or energy for your own needs. These are very natural feelings.

Breaking the cycle of negativity

The knowledge that your tension and frustration can be communicated to your baby will only increase your anxiety, which will in turn make your baby feel more insecure. It's very easy to become locked into a vicious circle of negativity. Your baby will express this in the only way he knows, by crying, and his crying will further unnerve you. This circle must be broken.

Talk to someone Pick up the phone and call someone you can confide in; just getting your feelings out in the open will help to put everything into perspective. Talking to other parents in the same situation is often useful— you'll realize that how you feel is very normal. You should also talk to your partner, but remember he or she may also be feeling exasperated; try to talk to each other when you're able to go out without the baby or when the baby is asleep. If none of the above is possible, speak to your doctor.

A change of scene If you're alone with your baby during the day, find an excuse to get out of the house together. The change of scene will help to relax you, and being driven in a car, wheeled in a stroller, or walked in a sling can often soothe a baby. In the short term, if you feel yourself being engulfed by anger, leave the room or put the baby in another room until you feel calmer. When your baby is older, make sure you have adequate time away (see p. 134).

If your baby is difficult to love

Just like both of you, your baby has his own personality. He may be happy and smiling all the time, or he may be reserved and seemingly unsociable. He may be independent and not very affectionate, or clingy and easily upset. Remember, your baby doesn't choose to behave in a certain way to spite you—it's just how he's made. As with all relationships, you need to keep the communication channels open with your baby. You have to get to know what makes him tick and accept that you're not going to have an easy relationship with him all the time.

Maintaining affection

Some babies don't like to be handled or cuddled very much; others go through phases of being unsociable. If a baby doesn't want attention, he will tend to stiffen his body and cry when you hold him. Most babies will become more sociable with time, but if you're worried, seek advice from your doctor. Try to do the following:

* Accept that babies are sometimes just difficult and don't blame yourself.
* Don't thrust unwelcome attention on him—it may make matters worse.
* If your baby is more affectionate with your partner, be grateful! Don't take this personally; babies often go through periods when they prefer or cling to one partner and this will pass with time.
* Remember, your baby will respond to you so make sure you're smiling and being affectionate toward him.

When your baby misses you

If you have invested time in your baby and bonded closely, you'll have created a feeling of rightness when you're together that is shattered when you're apart. An upheaval, such as returning to work, the preferred parent being away for a while, or the introduction of a babysitter or nanny may make your baby unsettled. This is most likely to reveal itself in his being fretful, fussy, and needing more hugs than usual, and a change in his eating and sleeping patterns. If your baby appears to be unhappy, reassess the situation; for example, it could be that he's unhappy with his babysitter. To help your baby if you're away:

* Call frequently.
* Ask your partner or babysitter to talk about you to your baby.
* Leave an item of your clothing for your baby to hold and some pictures of yourself.
* Tape yourself singing and talking to your baby.

▶ **KEEP IN TOUCH**
A baby will love to hold the phone, hear Daddy's voice, and "talk" to him when he's away from home.

A fretful baby

Most parents experience a period when their baby is consistently fretful and demanding for no apparent reason. The inability to communicate what's wrong can be very frustrating for both of you and your baby.

Why he may be fretful

* He may not be receiving as much stimulation as he needs. Babies who can sit up and who would like to explore their surroundings, but who can't yet crawl, can become frustrated.

* If your baby is teething, he may be experiencing discomfort or even pain (see p. 109).

* If you're particularly stressed, your baby may be picking up your heightened tension.

Getting through it

* Remember, your baby's behavior is normal. Much of your frustration stems from his inability to communicate. This is natural and not a failing in him or you.

* It doesn't mean that you're inadequate if your baby is going through a bad patch. Most parents experience difficult periods.

* Try to accept your feelings rather than getting angry with yourself, and you'll find it easier to keep an overall positive attitude.

* Try to keep things in perspective by sharing any negative feelings with each other or a friend.

* There are particular ways that a crying baby can be comforted. Try some of the suggestions outlined on pp. 104–109.

Feeling low

Helping each other

In the days after the birth, when the "baby blues" may be rife, you'll both need to support each other. Just sharing the day-to-day care of your baby and listening and being there for each other will help.

What fathers can do

✳ Encourage your partner to talk about the things that are getting her down. Give her lots of affection.

✳ Boost her self-esteem. She may feel unattractive and dislike her body—tell her often how much you love her and that she's beautiful.

✳ Take her shopping for clothes. Be patient and compliment her. Don't push her to lose weight.

✳ Encourage her to join a mother-and-baby support group and make it easy for her to go.

✳ Encourage people to visit if that's what she wants, but, if not, help to maintain her privacy.

What mothers can do

✳ If you've got the blues, try your best not to take out your tensions on your partner. Try to express how you're feeling. If you need a hug, tell your partner.

✳ Remember that your partner also has some big adjustments to make and may be finding it difficult, too.

✳ Make sure your partner has time with the baby. It will create problems if he feels left out.

✳ Try to limit visitors. Your partner may feel excluded if your house is full of female friends and family.

The "baby blues" usually last a few days, but in some mothers they go on for months due to postpartum depression. A partner needs to know the difference between the "blues" and depression so that he can help and knows when to seek medical advice.

Baby blues

The "baby blues" are mood swings caused by hormonal changes. In all likelihood this period of feeling low one minute and euphoric the next won't last beyond the first week, but you'll still need a lot of support to get through it. Maybe the "baby blues" are a natural sign to those around you that you need time and space to come to terms with being a mother. That's certainly how a concerned partner, relative, or friend should deal with it; although you'll find that because your hormones are all over the place, you'll also cry when someone's nice to you!

Why you get the blues

Your hormones, progesterone and estrogen, were high during pregnancy. After childbirth, these hormone levels drop and your body may find it difficult to adjust. This drop can have a marked effect on your emotions. With hormonal changes, exhaustion from labor, and lack of sleep, it's not at all surprising that you may not be feeling on top of the world.

What you can do

✳ Give yourself time. Accept that you'll feel like this for a short time and that what you're going through is incredibly common. Accept offers of help and don't try to do everything yourself.
✳ Try to talk about your feelings and have a good cry if it helps.
✳ Tell your partner you need a lot of love and affection, but remember this is a time of upheaval and change for him, too.

When fathers get the blues

Most fathers feel an anticlimax after the birth. There are so many changes—and if your partner is feeling low, you'll be called on to be a tower of strength, which can be a huge strain. Try to think of the first few months as a period of rapid change that is trying for both of you; when you come through it, you'll be closer than you were before. If you feel truly unhappy, talk things over with your doctor or a close friend.

Postpartum depression (PPD)

If symptoms that started out as the common "baby blues" don't go away and, in fact, start to become worse, you could be suffering from postpartum depression. This is a temporary and treatable condition that varies from woman to woman. It can develop slowly and not become obvious until several weeks after the baby's birth, but if it's diagnosed and addressed early enough, there's a good chance of a fast cure. Doctors are trained to recognize the symptoms, and treatment ranges from something as simple as talking to a friend or doctor about how you feel, to taking medication, such as antidepressants, in more severe cases.

Why postpartum depression happens

There are many reasons why postpartum depression occurs. It depends on you as a person, your personal circumstances, and the way your baby behaves. Research shows that the following risk factors may make you more susceptible to postpartum depression:

* If you enjoyed a senior position at work or high-flying career before the birth, it can be difficult to adjust to the status change.
* If you already have difficulties in your relationship, the baby may make them worse; this in itself may lead to disillusionment and low self-esteem.
* If you had an unexpectedly difficult birth experience (see pp. 50–53), you could easily feel demoralized and feel that you've failed in some way.
* If you've had depression in the past.
* A very demanding, sleepless baby can trigger postpartum depression from sheer exhaustion.
* If you have particularly difficult living conditions and no support network, this can make postpartum depression worse.
* If you've bottled up your emotions and not sought help early on.

Seeking help

Many women are too embarrassed to admit how they feel, fearing that it will appear that they've somehow failed. Talking about how you feel is the most important thing you can do. Once you accept that you're not "crazy" and that there are things you can do to help yourself, you are one step ahead on the road to recovery. Once you seek help, you may be guided to:

* Understand how you feel and learn to express this.
* Learn to prioritize, devote more time to yourself, and find ways to relax.
* Visit your doctor more regularly and seek support.
* Begin taking medication if your postpartum depression is extreme.

What fathers can do

You may feel helpless if you don't understand postpartum depression. Remember, it's temporary and treatable, so try to be patient. You can be a huge help if you make an effort to understand and do the following:

* Talk and listen to your partner. Never tell her to pull herself together—she can't. Don't assume she'll snap out of it—she won't.
* Mother the mother—encourage her to rest and eat and drink well.
* Encourage her to be with the baby as much as she wants so that she can take things slowly and gradually work out how the baby will fit in.
* Make sure she's not alone too much as she'll fear isolation.
* Go to see the doctor first for advice, since your partner may refuse to accept that she's not well.

PPD signs to look out for

Signs and symptoms may include:

* Anxiety—in particular, a mother may worry about her baby and refuse to be parted from her.
* Irrational fears, such as anxiety over being left alone.
* Loss of appetite.
* Insomnia or fatigue.
* Lack of concern with appearance.
* Making mountains out of molehills.
* Withdrawal from social contact.
* Feeling negative and inadequate.
* Growing feelings of despondency and helplessness.

Postpartum psychosis

Postpartum psychosis is the rarest and most serious form of PPD. It affects about one in 1,000 women, usually in the first three months after the birth. Urgent medical help is needed. Symptoms include:

* Sleeping all day.
* Crying for long periods.
* Feeling tense and anxious.
* Being manically "up" and behaving oddly.
* Being paranoid and hallucinating.
* Thinking about harming herself and the baby.

Taking time out

You need time out, but don't forget so does your partner. He needs his own time with your baby, time alone with you, and a chance to relax away from work and home.

How to help your partner

❋ Encourage him to have an occasional night out with friends or time to continue a hobby, even if he's been out at work all day. It's good for anyone who works to relax this way, as long as it doesn't take over his life to the exclusion of you and your baby.

❋ Make the most of your time at home with your partner. He may feel left out, so make the effort to make him feel special, particularly when the baby is asleep.

How your baby benefits

Spending short periods away from your baby can make you a better parent, so don't feel guilty!

❋ You'll appreciate your baby more when you see him again.

❋ A break will help you feel relaxed and rested so you cope better.

❋ It's good for your baby to get used to your going out—and see that you always come back. He'll gain confidence and develop his social skills by having to relate to others.

Being a new parent is undoubtedly a tiring and time-consuming experience, but you need to have time out for you and your partner—individually and together. Making time for yourself is not a luxury, it's a necessity. You'll need to be well organized, but it'll be good for your relationship and good for your baby.

Make time for yourself

❋ If you're the primary caregiver, incorporated into your daily timetable should be at least half an hour devoted entirely to yourself, when you can have a bath, read a magazine, or see a friend.

❋ When your baby is asleep, take the opportunity to rest; if you're feeling tired, taking a catnap is more important than cleaning the house. Don't be hard on yourself—it's okay to sleep in the middle of the day, especially if you're having to get up during the night.

❋ Time away doesn't only mean half an hour away from your baby when he's asleep; it means time away from the home environment. If you arrange to see a friend, suggest that you visit her or meet her somewhere. If you're at home you're more likely to become involved with your baby.

❋ Arrange a "baby swap" with other parents: They take care of your baby along with their own on a particular day or evening, and then you do the same for them. Ask friends and relatives to help out, if they live nearby.

❋ Find out if the local gym has a childcare facility—and use it!

Be flexible with your daily routine

You can roughly plan your day, but don't be too regimented and inflexible. The needs of a young baby change all the time, and if your baby wakes up unexpectedly you may not be able to have the half an hour you wanted. Try to be relaxed about it and take a break later in the day.

Accept help from others

It will be much easier to make time for yourself if you learn to accept offers of help. Don't be stoic and don't feel you're somehow a failure because you let someone else look after your baby. Just say yes, gracefully, and then do your own thing—you deserve it. It's normal to feel strange about leaving your baby for the first time, but this will pass with time once you've learned to trust your helpers. Your baby will also benefit in many ways by not being only with you all the time (see left).

Spending time together as a couple

An important part of keeping the communication channels open with your partner is to find time when you can be alone together. Doing this is possible, but may require planning. It may seem odd to book a time to see your partner, but if you try to be spontaneous about it, you'll always find an excuse or decide that your baby is more important. Sometimes it may only be possible to spend time together in the house, but try to find times when someone else can take care of your baby so you have the opportunity to go out and have uninterrupted time as a couple.

At home
✳ Try to continue any rituals you had before your baby was born, such as having a drink together in the evening, sharing a bath, or doing the crossword puzzle on Sundays. Try not to talk about your baby all the time.
✳ Snuggle up together for half an hour on the sofa; this precious time together will help you keep some semblance of normality and act as a reminder that you're still a couple, as well as being parents.

Going out
✳ Don't turn down invitations and, if possible, try not to take your baby with you all the time (although it may be easier to do so in the first six to eight weeks). Find a reliable babysitter and, if you're breastfeeding, express milk (see p. 83) so you don't have to cut your evening short.
✳ When your baby is a little older, find people you can rely on—such as grandparents—to take care of him for a longer period of time so that you can have a weekend away together.
✳ Continue hobbies you enjoyed together before the baby was born, such as playing sports (see p. 66). If you can't find a babysitter, go swimming—it's something you can all enjoy together (see p. 139).

Grandparents
Your baby's grandparents can loom large in your life both positively and negatively. If they respect your privacy and your right to bring up your children your way, grandparents are unquestionably the best friends, helpers, and supporters you and your baby will have.

Making the most of grandparents' help
Grandparents are the people most likely to encourage you to have time off, not least because they'll want to spend some time with their grandchild. Make the most of this. Let them be a part of your baby's life and have their own relationship with him—the bond between grandparents and grandchild can be priceless for your child and for them. It is, however, important to get the balance right, as much as anything because you don't want to fall out with the people who are your best helpers:
✳ Don't let bossy parents or parents-in-law take over, drop in every five minutes, or turn up uninvited. If they live nearby, try to get into a routine that suits everyone; for example, choose a particular day of the week for them to care for your baby.
✳ Be clear from the outset about how you want to bring up your baby to prevent any misunderstandings later on. Make sure that grandparents do things the way you like them done, and not the way they think best.

✳ JUST FOR DAD

Sharing the care of your baby will help you understand how your partner feels and how important it is for her to have some time off.

How to help your partner
✳ Take your baby out shopping or just out for a walk on the weekend to give your partner some space.

✳ Be fair to your partner—if she has stayed in with the baby while you've been out with friends, offer to do the same for her.

✳ Share the cooking, even if you've been at work. Treat yourselves to takeout occasionally.

Babysitters

Use a babysitter who has experience with babies and young children, and preferably one recommended by friends. Don't use someone under 16 years old in case a problem arises that he or she may not be able to handle. The babysitter will need:

✳ Telephone numbers for you and a relative or neighbor.

✳ The location of your first-aid kit and an explanation of how to use the baby monitor.

✳ An idea of your baby's routine and what to do if he wakes up.

✳ Feeding equipment and details of what your baby should be fed.

✳ Diaper-changing equipment and a change of clothes.

Sex and parenthood

Given your new responsibilities and possible physical discomforts (see below right), having sex is unlikely to be a high priority.

Your body image
You may feel unattractive if you have stretch marks and feel bloated, but your partner is probably less bothered about these things than you think. However, you do have to start liking yourself again before you can enjoy sex. Consider exercising (see p. 66); if nothing else, you'll feel better about yourself. If you're breastfeeding, you may be uncomfortable about your partner touching your breasts. Tell him—he may share your feelings.

Your baby
You're likely to be completely preoccupied with your baby and having sex may be the last thing you want to think about. This is normal, but once you decide to make love again, try to put the baby to the back of your mind.

Your partner
Don't put up with uncomfortable or painful sex because you feel you must. Your main priority is your baby and, although your partner needs to feel loved, you can show that in other ways. Remember, although you're preoccupied and fulfilled by your baby, your partner may not be to the same extent. Talk about this and how it affects your feelings about sex.

Your sexual relationship will, for a short time, be one of the many aspects of your partnership that has to adapt. Talk openly to each other about your sexual needs and expectations so this doesn't become a difficult issue.

Your feelings about sex

Don't just have sex because you think it's what your partner wants, and don't expect to have sex after a certain time. It's normal to feel sexually different now that you're in the dual, contradictory roles of being a parent and a lover. You may even feel guilty about wanting or thinking about sex because you feel you should be thinking about your baby. Don't take sexual rejection personally. Talk to each other and try to understand the reasons for wanting or not wanting to resume intercourse. Sex can only become a problem if you let it, and it should be easily resolved if you keep talking to each other about how you feel.

How sex can help Taking care of a baby can cause tensions and problems. Having intercourse at the right time, when you're both ready for it, may be just what you need to reaffirm your desire and affection for each other.

Physical considerations

You can generally resume sex when you both feel ready (unless you have been advised to wait for any reason), but there may be physical problems that will deter you from resuming sex in the first weeks after the birth.

Vaginal discomfort It's normal to feel too sore and tender to resume penetrative sex. The vagina will be bruised, making sex painful, even if the childbirth was free of intervention. If you had an episiotomy (see p. 46), you may not be able to tolerate anything rubbing against the site for many months. Also, the glands that normally lubricate the vagina will not function effectively because of hormonal changes after pregnancy, so it's advisable to use a lubricant.

Lochia (see p. 64) Don't resume penetrative sex until this discharge has stopped, which may not be for up to six weeks.

Breastfeeding Your breasts may leak milk during intercourse, especially when you orgasm, which can be a shock unless you're both prepared for it.

Tiredness Given the choice between having sex or sleeping, most new parents would choose the latter. Until you have more of a routine, and have found ways to have time to yourselves, it's difficult to resume a normal sex life. Try to be understanding if either one of you is too tired to make love.

Libido It appears that the sex drive in both new parents is much lower than normal, but it returns slowly over a matter of months.

Cesarean Although you won't have any vaginal discomfort, a cesarean is major abdominal surgery. You're likely to feel very tender for around six weeks and should wait to resume sex until you're fully recovered.

Contraception

The last thing you're likely to want when you're looking after a newborn baby is to find that you're immediately going to be parents all over again! Your doctor or midwife will talk to you about contraception in the hospital and/or at your six-week check (see p. 64). You can become pregnant even if your periods have not started, and you can be fertile as early as three weeks after the birth of your baby.

Breastfeeding While this does reduce fertility, you have to be feeding very regularly (at least every four hours, and more often for some women) to prevent ovulation. Breastfeeding is not a contraceptive.

Having sex

Without it being an automatic prelude to sex, you should both feel that you can engage in physical contact whenever you feel like it. It's important that you continue to enjoy sex and find what is right for both of you—talk about your preferences and be open to trying new things.

Foreplay It's good to build up your sex drive through foreplay—touch and caress each other, try massaging each other with aromatic oils, and/or take a bath together.

Non-penetrative sex For the first few times, maybe quite soon after the birth, try bringing each other to orgasm through gentle manual and oral sex. Consider being experimental; for example, try using some sex toys, such as a vibrator.

Comfortable positions Once you feel confident enough to try penetrative sex, experiment with different positions to find the ones that put least pressure on the sore areas. Stop at any time if you feel discomfort.

✳ Methods of contraception

Type	Advice
Pill	Those containing estrogen are not prescribed for women who are breastfeeding because they reduce milk production.
Mini-pill	These contain only progesterone, which does not inhibit milk production, but they may worsen postpartum depression (see p. 132) by inhibiting natural production of progesterone. They are taken at the same time each day.
Condom (male and female)	These should be used with a contraceptive gel for comfort and security. A female condom may cause discomfort if you're bruised and sore after childbirth.
IUD (inter-uterine device), Mirena or diaphragm	Your cervix may have enlarged and won't return to its normal size for two to three months. If you used a diaphragm or had an IUD or Mirena device before you were pregnant, you'll need a new one. Some doctors will fit this at your six-week check (see p. 64), though others prefer to wait a bit longer.

✳ JUST FOR DAD

It's natural to have a low sex drive (see below) for a short time after your baby is born. It's often a good thing because it allows you to concentrate on your baby. Many men, though, do want to resume sexual activity sooner than their partners.

Reasons for a low sex drive

✳ Being too tired and preoccupied with the baby.

✳ Having witnessed the birth.

✳ Sharing a bedroom with your baby.

✳ Feeling that your partner's body (especially her breasts) belongs to the baby and finding it difficult to think of her sexually.

✳ Being frightened of physically hurting your partner.

Understanding your partner

✳ Start being closer and more affectionate gradually and you'll soon begin to see your partner as your lover again.

✳ Don't expect too much from your partner too soon. Sex will be much less enjoyable for you if she's not ready or comfortable.

✳ Your partner may find it difficult to relax during sex as she will be listening for your baby's cry. Be understanding and try to find time when you can be alone without your baby (see p. 134).

✳ If your partner kisses you or you're just being affectionate with each other, don't assume you will have sex. This will only upset her, disappoint you, and probably cause an argument.

Your new world

Playgroups and classes

Playgroups and classes range from informal arrangements between several parents to professionally organized sessions, where a trained supervisor offers a wide variety of play-based activities.

✳ The playgroup gives you a chance to meet other parents, and your baby an opportunity to make friends with other children and adults.

✳ A child of two and a half can be left at some playgroups for a couple of hours; many also have a mother-and-baby group where parents go with their babies.

✳ Some malls, community centers, and supermarkets have supervised playrooms where babies and children can be left for a couple of hours. You must, however, stay in the vicinity in case you're needed.

Being a parent becomes a huge part of how you see yourself and how others see you. Your priorities change, and this takes some getting used to. Caring for your baby is easier and more fun if you meet other parents and use the facilities available to you.

Other parents and children

Being a parent will extend your range of friends to include those who have children. As well as counteracting the demoralizing effect of mid-morning and early-afternoon isolation that can be the curse of solitary childcare, making friends with other parents benefits you in many ways:

✳ You mix with other people who are equally focused on being a parent.
✳ It's a good way to introduce your baby to relationships outside the family, which helps to develop her social skills.
✳ Parenting is a learning process—you'll be breaking new ground every day and be able to exchange tips with the friends you've made.
✳ You'll have people who understand the difficulties you're going through because they're going through them too.

How to meet people

A good way to make friends who have children is to stay in touch with some of the parents you met while pregnant, particularly if you live in a rural area where there may be fewer activities. If you have a spring or summer baby, you'll probably meet people in the park or playground. If your baby is born in the winter, find out about activities from your pediatrician's office or local library.

▶ **MEETING PEOPLE** Forming friendships with other parents and their babies can be hugely beneficial to you and your baby.

When parenthood is not enough

It used to be thought that being at home with a baby was a satisfying way for a woman to spend her most creative and active years; the same would rarely be thought of a man. But nowadays many mothers and fathers are far from fulfilled by simply being a parent. Some who've tried to do it, because they believe that it's the best start they could give their child, have found the experience quite limiting.

Learning to adapt

In a society where the worth and freedom of the individual, the opportunity for self-development, and an obligation to be oneself are constantly cited as legitimate goals, it's not surprising that most people are ill-prepared for the narrowing of horizons that comes with caring for a baby. You and your partner simply won't have as much of yourselves left over as before, and this doesn't sit easily with the kind of ambitions bred by modern society.

Finding fulfilment Women who want to take an active part in the wider world, and have been educated and trained to do so, can hardly be expected to substitute an intimate relationship with the washing machine for the stimulation and satisfaction they derived from their work. The thousand joys of nurturing babies and children don't, for some women, compensate for the loss of a life outside the home, as the joys are not the same. You can't make up for a lack of vitamin A by taking large doses of vitamin B. It goes without saying that full-time parenthood is a worthwhile career for a person who is happy in it, but anyone who hankers for more than pure domesticity shouldn't feel ashamed. Just because you have interests beyond day-to-day childcare doesn't mean you don't love your baby.

Avoiding isolation Many people decide to become parents with the view that it will be a temporary—never total—denial of their needs and ambitions. This is why it's important—and, ultimately, in the baby's best interest—that you don't feel trapped by your parenting role. What most of us understand as isolation is the absence of other people and for those who spend their days caring for children, this means other adults. However much you love your baby, it's important to have the stimulation of adult interaction, which is why you need to get out and meet people.

Working from home

To make the transition to being a parent easier and less of a shock, some women try to keep some of their old self by working from home. The information technology revolution has made this more possible than ever before, but it's not as easy as it sounds, especially if it's attempted too soon.

✳ You must have a routine with your baby in order to do justice to your work and to make sure you don't end up working in the evenings.

✳ It's important to make sure you're not just dividing your time between work and your baby; you need time for yourself and with your partner.

✳ You'll still need to organize some form of childcare (see p. 172), which could mean that you miss out on time with your baby in her early months.

Activities at home

You'll be at home for some of the time, so getting together with other parents to host activities at home is a good idea. It's also a good way for your baby to get used to different people. Here are some ideas:

✳ **Coffee morning:** this is a fun and affordable activity, giving you the chance to chat as your babies play.

✳ **Lunch party:** provide simple snack food, so that you can eat and baby-watch at the same time. Ask friends to bring a contribution (especially for their babies) or just take turns hosting.

✳ **Home-selling party:** this is a good way to be sociable and earn some money. It involves presenting and taking orders for products, such as household goods or books, and earning commission on what you sell. Before you start, always check that the company you're working for is a reputable one.

Community centers

One way of getting out is to join a community center or gym. Find one that has childcare facilities (see opposite) so you can take your baby with you—some have a "soft room" where your baby can play. Most swimming pools offer parent-and-baby sessions, and your baby will enjoy the water once she hold her head up (around four months). Remember, avoid high-intensity exercise for the first nine months and while breastfeeding.

Single parents

Accepting help

Most couples struggle to bring up a baby without help, so as a single parent don't think you have to do it all yourself. Having guaranteed time on your own during the week is good for both you and your baby:

✳ Try to build up a small network of people you can depend on.

✳ If you have several helpers, spread their time with your baby throughout the week if you can.

✳ Ask a relative or friend who's not working to stay over once a week so you can get a good night's sleep, especially if you're working.

✳ Seek the help of voluntary organizations (see p. 187) if you don't have people you can rely on.

✳ Make sure you're getting all your financial benefits and any support payments from the absent parent, if applicable.

✳ If you know other single mothers, "baby swap" with them so that you all get a chance for some time to yourselves.

✳ Don't be embarrassed or too proud to accept gifts—people would probably have given you these even if you weren't single.

Negative reactions

Some people may judge you and your ability to bring up your baby. Dealing with this can have a positive effect— many single parents become determined to prove that they can raise a happy and contented child. Criticism can also put pressure on you, making you feel that you can't ask for help, but you can, so try to remember this.

Being a single parent and being without a good support network can be physically and emotionally exhausting, but the knowledge that you've done it alone can be hugely rewarding for you and good for your baby.

Single parent by choice?

If you've chosen to be a single mother, you may be more prepared emotionally, practically, and financially to take care of a young baby and look forward to the prospect. If you've separated with your partner during the pregnancy or soon after the birth, you may have more difficulty. Coping with the emotional problems of ending a relationship while caring for a young baby is bound to have an impact on your ability to cope. In this situation, it's even more important for you to ask for and accept help from family and friends.

Single parenting can be positive

Being a single parent is by no means all doom and gloom. You and your baby can benefit in many ways from the special relationship you'll form:

✳ Single parents tend to develop a very strong bond with their babies; they don't have to share their love between a partner and a child.

✳ Extended family—grandparents, aunts, and uncles—often get more involved when there's only one parent. The baby can greatly benefit from this network of support and love.

✳ Taking care of a baby alone is a great achievement. You'll strengthen as a person as you watch your baby develop.

✳ If you're single because your relationship has broken down, you've made the right decision; it's better for the baby to live with one fairly contented person than two people who are at war.

Balancing your relationship with your baby

I believe in showing boundless affection to babies, but you do need to balance your relationship with your baby—some single parents may invest all their emotions and energies in their baby and use him as an emotional crutch. You don't have to be a mother and father; being a responsive parent is good enough. Your baby has no notion of lacking a second parent; he's happy with you, so you don't need to overcompensate.

You and your baby will have a very close and important one-on-one relationship and no one can take that away from you, but babies need and thrive on exposure to others and should be encouraged to interact with a wide range of people. Introduce him to other adults, and children, so he gets used to being without you now and then. This will make it much easier for you and him if you have to introduce a babysitter. As your baby develops new skills (see p. 146), don't be afraid to share your joy with your relatives and friends—if they're close to your baby, they'll love to hear about it. Keep your own record of when each milestone occurs; when there is only one of you it will be more difficult to remember them.

Having a social life

All single parents are bound to experience feelings of loneliness and yearn for adult company. It's important for you to have a social life away from your baby and, of course, if you want to build future relationships you have to get out and meet people:

* If it's difficult for you to go out for financial or childcare reasons, invite people to your house for a meal—ask your guests to bring a course.
* Get to know other mothers—they'll probably be glad of the company.
* Ask people if they will babysit—you don't know unless you ask.
* Find hobbies, classes, and events that have childcare facilities.
* Find out about local activities so you can meet other parents.

The absent parent

Try to keep in touch with your ex-partner and agree on visitation arrangements and on how you want to raise your child. Ensure that he or she is clear about financial support required. Seek legal advice if necessary. Try to spend time together as a family occasionally, and, if appropriate, encourage the other grandparents to see your baby.

JUST FOR DAD

The single father

There are few men who are the sole caregivers for a young baby, but for those who are, the pleasures and most of the problems will be the same as those of any single mother. Remember that fathers can do everything mothers can do except breastfeed.

The benefits

Although being a single father isn't ideal, a single father may benefit in ways that wouldn't have happened had he been sharing the care with his partner. Research has shown that single fathers are more satisfied parents, feel closer to their child, and are more confident and effective than the average father.

The problems

Isolation may be the main problem experienced by the single father. Like a father who stays at home while his partner works (see p. 176), a single father may find the female-dominated environments that he is faced with difficult and, sadly, there may be those who question his ability to bring up his baby properly.

Potential difficulties

Problem	How to deal with it
Financial	With only one income, you're more likely to struggle financially and be unable to provide your baby with as many toys and clothes as you would like. Make sure you're getting all the benefits to which you're entitled, especially from your ex-partner. Remember that material possessions are not the most important things you can give your baby.
Fatigue	If you're caring for your baby alone, the physical and emotional strain will be more of a problem. Nap whenever your baby does. Try to take proper breaks and ask for and accept offers of help.
Concerns about the baby	If your baby becomes ill, you're unlikely to have someone there to reassure you and help keep things in perspective. Look at pp. 120–123 and consult your doctor as early as possible to minimize your worries.
Childcare	Affording childcare (see p. 172) can be a struggle for single parents. Look into subsidized and public daycare facilities in your neighborhood or consider sharing a nanny. Some churches, temples, schools, and community centers offer daycare, either free or for a reasonable rate.

The instant family

Questions and concerns

Adopting a baby is a big decision. You're bound to have doubts and fears about this new responsibility.

What if I can't cope?

All new parents have days when they can't cope (see p. 130). As an adoptive parent, you may have the added pressure of feeling that you're responsible for someone else's child and may have had less time to prepare. Don't be afraid to ask for help; use the adoption services, which are there to help.

What kind of child will I raise?

No one can predict the kind of person any child will turn out to be. Each individual is unique, so even biological parents have no idea whether their children will resemble them physically or in terms of personality.

Will I be a good enough parent?

Your motives for wanting to adopt and your suitability will be analyzed before you're accepted as adoptive parents. It's natural to question whether you'll be good parents, but I think the most important aspects of being parents have nothing to do with being the birth parents. These are:

✱ Your feelings and actions toward your child.

✱ Your sensitivity to your child's individual needs.

✱ Being consistently loving and accepting.

✱ Being fair and firm in setting limits for your child.

An "instant family" may be created through adopting a baby or by joining a ready-made family. A new baby brought into either situation can raise important issues that aren't present for most new parents.

Adopting a young baby

If you're fortunate enough to adopt your baby when she's very young, then everything said about bonding in earlier chapters applies to you. Babies come equipped with a strong urge to bond with their parents, or to anyone who gives them loving care, so you'll be off to the same promising start as everyone else. What may be difficult is that you won't have had the nine-month buildup to the birth and the internal bonding in the same way as a pregnant mother. On the other hand, as an adoptive parent you may have a stronger yearning for a baby than a natural parent. This makes you ideally placed to be a generous and loving parent, so be confident.

Adopting an older baby

If you adopt a baby when she is a few months old, it's really important that you find out as much as possible about the circumstances of her life up to the time when she came to you. This will help you to compensate for any experiences on which she has missed out and for any delay in the developmental stages you would normally expect her to have passed through. Don't, however, worry about her development too much; your baby may not have been affected at all by not being with her natural parents. Even if it has affected her, in the right loving environment your baby will soon be able to catch up.

▼ **BABIES NEED LOVE** Birth children, stepchildren, or adopted—all children need their parents' wholehearted love and support.

Bonding with an older baby

Trust is the basis of all good relationships between babies and their parents. If you have adopted an older baby, you may have to work harder to establish this trust than parents who have had their babies with them from birth. An older baby is likely to have been placed with foster parents for the first few months of her life and will have formed a strong attachment to them. Your baby may not immediately react as you had hoped; she has to learn how to respond to and accept your love and affection, and this takes time. Be reassured, however, that if you are relentless in offering your baby love, comfort, and affection, she will eventually learn to trust you and to accept and reciprocate your feelings.

A new baby in the stepfamily

If partners with a stepfamily decide to have a baby of their own, the dynamics of the family will change. While the baby may act as a uniting force within the family, her arrival may equally provoke some of the anxieties and tensions that were present at the formation of the family.

How stepchildren are affected

Your stepchildren's reaction to your baby will depend on how old they are, their relationship with you, and their past experiences. If their parents have split up recently, it may be more difficult; they're again being asked to adjust because of the actions of their parents.

Insecurities The news of the baby may remind the children of a previous breakup, and feelings such as rejection and fear of losing a parent may resurface. They may worry about the baby being seen as more precious and more desirable because she is a product of the present (your preferred) relationship, rather than of the past (your rejected) union.

Realization Many children from broken marriages live in hope that their parents will reunite. A new baby is a clear sign of commitment between their parent and stepparent, which often brings the truth home.

Relationship with stepparent If you and your stepchild have already established a good relationship, the arrival of your baby will cause fewer problems. If there are underlying tensions, the new baby may be the catalyst for resentment and anger.

Second time around A man who has a child later in life may change his priorities and be a more devoted father. Older children may resent not getting this attention when they were growing up. It's also common for children to find it distasteful for a parent to start a new family.

How you can help

Once the baby is born, your stepchild may become more accepting. To minimize problems, talk to him as early as possible. Ask him to tell you his concerns and reassure him that you still love him and that there's space and time for everyone to enjoy the baby. Encourage him to develop his own relationship with your baby. He may enjoy some responsibility, but don't abuse this—older stepchildren may resent being used as babysitters.

Deciding to have a baby

A couple may decide to bring a new baby into the stepfamily for a variety of reasons. One partner may be childless and want a baby of his or her own. The other partner, who is already a parent, may feel less of a need. Even if they both have children, they may feel that a baby will make them and also the whole family closer.

Planning ahead

* There may be financial obligations to an ex-partner and children from a previous relationship that can make affording another baby more difficult. Also, be aware that stepchildren living with you may resent having to sacrifice new clothes or going out because of the baby.

* Do you have room for a baby? Will it mean that stepchildren will have to move out of, or share, a bedroom? Discuss this as a family rather than just telling them it will happen. If you have to move to a new house, will it make it more difficult for visiting stepchildren to stay?

Telling an ex-partner

It's always better for your ex-partner to hear that you're having a baby from you rather than from someone else, and he or she definitely shouldn't be told by the children. Some people are shocked at their feelings when they hear the news and worry that their own children will lose out. However, if you have a good relationship with your ex-partner and he or she reacts positively to you having a baby, this could also have an effect on how your children handle the news.

Your baby's development

Your baby is developing from day one and it's one of the most fulfilling aspects of parenthood to watch him grow and learn. You'll become fascinated by his skills and amused by how he tries to copy you. In his first year, he'll change from a tiny helpless newborn into a sturdy and sociable toddler who very much has a mind of his own. Your role as parents is crucial in your baby's development: You are his first teacher and friend, and by being aware of the stages of development you can encourage certain skills at certain times. It's important, however, to remember that your baby's physical and mental development is individual to him, so never push him beyond his capabilities. Your baby mainly learns through play: He'll love it if you're his playmate and, although you should show him how things work, it's essential to his sense of self and independence that he find out how to do things for himself. He also learns by watching others, so encourage his social skills; getting to know other people is crucial to his development.

How babies develop

New skills

You'll see clear signs when your baby is close to acquiring a skill—a "milestone." Watch for the signs and only then match your efforts to her development and give her games to help. With correct timing, she'll acquire skills at 100 percent of her potential. If you push her too early or leave encouragement too late, she'll acquire the skill, but not at her full capability. Main milestones are:

✳ Smiling at a distance (six weeks).

✳ Discovering her hands and feet (three to four months).

✳ Blowing bubbles—the first sign of real speech (five months).

✳ The ability to transfer an object from one hand to the other (six months).

✳ Knowing her name (six months).

✳ Sitting unsupported (seven months).

✳ "Getting" a simple joke like peekaboo (eight months).

✳ Wanting to feed herself (nine months).

✳ Crawling (nine months).

✳ Pointing to an object with her forefinger (10 months).

✳ Picking up objects with her finger and thumb (10 months).

✳ Swiveling around while sitting to reach a toy (10 months).

✳ Putting things into containers and taking them out (11 months).

✳ Saying her first word with meaning (11–12 months).

✳ Walking unsupported (12–13 months).

One of the most fulfilling aspects of parenthood is watching and sharing in your baby's development. Encourage her to learn new skills, while allowing her to develop at her own pace.

Newborn babies

Your baby starts to develop from the very second she's born and she'll be longing to learn. She enters the world in a state of "quiet alertness" and this state of intense focus on her surroundings lasts up to an hour. She's a sponge ready to soak up information about her new environment:

✳ She recognizes your voice—and your partner's—immediately. She's heard these voices for months and switches on to them instantly.

✳ Your baby is born with her sight at a fixed focus of 8–10 in (20–25 cm); if you hold her at this distance from your face, she can see you and she'll smile.

✳ She has an acute sense of smell and will be able to inhale and register the natural scent (pheromones) from your body.

✳ She'll "mouth" in response to you if she can see your face and your lips moving (at a distance of 8–10 in/20–25 cm); she's attempting conversation.

Stimulating your baby

Both of you are your baby's first teachers and playmates. You must feed her with all kinds of stimulation, through play and through the way in which you interact with her, if you want to help her develop to her optimal

▲ **BEING A PLAYMATE** Spend time with your child; read books and play together—you are her best playmate. She'll enjoy your participation in her conversations and games.

potential. Your job is to teach her to be imaginative, adventurous, curious, helpful, and generous. There is no limit to the amount of praise and encouragement you should give her as she begins to discover her world.

Rules of development

Your baby develops to her own timetable and it's pointless trying to set a different one. Remember the following:

✳ No two children develop at the same rate so don't compare your baby to other babies—even if they do walk or talk before her.

✳ Development is continuous, although certain skills will be acquired in a spurt while other skills slow down. For example, when a child is mastering walking, she may turn into a sloppy eater.

✳ Development of the whole body depends on how mature the brain is and whether or not brain, nerve, and muscle connections have grown. Your baby can't learn a skill like walking or talking until all the connections are in place. Bladder control is not possible until 18 months (see p. 181). If you expect her to use the potty any earlier, this is likely to lead to failure and could slow down your baby's progress later.

✳ Development proceeds from head to toe (see p. 150) so a baby can't sit until she can control her head and she can't stand until she can sit.

✳ Skills gradually become finer; for example, at about five months she "grasps" with her open hand; at eight months she can pick things up with her fingers, and, when all the nerves and muscles have connected, she can pick up an object with her index finger and thumb.

✳ Overstimulation is as bad as understimulation; if there is a constant barrage of noise, your baby may become very confused and gain very little.

Positive discipline

Teaching your baby right from wrong starts at the very beginning, but it's the way you teach her that will affect her physical and emotional well-being:

✳ Praise and reward her good behavior and ignore bad behavior, especially if it occurs at meal times.

✳ Discipline her through love, praise, as well as encouragement. Never use anger or spanking—this can have a damaging effect.

✳ Set tasks to help her understand the discipline of a daily routine—for example, encourage her to feed herself and brush her hair.

✳ Hold your finger up and say "no" firmly if she's likely to harm herself, others, or cause damage. She'll begin to understand this from around the age of four months.

✳ Helping your baby to develop happily

What to do	How it helps your baby
Set realistic goals	Set appropriate goals for your baby; for example, don't expect her to be able to play properly with toys designed for older babies. If you do this, it will outstrip her skills and she will become unhappy, frustrated, and demoralized. Always concentrate on accomplishments, not deficiencies, and praise your baby with theatrical gestures.
Be a playmate	You are your baby's first playmate as well as her teacher. Make time to play with her whenever you can—even if it means the dishes have to wait! Babies have to be shown how to do things, so get down there and join in—your baby will love it. But don't interrupt when she's engrossed in something; it's hard enough for her to concentrate and see a job through to completion without distraction.
Encourage speech	Encourage her to "talk." Keep her eyes 8–10 in (20–25 cm) from yours when she makes noises, especially when feeding and talking to her. It's her first experience of feeling valued, and a valued baby will grow into a child who talks to you about everything—good and bad.
Repeat everything	Repeat words and actions over annd over until you're sick of it. Tell your baby the same thing over and over again—using the same even tone of voice—and show her how to do things. It will all be worthwhile once she understands and begins to copy.

Boys and girls

Newborn babies

The differences in behavior and development of boys and girls begin at birth and continue as they grow and develop (see p. 182). In newborn babies, the differences are mainly in the way they use their senses to perceive things and in the kinds of things in which they show an interest.

Hearing

Hearing in boys is less acute than in girls, which means they have more difficulty in locating the source of sounds. Girls are more easily calmed by soothing words because of their acute hearing. Whisper close to your baby boy's ear to stimulate his hearing and to help calm him.

Speech

A baby girl uses her voice to get attention earlier and more often than a boy. If a newborn boy hears another baby cry, he'll join in but will stop crying quite quickly, whereas a girl will cry for longer.

Sight

A newborn girl responds enthusiastically to visual things. A boy quickly loses interest in a design or picture and requires much more visual stimulation up to the age of about seven months.

Social skills

Boys are as interested in things as they are in people, while girls show a clear preference for the human face. This female trait continues into later life as an ability to intuitively read facial expression. Encourage your son to develop his social skills by holding him 8–10 in (20–25 cm) from your face so he can see you clearly.

It's a biological fact that there are differences in behavior and development between boys and girls from birth. Don't enforce stereotypes, but you can help your baby to develop skills that don't come as naturally, such as language for a boy and spatial skills for a girl.

Differences in brain development

Gender differences stem from the way the brain develops in male and female embryos. For a baby to learn and develop, certain connections have to have taken place between the right and left halves of the brain. Girls grow these connections earlier than boys (many are already in place when girls are born), which enables them to adapt faster to their new environment after birth. Connections form in a boy's brain more slowly and because of this later development, a baby boy will need slightly more help from you to reach his milestones (see p. 146).

Avoiding stereotypes

Stereotypes influence children and, worse, they tend to make people label certain qualities as inferior and superior—the latter usually being attributed to males. When children are taught to think, feel, and act in line with a stereotypical model, it can stunt their personal growth. Individuality should be encouraged, regardless of gender.

▲ **SPATIAL SKILLS** Help your daughter to develop her spatial skills by encouraging her to play with practical toys, such as a baby work bench, or cups or blocks to stack.

▲ **BEING A ROLE MODEL** You can positively influence your son's gentle, caring side by actively joining in with pastimes traditionally associated with females.

Gender differences up to age six

What develops	Girls	Boys
Natural ability	Girls are better at language skills like talking, reading, and writing and they tend to keep this ability.	Boys are slower to develop language skills, but from a very early age they show superior spatial skills.
Social skills	Girls are more sociable than boys—they're more interested in people and feelings and display this regard for others even in their first year.	Boys are generally more interested in objects than people and feelings. They tend to keep to themselves rather than playing in groups.
Behavior and personality	Girls cope better with stress and are more conciiatory. They tend to have fewer behavioral problems than boys.	Boys tend to be more aggressive, competitive, and rebellious than girls. They're more likely to develop behavioral problems.
Physical growth	Girls walk earlier than boys. They grow faster and more steadily, rather than in growth spurts. They also gain bladder and bowel control earlier.	Boys shoot ahead physically after five years. They develop faster during growth spurts, when many skills tend to emerge over a short time.

Discouraging gender stereotypes

Stereotypes of male and female roles will inevitably influence our children as they grow up if we're not sensitive to them and don't take appropriate preventative action. Research has shown that we even speak in a different tone of voice to boys and girls, and all too early, our children can become affected by stereotypical concepts of appearance, including body build, facial features, and clothes. There are also stereotypical concepts of behavior and role-playing. As parents, we all have to be vigilant if we want our children to escape stereotyping. Stereotypes are dangerous; once accepted, they are used as yardsticks against which our children are judged—good and bad, successful and unsuccessful, appropriate and inappropriate. It's far better to encourage individuality and originality.

Worse, stereotypes can be used as guidelines for training children. You need to act carefully from day one if you are to encourage a girl to be adventurous and strong, and a boy to be caring, able to show affection, and act as a peacemaker. Encourage more physical activities associated with boys for your daughter and don't always play over-boisterous games with your son. Traditional stereotypes have little to recommend them, whereas egalitarian gender roles offer massive scope for self-realization. Regardless of gender, each child needs to be able to reach his or her own potential.

❋ FATHER

Think about your attitudes and the type of activities you're encouraging, since all of these influence how your child develops and comes to see him- or herself.

Influencing your daughter

As a father, you may consciously or unconsciously reinforce your daughter's femininity. Fathers often involve boys in "rough-and-tumble" games, whereas they'll be more gentle with girls. Expose your daughter to all kinds of activities and let her choose—rather than limiting her to traditionally feminine pastimes like ballet and drama, introduce other activities like football too. Don't fall into the trap of believing some behavior is acceptable in boys and not in girls—you diminish your daughter if you do this. Try to be aware that your daughter is likely to feel devalued if she sees you devaluing her mother.

Influencing your son

Research shows that boys learn how to behave from their fathers. You can encourage your son to develop the more attractive male qualities (such as gentleness and a sense of responsibility) rather than the less desirable ones (such as being aggressive, dominant, and confrontational) simply by the way in which you behave. Your son will watch your actions and will imitate you in every respect. The quality of fathering that he receives from you is the most critical factor in how he views himself as a male.

How your baby grows

Concerns about weight gain

A baby's growth is an important indicator of health and well-being, but don't become obsessed with weight gain—it isn't the only issue. Any real discrepancies between length and weight should be picked up at your baby's well-child checkups (see p. 155), but, if you're concerned, speak to your doctor.

What if my baby isn't gaining weight?

Some babies remain the same weight for a while and then have a growth spurt. So don't worry if your baby doesn't gain weight over, say, one week or appears to have lost weight. Don't be tempted into switching to bottle-feeding (or adding to his bottle) in the hope of improving "slow" weight gain. In fact, breastfed babies typically grow faster, especially in the first few weeks.

What if my baby is overweight?

Some babies are naturally fatter than others, which may lead to some physical development happening slightly later. If you're concerned that your baby weighs too much for his age, seek medical advice, but don't reduce his intake of food as this could affect growth and development. The aim should be to maintain his weight at the current level until his length catches up. Research does, however, show that the pattern of heart disease and adult obesity can be set very early by being overweight from overfeeding. You should never push your baby to finish off the last drops of a feeding if he doesn't want it, or add extra formula to his bottle.

Your baby's physical development will be monitored closely at his well-child checkups (see p. 155): Growth (percentile) charts, which show the rate of growth expected for your baby's weight and gestational age at birth, will be used to map his progress. In the first year he will grow faster than at any other time in his life. Physical development starts at the top, which is why his head looks large, and from the inner parts to the extremities, which is why his hands and feet look tiny. Remember, your baby's development is individual to him; don't worry if he appears to be growing faster or slower than other babies. All babies grow at their own rate.

Weight

When a baby is born, the question "What does he weigh?" is second only to "Is it a boy or a girl?" Although people will place importance on your baby's weight, it is not the only sign of growth and it is important not to use this as the only way to judge his well-being (see left). Your baby's weight will be monitored at his checkups (see p. 155). Babies are normally weighed naked or wearing only a dry diaper.

One feature that all babies have in common is chubby arms and legs; this is due to uneven fat distribution, which remains uneven until he begins to use his limbs and becomes active. He may not lose it until he starts crawling, and possibly not until he's walking.

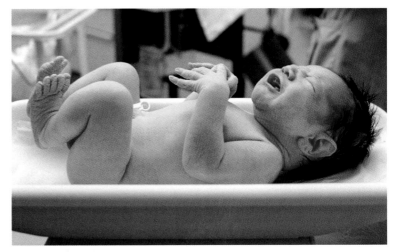

▲ **YOUR NEWBORN** At first, a newborn baby is floppy and has poor head control. As his bones and muscles develop over the next few weeks, your baby will learn to control his head. Amazingly this is the first step toward his being able to walk.

AT SEVEN MONTHS Once your baby learns to control her head, she will learn to sit. At first she'll need to be propped up with pillows, but soon she'll sit unsupported.

12 MONTHS At around one year your baby should be able to stand unsupported and perhaps be ready to take his first steps.

The normal pattern of weight gain

✳ In the first few days it's normal for a baby to lose up to ten percent of her birth weight. By the tenth day, she'll have regained her birth weight.

✳ In the following six months she'll gain weight rapidly, at a rate of about 2 lbs (1 kg) each month.

✳ In the second six months weight gain slows down and she'll put on around 1lb (500 g) each month.

Length (height)

Your baby's size is partly due to inheritance—if you're both tall, chances are you'll have a long baby. The biggest increase in length occurs in the first six months, after which growth slows down. If your child appears well and healthy, there's no reason for you to worry about her growth rate; any pronounced disproportion between length and weight will be investigated at her regular checkups (see p. 155).

An approximate guide to a baby's growth rate

✳ A newborn full-term baby is on average 20 in (50 cm) long.

✳ Her length will increase by 10–12 in (25–30 cm) in the first year.

✳ On average, boys tend to be taller than girls for the first two years.

Head size

A newborn baby is top-heavy, with a disproportionately large head—this gradually alters over the first four years. Head circumference is monitored at her regular checkups; if the proportions don't even out, it could alert doctors to certain rare medical conditions.

✳ A newborn baby's head circumference is about 14 in (35 cm), which is disproportionately larger than the rest of her body. By the time she is 12 months old, the size of her chest and head should have evened out.

✳ When a baby is born, her head makes up one-quarter of the length of her body, compared to an adult's head, which makes up around one-eighth.

How the senses develop

During the first year, your baby will begin to discover her world through her senses.

Vision

Your newborn has limited, but excellent, vision. At a distance of 8–10 in (20–25 cm) she sees clearly, so keep your face at this distance from hers when talking or smiling and she'll respond. At six weeks her eyes focus at any distance and both eyes work together. By three months she has full perception of colors; at six months she can see more detail; by one year her vision is well developed.

Hearing

She recognizes your voice and your partner's from birth, and will turn her head when you speak, so talk to her from the very first day.

Touch

Babies begin by "feeling" the shape and texture of objects. Initally they do this with their lips and tongue and then they explore with their hands.

Taste and smell

Newborn babies have a complete set of tastebuds and can recognize their parents' smell. They like only sweet tastes and smells, which is why they love breastmilk, but they gradually accept different tastes and make their likes and dislikes known.

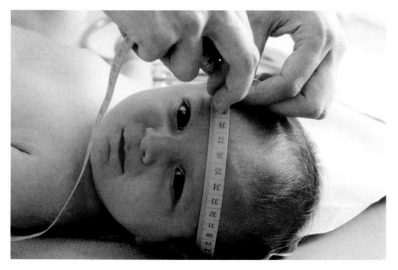

◄ **HEAD CIRCUMFERENCE** Your baby's head circumference will be measured at birth and again at her checkups. The growth of her head reflects the growth of her brain.

Nerve and muscle development

What develops	How it develops	What it means for your baby
Nerve connections that control limb muscles	Nerves extend from the brain and spine to reach the different muscle groups in the limbs. In a newborn, connections, or pathways, within the the brain that control nerves have not been formed, so a baby's movements are uncontrolled and crude. As the connections are forged, movements become finer and more precise.	Your baby progresses from picking things up with his fist at four months, to being able to pick up objects with his finger and thumb by ten months. As the nerve pathways develop, your baby will achieve head control and then he will sit, crawl, and then stand, before finally he starts walking.
Nerve connections that control bladder muscles	It takes at least 18 months to complete the nerve pathways that affect the bladder. Prior to that your baby can't have any control over how his bladder works—so don't expect it.	Once nerve connections are in place, your baby has to "train" his bladder muscles to hold urine and then let go. This takes several months and can't be hurried.

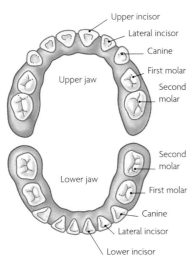

Upper incisor
Lateral incisor
Canine
First molar
Upper jaw
Second molar

Second molar
Lower jaw
First molar
Canine
Lateral incisor
Lower incisor

▲ **THE ORDER IN WHICH TEETH APPEAR** The age when teeth are cut varies, but they always come through in the same order: incisors, first molars, canines, and finally second molars.

How your baby's teeth develop

Your baby's first tooth is an exciting milestone. Teeth usually start to come through from six months, but the age varies from baby to baby (a few babies are born with a tooth already through, while others are still toothless on their first birthday). During teething, your baby may be more irritable and more wakeful than usual (see p. 109).

How teeth come in

✳ The first tooth to appear is usually a lower incisor, followed straight away by its neighbor.

✳ The next teeth to come are the upper incisors, followed first by the upper lateral incisors, then by the lower lateral incisors. There may be a delay before the first molar appears.

✳ Next come the canines, and finally the second molars appear.

▶ **BRUSHING HIS TEETH** Once your baby has his first tooth, start helping him to brush his teeth. Give him a toothbrush of his own and encourage him to copy you. Get into a routine of brushing his teeth morning and night, and after meal times.

Preventing tooth problems

You can help prevent your baby from developing any teething problems. Give him firm-textured foods such as a carrot to chew while he is teething. Make sure he has his own small, soft toothbrush and get into the routine of brushing his teeth in the morning, at bedtime, and after meals. Don't give him drinks and snacks that contain added sugar. Give him water to drink instead of juice; try to keep juices to meal times. Dilute his fruit juice and never add sugar, and give him juice in a cup rather than bottle.

Checkups

You'll be asked to take your baby for a checkup periodically, for example at six to eight weeks, and then throughout his first year. As well as discussing any issues with you, the nurse will weigh your baby, measure his length and head circumference, and then a doctor will check the baby's general health and carry out specific medical checks (see right).

What is the purpose of the checkups?

Many health professionals feel that "testing" babies at certain stages to see whether they are "up to the mark" is crude; now they are much more interested in the well-being of the whole child. At your baby's checkups, you'll be asked a series of questions to establish how you're all getting along, how you are managing, and whether you've noticed any specific problems with your baby. You should think of it as an opportunity to discuss any aspects of your baby's life (not just his development), or of your life with him that seem relevant: Baby checks aren't, or at least they're not supposed to be, just about checking off boxes.

Prepare yourself before you go

Make a list of questions and concerns you'd like to discuss. For example, you may have problems feeding or difficulty coping with sleepless nights. Don't be afraid to highlight problems—being a new parent is not easy for anyone, and you should take the opportunity to get expert advice.

What if my baby has a problem?

It's worrying to have doubts cast over your baby's development (see p. 124). If you have any concerns or a problem is found:

* Ask for time to sit down and talk through exactly what is wrong with your baby. Ask as many questions as necessary, especially if it isn't clear what the doctor is saying. Don't allow yourself to be brushed off by being told the doctor doesn't have time at the moment or that you are worrying for no reason.

* Don't accept that you should "wait and see"—if there's any question of a problem, your baby should always be referred for tests or to see a specialist right away.

* Get a second opinion if you're not satisfied or are still concerned.

Your baby's checkups

Six- to eight-week checkup

Heart and lungs The breathing and heart sounds are checked, particularly to rule out a heart murmur.

Palate The palate is checked at birth, and now, for completeness and to test the sucking reflex.

Vision Your baby will be tested to see if he can follow movement and look toward light.

Hearing Your baby will have had his hearing tested in the first few days after birth.

Mobility Your baby's hips are checked for displacement and any correction needed. Head control is checked.

Testes If you have a baby boy, the doctor will check to ensure that his testes have descended.

Later in first year

Speech Your baby should be making a range of sounds by now and his ability to do this will be noted.

Vision Any problem should have become apparent, but your doctor may check that eyes are aligned.

Handling The doctor may give your baby a toy to hold so that he can check his handling skills.

Mobility The doctor will check that your baby can sit up and is able to stand supported.

Testes A baby boy's testes may be checked again. If they still haven't descended, an operation may be needed later.

Baby development
0–1 month

❋ What to look out for

What develops	How she progresses	How you can help
Her mind	❋ She can see clearly at a distance of 8–10 in (20–25 cm). ❋ She will respond to your voice by moving her eyes and turning her head. ❋ She will gaze at you and recognize you. ❋ She will become quiet when you speak soothingly and distressed when you are loud.	❋ When talking to her, hold your face 8–10 in 20–25 cm) away from hers. ❋ When you speak, let her see your mouth moving. Smile and make eye contact at 8–10 in (20–25 cm). ❋ Use your voice: speak in a sing-song voice, sing lullabies, and laugh a lot.
Her mobility	❋ She will turn her head: This control is the first step towards learning to walk. ❋ By the end of the first month, the most she may be able to do is lift her head about an inch off the surface when lying on her tummy.	❋ Do gentle exercises to make her aware of her body (see p. 61). ❋ Her neck and back muscles are too weak to lift her head so give her something to look at when she is lying on her back.
Her handling skills	❋ Your baby is born with a "grasp reflex"—she'll keep her fists tightly closed and grasp anything put into her fingers (see above). ❋ If she's startled, she'll spread her arms, fingers, and legs to protect herself.	❋ Your baby can't purposely hold on to anything until she loses the grasp reflex. ❋ Gently open her fingers one at a time. ❋ If she grasps your fingers, she'll take her weight if you pull her up a little.
Her social skills	❋ Your baby is born ready to love other people and asks for love. She longs for company and takes immediate delight in you. ❋ She'll respond instantly to your voice and your smell. She is upset by a harsh-sounding voice.	❋ Let her have contact with other people from when she's very young. ❋ Be physical: Make skin-to-skin contact with your baby; use your body to express love; rock, sway, and dance with her.
Her speech	❋ She "mouths" if you speak to her at a distance of 8–10 in (20–25 cm); she's trying to imitate your gestures and expressions. ❋ She's born longing to communicate and makes little burbling noises to show contentment.	❋ Talk to your baby all the time so she gets used to your voice. ❋ Make facial expressions to match what you're saying.

Stimulating play
❋ Stimulate her senses with songs and by talking to her. Hold her where she can see you, ideally at 8–10 in (20–25 cm).
❋ Move your fingers or a colorful toy through her line of vision so that her eyes and head follow your movements; put a mobile over her crib.
❋ Do gentle knee bends and straighten her legs when you're changing her diaper; this will encourage your baby to straighten out her body.
❋ Place a small mirror or a clear, cartoon-style drawing of a face in her crib where she can see it when she is lying down.

Baby development
1–2 months

✳ What to look out for

What develops	How he progresses	How you can help
His mind	✳ Your baby begins to smile at you from a distance and bobs his head when you talk to him (see above). ✳ He starts to be interested in his surroundings, looking in the direction of sounds and staring at objects as though "grasping" with his eyes.	✳ Prop him up slightly with pillows or put him in a baby chair. Place lots of brightly colored toys within his view. ✳ Put a mobile over the crib—it's good if it makes a sound or has a musical box.
His mobility	✳ He can raise his head to 45 degrees when he's lying on his tummy. ✳ By the end of this month he can support the weight of his head if you hold him upright with your hands around his chest.	✳ Hold a colored toy close to his head so he has to lift his head to see it. ✳ To teach your baby about balance, hold him upright on your knee so his legs take his own weight for a second.
His handling skills	✳ Your baby will no longer have a grasp reflex. ✳ His fingers are open most of the time and he's starting to become aware of them.	✳ Touch, tickle, and massage his hands. ✳ Give him toys and encourage him to bend his fingers over them.
His social skills	✳ He's starting to notice people, but knows you from all others. ✳ He smiles from a distance at six weeks and moves his whole body with excitement when he sees you.	✳ Make sure you give your baby frequent skin-to-skin contact and maintain eye contact when you're talking to him and, more importantly, when feeding.
His speech	✳ He will begin by answering you with small throaty sounds and by the end of two months he'll make grunts, cries, and move his whole body in his desire to communicate with you. ✳ He knows your voice—and your partner's—and turns his head and neck when he hears it.	✳ The more your baby is stimulated to talk by being talked to and encouraged to respond, the earlier he'll learn to talk and the better his quality of speech. ✳ Talk non-stop, be theatrical with your conversations, and ask questions.

Stimulating play

✳ Sing and make eye contact (see left). Sway while you hold him.

✳ Show him his hands and demonstrate how to wiggle his fingers. Play "This little piggy."

✳ Gently rub a soft brush over his hands and fingers, especially at the tips.

✳ Sit him up supported at an angle of 45 degrees—this helps increase his attention span. Use pillows or a bouncing baby chair on the floor. Let him touch toys or objects of different textures and shapes. Dangle, kick, or bat small soft toys within striking distance of his hands.

✳ Every day have a special walk, talk, and singing time with your baby. Carry him in a sling (see p. 77).

Baby development
2–3 months

✳ What to look out for

What develops	How she progresses	How you can help
Her mind	✱ She's becoming familiar with her own body, staring at her fingers and then moving them. This is her first lesson in cause and effect. ✱ She has a repertoire of responses to you: she smiles, mouths when you speak to her, nods, squeaks, yelps, and blows raspberries.	✱ Show your baby her fingers so she can study them. ✱ Answer her with responses that are theatrical and larger than life. ✱ Reward her attempts to relate to you with hugs, kisses, and squeals of delight.
Her mobility	✱ She can keep her head up steadily now when in a standing or sitting position or while lying on her front, but not for long (see above). ✱ When she's lying on her tummy, she can hold her head in line with her body.	✱ Encourage her to reach out for soft toys, especially when she's on her tummy. ✱ Teach your baby about balance: Hold her in a standing position with your hands around her chest, for a few seconds at a time.
Her handling skills	✱ She begins to discover her hand—she keeps them open and looks at them. ✱ She'll hold a rattle for a few seconds if you place it in her hand.	✱ Encourage her to look at her fingers and to hold a rattle. ✱ Put toys over her crib or give her a baby gym to encourage her to reach out.
Her social skills	✱ She turns her head to your voice and smiles because she is happy to see you. ✱ She expresses her joy in you by waving her arms and kicking her legs.	✱ Keep eye contact with her when nursing—it's heaven for her to have food and your attention at the same time! ✱ Respond positively to her overtures.
Her speech	✱ She will begin to make simple vowel sounds, such as "oh," "ah," and "uh." ✱ She has a repertoire of easily recognized cries to express how she is feeling: hungry, tired, frustrated, lonely, angry, impatient, or just wanting to be left alone.	✱ Imitate all the sounds she makes back to her. ✱ When your baby cries, it's her way of communicating with you—always respond to it (see p. 104).

Stimulating play

✳ Introduce her to small toys with different textures and describe out loud to your baby how they feel (see left).

✳ Act out nursery rhymes and play pat-a-cake.

✳ Play lots of simple physical games, such as gentle jerks, knee bends, arm pulls, and tickling feet.

✳ Lie on the floor opposite her while she lies on her tummy and looks at you—this will encourage head control.

✳ Encourage her to reach out for soft objects.

✳ Take her into the bath with you and encourage her to kick and splash. Make her aware of her hands by splashing them in the water.

Baby development
3–4 months

What to look out for

What develops	How he progresses	How you can help
His mind	✳ He's curious and wants to join in. ✳ He can recognize places and faces as familiar. ✳ He loves the breast or his bottle and shows it. ✳ He'll laugh by the age of four months.	✳ Offer a wide range of toys. ✳ Explain everything you see and do. ✳ Pin photographs of yourselves in his crib.
His mobility	✳ He loves sitting up now with a little support from you or pillows. ✳ If you gently pull him into a sitting position, he will bring his head up in line with his body. ✳ If he is lying on his tummy, he can look straight at you now.	✳ Sit him up with pillows for support. ✳ Pull him gently up into a sitting position to strengthen his back and neck muscles. ✳ Play games that make your baby swivel from the waist and offer him toys that he is able to reach easily when he turns.
His handling skills	✳ He's starting to control his hands and feet and will start reaching for his toes (see above). ✳ He moves his hands and feet together. ✳ He crosses his feet and puts a foot on the opposite leg.	✳ Put toys in his hands when he reaches for them or he will overshoot. Make him reach for things in every position. ✳ Give him rattles so that he can make noises with his hands.
His social skills	✳ He looks at and smiles at people who talk to him—he hasn't learned shyness yet. ✳ He knows you and your partner and people he sees regularly, such as grandparents. ✳ He loves company and cries when left alone for long. He knows warmth, love, and the opposite.	✳ Encourage his sense of humor. Laugh with him, share the joke, and imitate everything he does. Don't be afraid to over-act all your responses. ✳ Encourage emotional development: Laugh when he laughs and cry when he cries.
His speech	✳ He'll squeal with pleasure. ✳ He's learning all the basic tones of voices. ✳ He says "m," "p," and "b" when unhappy and "j" and "k" when happy.	✳ Repeat sounds back at him—"M, m, m you're not happy are you?" Speak in a tone of voice that is appropriate.

Stimulating play

✳ Gently pull your baby up by his arms when he is lying on his back to help his head control (see left).

✳ Play "peekaboo" and hiding-your-face games. When playing "peekaboo" stay slightly to one side so that your baby has to swing his body to find you.

✳ Put objects on a string over his crib so he can examine them—one day he'll reach out and knock one; make sure string is not long enough to present a choking hazard.

✳ Amplify his experiences by talking to him about what you see and do.

✳ Place a rattle in your baby's hand and shake it a few times. He will be intrigued by its texture and by the sound that it makes.

Baby development
4–5 months

✱ What to look out for

What develops	How she progresses	How you can help
Her mind	✱ Your baby loves games—she learns skills from them by copying what you do. ✱ Her concentration is expanding. She spends a long time examining things. ✱ She smiles at herself in the mirror. ✱ She moves her arms and legs to attract you. ✱ She pats her bottle when feeding.	✱ When she attracts your attention, respond to it; this will encourage good behavior. ✱ Turn your body theatrically toward her. Let her know you're attending to her by focusing on her: Move towards her, bend down, and make eye contact. ✱ Call her by her name all the time.
Her mobility	✱ She has now mastered full control of her head. Although it's quite steady, it may wobble if she moves suddenly.	✱ Give her plenty of rocking motion. This will promote head stability and aid her when she begins walking.
Her handling skills	✱ She puts things such as toys, her fist, and her feet into her mouth as it's the most sensitive area (see above). ✱ She grasps large toys with both hands and begins to use the little-finger side of her hand to grip things. She sometimes can't let go.	✱ Don't try to stop her from putting her hand in her mouth—it's natural. ✱ Play with her toes and guide them to her mouth. ✱ Play give-and-take games with toys.
Her social skills	✱ Your baby is beginning to be shy with strangers (this is the first sign of her emerging "self"), but she still smiles at people she knows.	✱ Introduce her to all visitors so that she gets used to strangers and the concept of friends.
Her speech	✱ Her language is very colorful: she tries to "talk" by blowing, babbling, squealing, laughing, and she says "ka" in an attempt to sound like you. ✱ She uses different facial expressions to communicate with you.	✱ Imitate all her sounds with changes of pitch and volume. If she listens, stimulate her with new sounds and name them.

Stimulating play

✱ Play rocking games while she is sitting on your lap (see left).

✱ Play lots of games with her, especially those that involve clapping.

✱ She loves crumpling paper—give her sheets of old packing paper or lots of tissue paper that crackles.

✱ Hide her face under a towel for a second then whisk it away and say "peekaboo!"—she'll squeal with delight.

✱ Look out for your baby holding her hands up and her arms wide—this means that she wants to play.

✱ Encourage her to open her fingers by playing giving and taking away games. Always give her the object when she reaches out.

Baby development
5–6 months

✳ What to look out for

What develops	How he progresses	How you can help
His mind	✱ He gets excited if he hears someone coming. ✱ He expresses his discomfort or insecurity. ✱ He makes lots of attention-seeking sounds and raises his arms to be picked up.	✱ Respond to his call as soon as you hear it. Shout out that you're coming, then go toward him and say his name. Hold out your arms as you approach him. ✱ Keep using his name every time you speak to him.
His mobility	✱ He's now strong enough to take the weight of his upper half on his arms. ✱ He can sit for a few minutes supported on the floor with lots of pillows (see above).	✱ Play bouncing games with your baby. Get a baby bouncer if he likes it. ✱ Lie next to him on the floor and crawl around. It will encourage him to copy.
His handling skills	✱ He now has the ability to transfer objects from one hand to another. ✱ Holding one toy in his hand, he'll drop it to take hold of another. ✱ He'll hold his bottle.	✱ Show him how to let go and drop things and how to pass a toy from hand to hand. ✱ Play give-and-take games—this will also encourage him to share.
His social skills	✱ He starts to make assertive advances: pats on your cheek, scratches, and slaps. ✱ He explores your face with his hands—it means "hello," so say "hello" back and smile. ✱ He's possessive of you and may be very wary of people he doesn't know.	✱ Show your baby new gestures, stretch out your arms to him and he'll lift his too. ✱ Make expansive gestures and pitch your voice to match. He will copy you. ✱ Avoid leaving him in a room with strangers.
His speech	✱ He blows bubbles (this is his first real speech). ✱ He now says "ka," "da," and "ma" all the time and a new sound emerges: "ergh." ✱ He understands some of what you say.	✱ If he appears to understand you, ask if he does, repeat what you said, and praise him.

Stimulating play

✳ Play weight-bearing games: These encourage him to take more and more weight on his legs, which helps to strengthen them. Hold him on your lap or on the floor, gently bounce him up and down, and feel him push himself off your legs (see left).

✳ Demonstrate cause and effect. Push a ball to him while he's sitting up and say "the ball is rolling."

✳ Blow "raspberries" on his tummy when you're changing his diaper—encourage him to copy the different noises you make.

✳ Reward him for holding out his arms by playing lifting games—squeal with delight as you lift him and swing him around.

Baby development
6–7 months

✳ What to look out for

What develops	How she progresses	How you can help
Her mind	✳ She starts off conversations and you'll understand many of her own sounds. ✳ She knows her name and who she is. ✳ She may want to feed herself. ✳ She anticipates repetition and imitates you.	✳ Encourage her sense of self by showing your baby her reflection in the mirror. When you are looking in the mirror repeat her name over and over "That's Lucy, that's you". ✳ Have conversations with her.
Her mobility	✳ She can now bear weight on one hand when she is lying on her tummy. ✳ She can lift her head when lying on her back. ✳ When you hold her up she can take all her own weight on straight legs and hips.	✳ To encourage her to take her weight, play lots of standing games. ✳ Place a toy above her while she's lying on her back and encourage her to lift her head to reach out for it.
Her handling skills	✳ She reaches out for objects using only her fingers now. ✳ She holds on to a toy if she reaches for another. ✳ She bangs the table.	✳ Let her try to feed herself from a bowl with her own baby spoon. ✳ Give her plenty of toys that are easy for her to hold.
Her social skills	✳ Your baby loves other babies and stretches out to them in friendship. ✳ She may cry if she's left with anyone other than you or your partner, especially if it's someone whom she doesn't know.	✳ Give her physical affection; she can't be loving to anyone (including herself) if she doesn't have a bank of love to draw on. ✳ Keep introducing her to strangers and give her time to adjust.
Her speech	✳ She now has very clear syllables with actions, "ba," "da," and "ka." ✳ Cries have high and low pitches and a nasal sound has appeared.	✳ Make every sound back to her to make her feel important.

Stimulating play

✳ Play touching games together: Use every opportunity to touch your baby and let her touch you. She'll love it if you let her explore your face with her hands (see left).

✳ Encourage her sense of self by playing games with her things and using her name: say "That's Lucy's dress," and "Whose teddy is this? It's Lucy's."

✳ If she's wary of strangers now, introduce them gradually.

✳ Develop her sense of humor with simple jokes like tickling; play "Round and round the garden, like a teddy bear".

✳ To encourage her to try to pull her tummy off the floor, play airplanes. Lie side by side on your front and lift your arms and body—and your baby's—off the floor.

Baby development
7–8 months

✳ What to look out for

What develops	How he progresses	How you can help
His mind	✳ He's showing signs of determination; he'll keep going after toys he can't quite reach. ✳ He concentrates hard on discovering what he can do with his toys—he's learning all the time about the properties of various objects.	✳ Encourage him to retrieve a toy for which he has to stretch. ✳ Play water games in the bath. ✳ Give him plastic containers to pour, empty, and fill over and over.
His mobility	✳ He'll sit rocking his body back and forth to try to reach a toy. ✳ He loves standing when supported. If you stand him on your lap, he'll dance around. ✳ Lying on his tummy, he'll try to inch forward.	✳ While he's sitting, sit a little way from him and hold your arms out. He'll try to shuffle along on his bottom to reach you. ✳ Hold him upright as much as possible. ✳ Get him to reach a toy while on his front.
His handling skills	✳ He loves making any noise by banging. ✳ He'll try to copy you if you clap. ✳ He can hold any toy firmly in his fingers. ✳ He'll point to objects—this is the first stage of learning the finger-thumb grasp.	✳ Give him spoons, pan lids, or a toy drum so that he can use his hands to bang and make a noise. ✳ When he's sitting on the floor or in his crib, make sure that he has lots of toys to reach for, pick up, and explore.
His social skills	✳ He will respond fully to sociable games such as "Pat-a-cake" or "This little piggy." ✳ He doesn't like it when you're angry and will respond accordingly. ✳ He's clear what "no" means and responds to it.	✳ Make him feel valued by using his name in every situation. This will help him to develop a sense of himself. ✳ When you need to say "no," say it firmly and use a different tone of voice.
His speech	✳ He plays games with his mouth and tongue, blowing "raspberries" and smacking his lips. ✳ He may combine two syllables such as "ba-ba" and "da-da," although not with meaning.	✳ Play sound games to convey meaning—"quiet" (whisper) or "loud" (shout).

Stimulating play

✳ Hold a mirror up in front of your baby so she can see herself, and say her name (see left).

✳ Play and sing word games to encourage her to vocalize. Say rhymes over and over again, always with the same emphasis, and move your body; she'll start to copy you and use hers.

✳ Play with all kinds of safe household items as toys—for example, plastic or wooden spoons, pans, and brushes. Banging games will be huge fun.

✳ Always answer her needs and cries; this fosters self-confidence and self-esteem in your baby.

✳ Sit with your baby on the floor and encircle your legs around her. Fill the circle with her favorite toys.

Baby development
8–9 months

✱ What to look out for

What develops	How she progresses	How you can help
Her mind	✱ Your baby loves familiar games and rhymes and laughs at the right times. ✱ She can anticipate movements. ✱ She will turn her head to her name and hold out her hands to be reached.	✱ Help her to understand life on a day-to-day basis by explaining all routines. ✱ Use meals and bath times as cues for special activities: "Now it's time for lunch"; "Now it's time to have your bath".
Her mobility	✱ She can take her weight on her legs, if supported. ✱ She can sit for ten minutes, lean forward and sideway, and stay balanced. ✱ She can roll from side to side, but can't get up from a sitting position to stand.	✱ Help her to stand from a sitting position, bend her hips and knees for her. ✱ Help her to cruise around the furniture by having pieces close together. Encourage her to hold on to a low piece of furniture.
Her handling skills	✱ Her movements are becoming more refined. ✱ Her fingers are used for exploring—she puts things in her mouth much less often. ✱ She has the ability to lean forward and pick up small things easily (see above).	✱ Show her how to stack blocks on top of one another or side by side—she's learning about volume as well as fine movements. ✱ Give her a soft cooked pea to pick up between her finger and thumb.
Her social skills	✱ She's shy with new faces and may be reluctant to be picked up by people she doesn't know. ✱ She remembers people she's gotten to know well, even a few days later.	✱ Talk to her on the telephone if you have to be away from home at all. ✱ Get her a toy telephone to play with. ✱ Help her get to know the babysitter.
Her speech	✱ She's understanding more and more of what you say so repeat "Yes, that's what daddy means: it's cold outside, brrrr." ✱ She'll start to add "t," "d," and "w" sounds. ✱ She might make one animal sound if you do.	✱ Repeat words that start with t, d, and w. ✱ Repeat all her sounds back to her. Name everything. ✱ Read animal stories and make the noises.

Stimulating play

✱ Get lots of noisy toys (wooden spoons, metal pots and pans, or a toy drum). It helps her to understand how to exert some control over things and herself and develops her understanding of cause and effect (see left).

✱ Read a book or magazine. She'll love a commentary from you.

✱ Name parts of your body and ask her to copy.

✱ Crawl alongside your baby and imitate her movements to encourage her to do the same.

✱ Show her how you can put one block on top of another. It takes great skill and she won't achieve it by herself for at least another month or so, but she'll enjoy knocking the bricks over and scattering them about!

Baby development
9–10 months

✳ What to look out for

What develops	How he progresses	How you can help
His mind	✳ Your baby is getting used to rituals; they order his life and make him feel secure. ✳ He'll wave bye-bye. ✳ He'll put his foot out for a sock—he's longing to be helpful! ✳ He knows his teddy bear and doll. ✳ He'll look around corners for a toy.	✳ Try to keep to some sort of routine so that your baby can get used to it. ✳ Show him how to dress and undress, so that he can begin to understand the concept of a daily routine. ✳ He should have toys such as teddy bears or dolls that are "like baby."
His mobility	✳ He's discovered mobility. ✳ He moves forward on his hands and knees and loves changing positions (see above). ✳ He can twist his trunk around quite confidently.	✳ Hold out your arms, call his name, and encourage him to crawl to you. ✳ Offer your fingers for him to pull himself up on, then lift his foot on and off the floor.
His handling skills	✳ He reaches for objects with his index finger and will master picking up something small, such as a raisin, with his thumb and index finger. ✳ He'll let go of objects deliberately. ✳ He can build a tower of two blocks.	✳ Point to objects for him. ✳ Put toys on the tray of his high chair and encourage him to throw them over; you can tie them on. ✳ Ask him to roll a ball to you.
His social skills	✳ He shows affection by pressing his face and head against yours and hangs on to you tightly. ✳ He'll give you a toy if you ask him for it, but become angry if you take it away.	✳ Teach about hugs—"let's give each other a hug"—he's learning reciprocity. ✳ Teach sharing: Ask him for a bit of food and show him how nice he is for sharing it.
His speech	✳ He begins to make lots of consonant sounds. ✳ He chatters away in the rhythm of speech, without any meaning.	✳ Name absolutely everything. ✳ Face your baby when you speak to him so that he is able to read your lip movements.

Stimulating play

✳ Read to him each day: Read real story books and point out pictures. He'll learn to look at pictures the right way up and begin to recognize pictures of objects (see left).

✳ Rock him on your knee and pretend to drop him—he'll enjoy "falling."

✳ Play hide and seek by hiding yourself or a toy.

✳ Give him bath toys—plastic jugs, cups, sieves, boats, and ducks.

✳ Give him a doll and teddy bear and show how to dress and undress it.

✳ Give him squeaky toys, horns, and bells.

✳ Stack blocks or cubes of the same size on top of one another and side by side for him to see.

Your baby's development

Baby development
10–11 months

✳ What to look out for

What develops	How she progresses	How you can help
Her mind	✱ Your baby will point things out to you. ✱ She loves dropping toys off her high chair, then looking for them. ✱ She asks to be picked up. ✱ She learns through opposites: Keep showing her examples, such as in and out, here and there, and over and under.	✱ Read different kinds of books and magazines to her. ✱ Encourage her attention span by telling her a simple storyline. ✱ Pick her up if she reaches out to you. ✱ Keep demonstrating cause and effect, by pushing over blocks or splashing water.
Her mobility	✱ She's crawling or shuffling at great speed. ✱ If you support her standing, she'll lift one leg. ✱ She's completely balanced while sitting.	✱ Place a toy right behind her to make her twist around—it's okay, she's got the skill now. ✱ Position her so that she can crawl or shuffle.
Her handling skills	✱ Your baby loves taking things out of containers and putting them back (see above). ✱ She will hold something out to you if you ask her for it.	✱ Play giving things to each other and then taking them away, but don't force her to relinquish something. ✱ Take her hand and point to objects.
Her social skills	✱ She knows her name and who "Mommy" and "Daddy" are when you use the words. ✱ She's got a wonderful sense of humor: Play little jokes all the time and laugh at her attempts to make you laugh.	✱ Use laughter to show your approval and silence to mean the opposite: this is gentle baby discipline and she'll soon catch on. ✱ Demonstrate social rituals, such as kissing and waving good-bye.
Her speech	✱ Your baby is now beginning to imitate real speech sounds. ✱ She may start to attempt to say one word with meaning—"Dada" when Daddy appears is often the first. She will probably understand the word "No."	✱ Keep saying "Mama." ✱ Repeat "Dada." Use association—for example: "Dada has gone to work".

Stimulating play

✳ Play games with blocks: Make a tower of blocks and show her cause and effect by knocking them down and saying "all fall down" (see left).

✳ Play games using the hands, such as "Itsy-bitsy spider" and "Jack and Jill"—buy a book that shows you the movements.

✳ When reading, name several items on each page and go over them in the same order each time you read. Let her turn the pages.

✳ Encourage her to practice putting in and taking out by giving her a wooden spoon and bowl or blocks and a basket.

✳ Encourage her to pull herself up to standing by holding a favorite toy just out of reach.

Baby development
11–12 months

✳ What to look out for

What develops	How he progresses	How you can help
His mind	✳ He loves jokes and will do anything for a positive response like a laugh—this will make him feel good about himself. ✳ He knows about kissing and wants to kiss you.	✳ Laugh when he finds something funny. ✳ Let him kiss you, but don't ask him to kiss strangers. ✳ Talk enthusiastically about your activities.
His mobility	✳ He can walk if you hold one hand. ✳ He'll walk if he pushes a sturdy cart, or he'll hold on to furniture to steady himself.	✳ While he's cruising, encourage him to launch off by calling him. ✳ Make sure the furniture is steady.
His handling skills	✳ He is getting better at feeding himself. ✳ He can rotate his hand to turn toys over. ✳ He loves throwing things away. ✳ He makes lines with a crayon. ✳ He holds on to two things in one hand.	✳ Keep putting two blocks into his hand. ✳ Encourage self-feeding of soft but non-runny food with a spoon. Give him his own special dish and spoon. ✳ Give him crayons and paper.
His social skills	✳ He knows who he is. ✳ He becomes possessive of his toys and resents it when they are taken away. ✳ He loves social gatherings as long as you or someone he is familiar with carries him. ✳ He'll give you things if you ask for them.	✳ Introduce him to lots of babies. ✳ Encourage him to share. ✳ Encourage affection by cuddling his doll. ✳ Leave him with a babysitter occasionally. ✳ Sit him in his high chair at the table or playpen in the room in which you're sitting.
His speech	✳ He follows conversation and makes sounds in the gaps. ✳ He may say one word, such as "dog," with meaning. ✳ He can make you understand he wants something and what it is.	✳ Teach him "thank you." ✳ Congratulate him when you understand what he's saying.

Stimulating play

✳ Give him non-toxic colored crayons and large sheets of plain paper on the floor, to encourage him to draw (see left).

✳ Read simple stories about animals and their young to encourage his interest in other "babies." All babies love this.

✳ Encourage him to stand unaided by holding him steady, then letting go for a second or two.

✳ Concentrate on the names of objects and name parts of the body. Point to parts of your body and he'll copy you.

✳ If he uses the furniture as support to get around, place it slightly further apart to encourage him to bridge the gap. Be ready to help.

Going back to work

No sooner than you've settled into being a mother and found a routine that's right for all of you, you may find yourself thinking about returning to work. For many women, this is a financial necessity and for some it's a relief after months of diapers and baby talk! Going back to work requires some reorganization and a change of priorities, and it's sensible to consider all the options soon after your baby is born. Try to decide as a family which arrangements suit you best. You may, for example, have the option to return part-time or work from home some days, or your partner may decide to give up work to care for your baby, especially if you earn more money. If you both work full-time, you'll have to arrange childcare and accept that on weekdays you're only going to see your baby for a couple of hours in the morning and evening. This is never ideal or easy, but as long as you maintain your baby's routine, and she has your undivided attention while you're with her, she won't suffer from having working parents.

Work and parenting

Make the return to work easier for you all by ensuring you've made good childcare arrangements and deciding how you'll adjust your routine. Remember that the changes may be unsettling at first, especially for your baby.

Aside from legal requirements (see p. 184), your baby's needs and your feelings will, to an extent, dictate when you return to work:

✳ If you want to continue breastfeeding, practice expressing enough milk for your baby's needs (see p. 80). If you intend to stop breastfeeding, you need to introduce the bottle in good time.

✳ Think carefully about whether you are physically and emotionally ready.

Work options

Look carefully at all your options.

Part-time/job-sharing
Part-time can be the best of both worlds, since you have time with your baby and the stimulation of work—but you also have the pressure of both. If you can job-share, you may be better able to continue to build your career.

Working from home
You need to be self-disciplined and you'll still need some childcare (see p. 172), as it's easy to be distracted.

Career break
You may decide to have a break. Make sure this is what you really want and think through all the implications.

Father at home
If you want to return to work full-time, your partner may become the main caregiver (see p. 176).

Making the decision
You may decide while you're pregnant that you want to return to work at the end of your maternity leave (see p. 184). Once the baby is born, however, it's normal to feel unsure about leaving him, especially as this is likely to coincide with the time that you're just settling into being a mother. On the other hand, you may find that you actually miss work and are ready, after a few months, to take a break from the domestic routine and return to an adult environment. Of course, there may simply be no decision for you to make—financially, you may have to work.

What to consider
Whatever you decided while pregnant, it's important to look at your financial and domestic situation once the baby is born and for you and your partner to talk about work options:

✳ What type of childcare can you afford? Have you checked what is available in your area?

✳ After covering the cost of childcare, does your salary leave enough extra to make it worthwhile? (Don't forget to take travel costs into account.)

✳ Is it feasible to return to your old job as it was and also devote enough time to your baby? For example, does your job involve lots of overtime or travel away from home?

Concerns
For the past months you've been focused on preparing for the birth and then looking after your new baby. Once you have to think about returning to work, you're likely to have concerns and mixed feelings.

Feeling guilty You may feel guilty (especially if you can't wait to get back to work), but don't. Just because you're a working mother doesn't imply that you're a bad mother. There's no point in staying at home with your baby if it doesn't fulfil you—it will be more beneficial to him if you're happy and contented when he does see you. Also, don't forget how your baby will benefit from the additional income.

Losing your confidence After a few months at home with your baby, you may doubt your ability to readjust to a working environment. Try to ease yourself back into work mode by catching up on what's been going on and by talking to colleagues. Nearer the time, go into the office (by yourself, if possible) so that it isn't such a shock when you return. You'll soon realize that not much has changed while you've been away.

Making the transition

Area of change	How to make it easier
Preparing your baby	Introduce your baby to the babysitter, starting with a couple of mornings each week and gradually building it up, or take him to the daycare for a trial run. You should also start to adapt his feeding routine.
Adapting to a change of routine	Trying to juggle work and looking after your baby can be difficult. Establish a routine in the mornings and evenings so that you are sharing the babycare and chores equally. You'll soon find a routine that works.
Coping with fatigue	No one who is consistently sleep-deprived can be expected to cope adequately with a job; you must take turns caring for your baby at night. Even if one of you works part-time, find a fair way to share the load.
Focusing on work	It's an acquired skill not to think about your baby while you're at work. If you've made the best arrangements you can for his welfare, any energy you now dispense on worrying is wasted and sells you and your employer short.
Helping your baby adapt	The fact is your baby will have to adapt and he will. What you can do is prepare yourselves for his reaction and, when he's with you, be reassuring and comforting. Make sure he has whatever comfort object he loves.

JUST FOR DAD

The routine at home will change if you're both working full-time. It will help if you prepare yourself for this.

How you can help

✳ Be supportive. Your partner is likely to find going back to work a strain and may be distressed by leaving the baby. Try to plan in advance as much as possible and give her time to adjust.

✳ Share the responsibility. Don't assume that your partner will handle childcare issues. The babysitter or daycare needs telephone numbers for both of you (including cell phones), so that you can easily share the responsibility if a problem arises.

✳ Share the chores. Your partner may have been doing most of the chores while she was at home, but now that she's back at work this should be more equal. Alternate doing the domestic work, getting up during the night, and picking your baby from the babysitter or daycare.

When you're back at work

It may take a few weeks to settle back into work. You'll just about have worked out a routine with your baby at home and then suddenly have to adapt to a different timetable and concentrate your mind on a different set of priorities. You'll also be doing your job while having to handle added pressures and responsibilities at home.

Career considerations

People often assume that a woman's first priority will be her child and, in some situations, they're right—when push comes to shove, it's quite often the mother's employment that takes the strain and not the father's. If your partnership is different, you're probably going to have to demonstrate this several times before it's recognized.

How your career is affected may also depend on your employer's attitude—set the ground rules early on by talking to your manager and telling him or her that you're committed to your job, but that your responsibilities at home mean you'll need some flexibility. Explain that you need to leave on time (although, ideally, picking up your baby should be shared equally with your partner), but that with sufficient notice you're prepared to work extra hours, if necessary.

Emergencies

Talk about a strategy for emergencies, such as your baby or the babysitter being ill. If you don't have a backup caregiver, one of you will need to take time off work to care for your child. If either of you feels strongly that your job takes priority, try to agree this in advance. This can save a lot of arguments.

Choosing childcare

Trial period

It's worth having a trial period before you return to work, so that you can settle your baby gradually:

✳ Your baby will have time to become familiar with her new surroundings and her new caregiver.

✳ You'll have an idea of the impact on your baby and be able to find ways of soothing her if she becomes unsettled.

✳ You'll be able to sort out any practical hitches.

✳ If you introduce your baby to her new caregiver gradually, the emotional impact should be less once you actually return to work.

If things go wrong

If the childcare doesn't work out, it can be disappointing and problematic, especially if your caregiver lives with you. Treat the problem professionally:

✳ Deal with issues quickly; ignoring them will only make matters worse and lead to resentment.

✳ Talk to your caregiver to reach a compromise. Agree to see how things go and, depending on the problem, set a time limit. If after this period, the matter isn't resolved, it may be best to end the employment.

✳ Decide on a set notice period. This benefits both of you—if your caregiver decides to leave, you won't be left in the lurch.

Finding and choosing a caregiver for your baby is mainly dictated by practical and financial considerations, but there are also emotional issues. It's hard to leave your baby with someone new, so you need to be as comfortable as possible with the care and caregiver you've chosen.

What to look for in a caregiver

Once you've decided on the type of childcare you'd prefer, you need to look around for the best provider. The earlier you plan your childcare, the more choice you'll have. Ask lots of questions of the person or institution you're considering to find out the type of care they provide, and thoroughly check the facilities. If you don't feel sure about any aspect, follow your instincts, and look elsewhere.

Qualifications and references Daycares should be licensed by the state. Nannies may have various credentials and references, depending on whether they came through an agency or not. Au pairs are not professionally trained. Ask a potential au pair or nanny for the name of another employer and at least two written references. Talk to her references on the phone to get a better idea of a person's suitability.

Level of care With a daycare or family-care situation, find out how many babies are looked after at one time and the caregiver-to-child ratio. Even if your baby will not be receiving individual care, she still needs enough care to be stimulated and to encourage her development. Check the space and resources available, such as the kitchen and sterilizing equipment, the play area, and the types of toys offered. Ask what kinds of activities your baby will be involved in on a day-to-day basis.

Interaction with your baby Always invite a potential caregiver to spend time with your baby, or take your baby to the daycare. Watch to see what a caregiver says while holding your baby and how your baby reacts to her.

Commitment It can be confusing and distressing for a baby to have a change of caregiver. Check that the person or institution will be able to provide relatively long-term care.

Your relationship with your caregiver

However sure you are about employing your caregiver, it's advisable to discuss and agree on all aspects of caring for your baby from the outset:

✳ A trial period before you agree to a full contract is a good idea.

✳ Write down your requirements so that you can agree some ground rules from the outset; especially with regard to telephone use and visitors for live-in nannies.

✳ Find out a caregiver's thoughts, or an institution's policy, on discipline to make sure they match your own.

The caregiver's relationship with your baby

Leaving your baby with a caregiver is likely to come at a time when you've just settled into being a parent and feel particularly close to your son or daughter. Your caregiver will also form a close relationship with your baby, but this doesn't mean you're any less important, and you're by no means replaced. Your baby is capable of being close to—and accepting the attention of—more than one person; in fact it's beneficial to her if this happens because the more love, attention, and stimulation she receives the better she'll develop.

Babies often go through periods of time when they favor certain people (see p. 131); if your baby seems closer to her caregiver, it's probably only a phase. Your baby may also seem unsettled now and then, but don't read too much into this. However, if she continues to be unsettled for more than a week or two, spend time with the caregiver and your baby together to try to pinpoint any problems.

Hidden costs

When thinking about the cost of childcare, it's worth considering:

* Are there transportation costs?
* Are your baby's meals provided?
* What are the additional costs associated with live-in care?
* If you have twins, would it be cheaper to employ a nanny?
* Are there hidden emotional costs, such as feeling indebted, if you're using a friend or relative?

Childcare options

Type of care	Description	Advantages	Disadvantages
Relative	You may leave your baby with a family member, such as a grandparent. Encourage him or her to involve your baby in activities, such as a playgroup.	* Usually a cheaper option. * Your baby is with someone who loves her. * You're less likely to have strict time restraints; don't abuse this.	* It can be difficult if there are disagreements. * You may worry about your baby forming a closer relationship with the carer.
Family daycare	Childcare is provided in a caregiver's home, often with her own children. Caregivers are usually untrained but often motivated and experienced.	* You can often pay by the hour to suit your budget. * Your baby will mix with other children, which will help to develop her social skills.	* May have limited resources. * You can't take your baby if she's ill.
Nanny	Nannies care for your baby and may live in your home. Interview a nanny together and observe her with the baby; you both have to like her.	* Nannies may be professionally trained. * Care takes place at home, which helps your baby adapt and is convenient for you.	* A nanny is expensive (you pay her tax and insurance too), but consider a nanny share. * Beware of domestic tensions if the nanny lives in.
Daycare	Your baby attends a daycare facility with other children. In some areas there may be wait lists for daycare centers. If you're very lucky, daycare may be available at your workplace.	* Your baby is with other babies and care is based around developing skills. * Centers must be registered and they often employ licensed caregivers.	* Can be expensive and there will be limited places. * You'll have to pick up your baby at an agreed time. * You can't take your baby if she's ill.
Au pair or mother's helper	This is a student from another country who lives with you as part of the family. Au pairs are allowed to work a limited number of hours per week.	* Care is provided in the home. * Cheaper than a nanny. * When your baby is older, the au pair may be able to teach her a second language.	* Not professionally qualified, so not suitable for the full-time care of a baby. * Works limited hours. * There will be live-in costs.

Special time with your baby

An hour a day

An hour playing with your baby each day is rewarding and fulfilling for all. A baby who has his parents' undivided attention for this time acquires self-esteem and self-confidence and becomes generous, loving, and well adjusted. It doesn't have to be all at once. He won't concentrate for long, so try 15 or 30 minutes at a time—as long as you give your full attention.

If you're working parents, the time spent at home as a family becomes not just important, but precious. Play is essential to your baby's mental and physical development, and he'll love the attention from you both while he plays.

The importance of play

As well as being a parent, you are your baby's playmate and best friend; this is especially true in his first year when he may not have much opportunity to interact with other children. Every game you play with him is magical and every lesson becomes worth learning, so time spent in games, no matter how simple, ensures that your baby is avidly learning and acquiring skills. Don't underestimate how important play is to your baby: It's his full-time job; a job that requires great concentration and expenditure of energy. It's harder than most adult work because everything is new and fresh lessons are learned all the time. These lessons, however, are made easier and are more fun if he can enjoy them with his favorite playmates—his parents.

Why play is essential

Your baby investigates his world through play.
* Play stimulates and excites him.
* For the first few years of his life, play is the only way he learns.
* Play is an integral part of his physical and mental development.

Getting the most out of play

Make the time to join in activities with your baby and encourage him in play that will stimulate his development.

Investing time Formal play isn't necessary, but some planning does reap dividends so try to make play a part of your morning, evening, and weekend routine so that your baby is getting at least an hour of playtime in total from both of you each day (see left). A baby has a very short attention span so don't expect him to sit playing happily while you cook dinner. Fifteen minutes invested in playing with your baby before you begin a task will pay off; if you only give him five minutes of your time, he's more likely to become attention-seeking when you're busy doing something else.

Stimulating development Babies start acquiring skills from the very moment of birth. These mental and physical milestones (see p. 146) emerge at particular stages as your baby's brain and body develop. It follows that these are optimum moments for you to introduce games that encourage particular skills to flourish, so make sure you vary the activities that you play with your baby; for example, physical games encourage mobility; singing helps to develop speech; playing with toys, such as building blocks, helps your baby to become more dextrous.

Maximizing your time

If you work full-time, try to take advantage of any spare moments you have to spend time with your baby. It helps if you're organized and can prioritize. If you're both in high-pressure jobs, it's easy to let work take over and work an extra hour at the beginning or end of the day, but this hour is invaluable time you could be spending with your baby (see box opposite).

Weekends

Don't bring work home with you; if it's not there you can't do it, which means you can spend time with your baby without feeling guilty. Try to get out as a family at least one of the days at the weekend; if you're in the house, you're more likely to get distracted with other things. Keep to your baby's weekly routine as much as possible—at around nine months he'll begin to understand that certain things happen at certain times. If one of you doesn't have much time on weekday mornings to dress or give your baby breakfast, he or she can try to make time to do this on the weekend. Your baby will enjoy the change and it gives your partner a break too.

Mornings

Most babies wake up early so use this opportunity to spend time together. If you don't have time for proper play, sing and talk to your baby as you change and dress him and get him ready for the day. Sit down and have your breakfast with him.

Evenings

Working full-time will make you tired in the evenings. Try to establish some sort of routine for when you get home; as well as having time with your baby, it's important that you both have time to yourselves and time together as a couple (see p. 134).

Leave work on time Try to leave work on time. It's unfair on your partner and the baby if either one of you is always home late. Don't take advantage of your nanny or babysitter—an extra hour in the evening is a lot when she's been looking after the baby all day.

Divide the chores One of you should cook and the other clean up afterward so that you both have time to spend with your baby.

Choose relaxing activities It will be difficult to get your baby to bed if he's very excited. Give him a bath, then read or sing to him to calm him down before you put him to bed.

Time-saving tips

To give yourself more time with your baby in the evening:
* Try to prepare some weekday meals ahead of time and freeze them.
* Record any early evening TV shows and watch them once your baby has gone to bed.
* Save any long telephone calls until after your baby's bedtime.
* Eat mid-afternoon sometimes so that it's possible for you to wait later for your evening meal.

✳ JUST FOR DAD

Your baby will look forward to you coming home in the evenings. Shower him with attention and show him how special he is.

What you can do

✳ Develop a special routine for when you get home from work. It could just be holding out your arms for your baby to crawl or to walk to you, or picking him up immediately, walking around with him, and telling him about your day.

✳ Try to find time each evening to spend 10 or 15 minutes playing a game with him.

✳ If you read the paper in the evening, read to your baby and give him some paper to crumple.

✳ You and your baby can relax with a bath together (see p. 95) before getting him ready for bed.

▲ **RELAXING TOGETHER** Play doesn't always have to be energetic. Settle into a comfortable chair in the evening and read a story to your baby. This is a relaxing and enjoyable activity for both of you.

Fathers at home

JUST FOR MOM

Being the breadwinner while your partner stays at home can lead to conflicting emotions.

How to help yourself
In general, society still pressures women to be the main caregiver, and it's difficult not to be affected by this. You may feel guilty and envy women who have more time at home. Try to be confident in (or accepting of) your decision and spend as much time as possible with your baby. Being the breadwinner can be stressful, so find ways to relax and try not to feel resentment.

How to help your partner
Make sure he has time to relax, see his friends, and spend time with you (see p. 134). Try not to leave all the household chores to him.

Reactions

Full-time dads are more common nowadays, but you may get some flak. Some traditionally minded men find it threatening that a "house-husband" is independent enough to flout the traditional social conventions—they like to hang on to these conventions, which give them security. But if you're a man who's strong enough to have made the decision to be a full-time parent, you'll no doubt be strong enough to take the flak!

It suits some couples best for the mother to return to work and be the breadwinner, while the father is a stay-at-home dad, caring for the baby and running the home.

Making the decision

For many couples, the decision to reverse roles is made because they feel that their baby will benefit from having a full-time parent at home. If the mother is earning more, it makes sense for the father to be that person—especially if his work is something he can do from home. When a parent stays at home full-time, a couple will be financially worse off than if both worked, but this is often compensated for by an improvement in their quality of life and is seen as a worthwhile investment in their child. A man may be forced to stay at home due to a job loss; even if this is only short term, it can often be an invaluable opportunity for him to spend time with his child and take on the role of primary caregiver.

A learning process

Those people who take a stand on the traditional roles of father and mother as being "natural" are missing the point, and to divide parental labor along the lines of gender is a groundless exercise. Caring for a baby is a learning process for all new parents, whether they're male or female, so don't let anyone tell you otherwise. Remember the following:
❋ Women are not born with an innate ability to change diapers and dress babies. Possibly, they appear more confident at it because they're made to feel that they should know what to do.
❋ Looking after and nurturing a baby is a learned skill and at the beginning, it's as difficult for a mother as it is for a father.
❋ Men are not at a disadvantage when it comes to caring for a baby. If you're a father who has decided to stay at home to be the main caregiver, you have as much chance at being good at it and raising a happy, confident, and intelligent child as your partner.

Parenting

If you're a couple who has chosen the father-at-home option, you are hopefully committed to parenting in general rather than fathering or mothering (see p. 11). It's only sensible to base your family setup on your mutual strengths rather than be captive to stereotypes that may well conflict with your personalities.

The advantages

As a father who chooses to stay at home, you'll form a close bond with your baby and have a chance to watch and enjoy her development at an age that most men miss out on. This role will enable you to express your affection and feelings in ways that are difficult when you're in the more traditional male role. Being the caregiver lets you change your priorities and releases you from the pressures of being the main provider for your family. This leaves you with more of yourself to offer your baby and partner, which can be hugely beneficial to the family as a whole.

How your child is affected

To a baby, mother and father are interchangeable. The baby only knows parental love and care—it doesn't matter who is doing the giving. The advantage of a man being the main caregiver is that he can offer a positive role model free from the commonest kind of stereotyping. A son will grow up feeling comfortable with the emotional side of his personality and follow his father's lead in having an independent spirit unpressured by prevailing social mores. A daughter, of course, will seek out the same well-balanced kind of men as her father—and that's not a bad thing.

Being the only man

The main problem for most full-time parents is isolation, and since a large proportion of people are working during the day, adult company is found largely with other caregivers. As these are usually women, this can cause a problem for the full-time father. It's pointless to pretend that people interact with the opposite sex in the same way as with their own, but it's likely that a man with enough flexibility and confidence to become the main caregiver will move fairly easily into this predominantly female world. While some mothers may be surprised to find their ranks as full-time parents joined by a man, few will be hostile. The surprise at the "house-husband" is usually a temporary phenomenon; his role will soon be taken for granted. Most men are welcomed, although some are victims of the "let-me-help-you-love" maternalism, which can be as irritating as the "leave-that-to-me-darling" paternalism practiced by some men.

An equal share

Some couples decide to both work part-time or one or two days at home so both have a mix of parenting and work. This is possible if the jobs can be done part-time or at home—new technology has made it even easier. It may mean that both of you put your careers on hold, but many feel that it's the right choice. At least it prevents either person having to give up their career altogether. The advantages include:

✳ Both of you have real quality time with your baby, which will mean you'll form an equally close bond with her.

✳ You'll both have a strong appreciation of the frustrations involved in being in sole charge of your baby and the problems of juggling work and home.

✳ The baby benefits from building a close relationship with you both.

✳ You become a real team by sharing things equally, and prevent the resentments that often build up when one parent is at home.

◀ **BEING ACCEPTED** Over time, a full-time father will stop being the token male and become just another parent, who shares the same pleasures and problems of parenthood as his female friends.

Looking to the future

Your constant role

A parent's role as nurturer means respecting your child, and offering support without forgoing your own principles. It takes many forms.

Comforter

You can only help your child to cope with emotional or physical pain by acknowledging it, and offering comfort when it's needed.

Playmate

Play is a serious business for your child, and the best play is with other people, the most important of whom are his parents.

Limit-setter

The first limits you set for your baby will be to prevent him from hurting himself; later, these limits will prevent him from hurting others as well. Never be apologetic about consistently setting reasonable limits, but try not to do so in a punitive or accusatory manner. Rather than saying "no" to him all the time, help him to understand your reasons.

Teacher or role model?

The role of teacher is crucial for any parent; but it isn't formal teaching: Do it by example. Your child learns about life from you, so you can't shrug off responsibility for an errant school child or a truculent teenager.

Authority figure

Don't confuse authority and power: Power results from the use or threat of force; authority comes from a person who has influence over, and receives consent from, others without force. Your child will accept your authority if he can also see that you are fair, competent, loving, and reasonable.

Your baby has now completed his first year of life; he's beginning to communicate with language, he's mobile, he's feeding himself, and asserting his personality as a full member of the family. He's growing up, so your roles as parents will be changing too, and they'll continue to change as he progresses on to school and ultimately to adolescence and adulthood. Under your care, he'll become more and more independent, but he'll always need you both as his permanent bedrock of security, sympathy, friendship, and love.

Your baby grows up

The main change you'll see, and must be prepared to accept, is that your baby is becoming a person in his own right, with personality, preferences, and a will of his own. He will gradually acquire a sense of place in the family, a sense of independence, and, most importantly, a sense of self-worth. Not all these changes are straightforward for you. On the one hand, they are all signs of growing maturity and so should be welcomed. On the other hand, some aspects of his growing up may lead to clashes with you and could result in a battle of wills that needs careful handling. Then again, his frustration at wanting to out-perform his ability may express itself as tantrums that leave you bewildered, perplexed, and sometimes helpless (see p. 182). Tantrums, though, are a crucial milestone; he can't become a reasonable, self-controlled child without experiencing them.

A hierarchy of needs

Keep in mind the basic needs that will help your child to grow and develop normally. Health, of course, is a prerequisite, but you also have to try to provide the right sort of environment for him to reach his full potential —

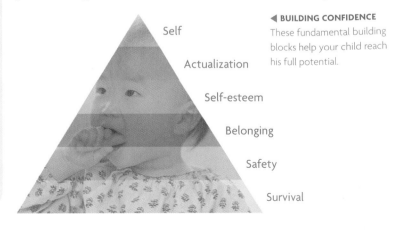

Self

Actualization

Self-esteem

Belonging

Safety

Survival

◀ **BUILDING CONFIDENCE**
These fundamental building blocks help your child reach his full potential.

physically, emotionally, socially, and intellectually. All children have a hierarchy of needs, starting from the very basic need for survival. You can think of your child's needs in terms of a pyramid (see opposite): The solid base is the provision of the food, drink, and shelter needed for survival; then comes safety—protection from harm; a sense of belonging—your child needs to feel wanted and secure; leading to self-esteem—no one can feel good about himself if he feels unloved. Near the top of the pyramid comes actualization, an understanding of his place in the world. Finally comes a fully developed sense of self, a pinnacle that can't be achieved without the other needs being met.

Becoming independent

Your child's burgeoning spirit of self-reliance is more important than you may think because so many good things can flow from it. Without a secure feeling of independence, a child can't relate to others. He can't share, be reasonable, outgoing, and friendly, have a sense of responsibility, and eventually respect others and their privacy.

Many other qualities stem from his belief in himself too—curiosity, adventurousness, being helpful, thoughtful, and generous. With such qualities people will relate well to him and he'll automatically get more out of life. What you pour in as love, expresses itself as self-worth and belief in himself. Love, of course, is not the only spur; you can encourage him practically as well.

GROWING UP Your baby is growing up. She's mobile and is beginning to know her own mind. As she gains independence, physically and emotionally, your role is also changing.

Being reasonable

This heading disguises a few personal comments on discipline in young children. I have to disguise it because what I believe to be good discipline has little to do with the usual punitive interpretation of the word.

Redefining discipline

Good discipline has nothing to do with a parent forcing a mode of behavior on a child; it's about encouraging reasonable behavior from a child. Your aim should be to create a desire to behave well most of the time, rather than to conform to an arbitrary adult code out of fear, weakness, or resignation.

Encouraging good behavior

Praise good behavior rather than penalizing poor behavior.

Start from the beginning

It's easier if you start how you mean to finish; discipline doesn't just happen at, say, three years old. It's something that's been building from birth and is based on reasonable behavior expressed by you.

Parental responsibility

All children are born with an overwhelming desire to please; if they lose that desire, my view is that we parents must take responsibility. If you think you're doing everything right but still have a difficult child, you may be going too easy on yourself. Look at what you think of as "right," and ask yourself if it is right for your child.

Being consistent

Decide on your joint attitude to discipline, and be consistent in your response. A child who gets different reactions from each parent will be confused about what her limits really are, and her behavior will reflect this.

Helping independence develop

Helpfulness Ask her to get things for you, such as the shopping bag or the dustpan, so that she can help and feels useful.

Decision-making Give her small decisions to make, like which toy to play with or which cup to use, so that she can use her judgment and rely on it. Let her choose what she wants to wear in the morning; dressing may take a bit longer, but it'll give her a real sense of achievement.

Sense of identity Ask questions about her preferences and solicit her opinion to give her a sense of identity and importance.

Physical independence Give her slightly more and more difficult tasks—like jumping up and down, or throwing or kicking a ball, so that she can feel proud of the strength and coordination of her body. Let her dress herself when she is able to. Choose clothes that are easy to put on, such as pants with elastic waists. Don't intervene unless she asks you to, or she is very frustrated. Praise all her efforts at new tasks.

Emotional independence Show her that she can trust you: you always come back after leaving her, you always comfort her when she's hurt, you always help her when she's in difficulties.

Cooperation "We can do it together" is a motto that you should keep repeating—it breeds faith in your baby's own efforts. When she overcomes an obstacle or succeeds in a task on her own, she'll experience the thrill of achievement—especially if you heap praise on her.

Achieving control of her body

Many parents believe that they can set a clock for their baby to achieve bowel and bladder control. Those parents are doomed to frustration. Your baby's timetable has nothing to do with your expectations – only with her speed of development. Bowel and bladder control are undoubtedly important milestones between dependent baby and independent child, but they can't be reached until other areas of development have been achieved. Until the nerve connections or pathways between her brain and her bladder and bowel are in place, she can't control her actions. Likewise she can't control her bowel or bladder until her muscles are strong enough. This is why I dislike the label "potty training"; no child can do something until she's ready for it and, once ready, no child needs training.

When she'll be dry

At around 18 months and no earlier, your child might start to tell you that she can feel herself passing urine. She can't hold it, she can't wait, she has no control over it. She'll give you a sign; she'll point to the diaper and vocalize to draw your attention to it. Then, and only then, do you start a gentle program of encouragement. The first step is to get her a potty of her own and put it in the bathroom. Let her sit on the potty when she wants to. If she does anything in it then praise her for it. You may also be able to encourage your child by giving her special pull-up diapers to wear during the day or night, so that when she does become more aware, you can take her diaper off quickly; she may even be able to do it herself.

Your daughter may achieve bladder and bowel control by the age of two, and be dry at night by three; it may take your son longer. Being dry all night can take some children a long time—it's normal for a boy not to achieve full control until he is four or five. Never scold your child for wetting the bed, or having an accident during the day, especially if she's been "dry" for a while. It could be a sign of illness or emotional distress, so think about the underlying causes. Being angry with your child for something over which she has little control will just upset her and make the problem worse.

Gender differences in development

Bladder and bowel control is one obvious area of development where there may be a marked difference between boys and girls (although there will always be exceptions to the rule). Many gender differences are imposed on boys and girls by adults' own prejudices about what boys or girls are expected to be like (see p. 148), so it's not always clear whether the recognized differences are solely due to nature or nurture. Differences in

Toilet tips

Here are a few tips that you might find helpful:

✳ Let your child develop at her own pace. There is no way you can speed up the process, just be there to help your child along.

✳ Never force your child to sit on the potty; let her decide.

✳ Praise your child and treat her control as an accomplishment. Always forgive and ignore any accidents.

▲ **"POTTY TRAINING"** There's no need for "potty training". Let your baby develop at his own rate. He'll achieve bowel and bladder control as soon as he's ready and not a minute earlier.

▶ **GETTING DRESSED** By the age of about two-and-a-half, your child will find putting on her clothes (and taking them off) becomes easier. As her independence develops, she'll be increasingly eager to do this for herself.

Temper tantrums

By the time he's about two, your child's will is well developed, but his ambitions far outreach his capabilities. The resulting combination of stubbornness and frustration can be explosive—the classic temper tantrum. There are ways to cope:

✳ Accept temper tantrums as normal. Better yet, see them as a cry for help. Having your child throw a fit of screaming, kicking, and crying is upsetting, but if you're firm, gentle, and have a steady nerve, you'll nurse him out of them; remember, he's not being wilfully bad—he just can't control himself.

✳ Don't shout, spank, or get angry. He needs you to help him regain control. A tantrum means he's saying, "Help me. Protect me from myself." Your very quietness should calm him down.

✳ A really upset child can frighten himself by the sheer strength of his emotions, so cuddle him close; be firm—he will struggle.

✳ Be businesslike; he's trying to elicit a dramatic response, but he'll calm down if you're cool.

✳ If this doesn't work, say you're going to leave the room. Go somewhere he can't see you, but you can see him. If you do as you promised, the screaming usually stops because he loses his audience.

✳ Try to stay where you can watch him and be ready to prevent him from hurting himself or others.

Caution
Some children develop breath-holding attacks that may be frightening to witness. Most are brought to an abrupt end by a firm tap between the shoulder blades.

the rate of development of certain skills between boys and girls throughout childhood and into adolescence have been measured by researchers (see chart below). Being aware of the differences between the genders may help you to understand your children better, which can then enable them to move forward at an appropriate rate and also help overcome any difficulties before they become problems. It can also help to avoid the sort of gender stereotyping that doesn't allow girls to be adventurous or boys to show affection.

Widening horizons

As your child grows and develops, he'll become increasingly sociable and need contact with other people in order to develop natural curiosity and intellectual growth. He'll get these from the everyday interaction he has with you, your friends, and their children, with grandparents and other

✳ Some developmental differences

Girls	Boys
As toddlers, girls are better at hopping, rhythmic movement, and balance.	At school age, boys are usually better than girls at running, jumping, and throwing.
Girls are slightly faster than boys at some aspects of early language ability. They generally learn to read and write, and grasp grammar and spelling, earlier than boys.	Most boys talk later than girls, and take longer to make complicated sentences. They have more reading problems by adolescence, and are less adept at verbal reasoning.
Girls are more emotionally independent than boys and are also more sociable and form close friendships from an earlier age.	Boys are more emotionally dependent than girls, and tend to have more behavioral problems before and during adolescence.
There's little difference in strength and speed between girls and boys until puberty, but from that time fat-to-muscle ratio is greater in girls.	At adolescence, boys become stronger and faster than girls and have more muscle and bone, less fat, and larger hearts and lungs.
Physical growth is faster and more regular; girls reach adolescence earlier than boys.	Physical growth tends to go in uneven spurts in boys; they reach puberty later than girls.
Girls may be slightly better at math than boys before they reach adolescence, after which the trend reverses.	At every age boys are better at spatial visualization and, from adolescence on, boys tend to be better than girls at mathematical reasoning.
In early childhood, girls generally appear to be more willing to obey adults' requests.	From toddlerhood, boys are more aggressive socially, and more competitive than girls.

relatives. But it's also a good idea to let him meet other children of his own age with you at daycare, classes, or parent-and-toddler groups, and to think about playgroups as a way of preparing him for formal schooling in the future. Although your child may not start to form strong attachments—real friendships—until he's approaching three years old, he'll enjoy playing alongside other children. This will enable him to start finding out about giving and sharing, and to begin exploring the enormous potential for creativity in joint imaginative play.

Extending your family

Once you're settled as a family with one child, it's natural to think about whether or not you're going to extend your family and, if so, how long to wait. As with all family matters, there's no hard and fast rule about this. It suits some couples to wait until their first child is old enough to attend Pre-K, or even until he's at full-time school. For others, a smaller gap seems better, but bear in mind that children have been found to benefit from a minimum gap of about two and a half years.

It's important, too, to take into account work commitments and financial considerations, as well as your own health; a mother who had a strenuous labor and birth or a cesarean section would probably want to feel that her body is completely back to normal and has had time to become "hers" again, before embarking on another pregnancy. Age also has significance, although nowadays this doesn't have as much bearing on the ability to bear and care for children. However, biology is against you: The older you are, the longer it will take you on average to conceive again (see p. 18), so you may not want to wait too long before trying for another baby.

The impact on your child

Whatever the length of time between the two (or subsequent) births, it's important that you think carefully about the impact on your older child, and that you introduce the idea to him sensitively and in good time. Even a teenager can feel displaced by the arrival of a new baby, something that may well happen if you've entered a new relationship and one of you already has children (see p. 142). Your decision to extend your family must always be inclusive: Your first child is a full member of your family unit and deserves to be treated as such, whatever his age.

A final word

Long after your child can cook himself a meal, iron his own clothes, and has set off on his own path in life, he'll still need both his parents to nurture him. True nurturing caters not only for his material wants, but also offers continuing and unconditional love, and it's a lifelong commitment. If this unconditional love is combined with reasonable limits and guidelines, you'll both help him to mature into an individual who is sensitive to the needs of others, but remains independent of mind, confident, and open to all the possibilities that life can offer.

Sibling rivalry

Jealousy is a normal emotion for a small child to feel if his security appears threatened by the arrival of a new baby. Although you can't guard completely against his feeling some jealousy, the best way to help him is to prepare him for the new arrival and keep showing him that his place in your affections is safe.

Before the birth

Talk to him about the new baby as soon as your belly looks really swollen. Let him touch your belly whenever he wants to, but especially to feel the baby kick. Refer to the baby as his baby, and ask if he'd like a brother or a sister to get him involved. If you know the sex in advance, tell him so he can start to identify with the new baby. Get him to show love and affection openly by reading parent-and-baby animal books together, encouraging him to be gentle with other babies, and exchanging lots of hugs.

After the birth

When he visits you in the hospital for the first time, make sure you aren't holding the baby—have your arms free for him and wait for him to ask to see the baby. Give him a present from the baby. Share bath and meal times so that he can show you how helpful he is and be praised by you. It's important to put aside at least half an hour each day when you give him your full attention. Keep telling him how much you love him.

The father's role

Reassure your elder child that you still love him. You're ideally placed to arrange special treats. With your attention and love, you'll enable your first-born to negotiate the choppy waters of sibling rivalry and you'll have cemented a lifelong friendship.

Useful information

Your rights

To be eligible for family medical leave (FMLA) benefits:

* You must have worked for a covered employer for a total of 12 months.

* You must have worked at least 1,250 hours over the previous 12 months.

* You must provide notice of your intent to take family and medical leave at least 30 days before leave is to begin.

* Upon return to work you have the right to be restored to your original job, or to an equivalent job with equivalent pay.

Social security

While you are learning about your rights as a new mother, find out what you need to do to apply for a social security number for your baby.

* A social security number is mandatory for any child over one year who is listed as a dependent on a tax return, and to apply for government services on behalf of your child.

* Apply for your child's social security number immediately after birth.

* You will find that most hospitals will apply for your baby's social security number at the same time they send in your baby's birth certificate.

Unfortunately, maternity rights and benefits in the U.S. are somewhat limited. Talk to someone in your human resources department at work about getting the full benefit of what your employer and federal laws allow.

Finding out about maternity rights

The important thing is to start asking questions and gathering information early on in your pregnancy—don't wait until you're 35 weeks pregnant to find out what the possibilities are. Every employer offers different options for maternity leave, so be sure to find out which ones apply to you. You may be able to negotiate terms if you begin the process early enough. To get the information you need about the maternity rights your company and federal law offer, make an appointment with your human resources department as soon as your pregnancy has been confirmed.

What you're entitled to

Regardless of how many hours you work or how long you've been employed, you are entitled to working conditions that are safe for you and your unborn child. The Occupational Safety and Health Administration (OSHA) requires emloyers to provide a workplace free of known hazards, while the Pregnancy Discrimination Act (PDA) requires employers to treat pregnancy as they would any other medical condition. This means that they must offer the same disability leave and pay. The PDA also makes it illegal to hire, fire, or refuse to promote a woman because she is pregnant. Your human resources department can provide you with additional information, so if you need clarification, arrange a meeting with the department.

Working women

Another major federal law that protects the health, safety, and employment rights of pregnant working women is the Family and Medical Leave Act (FMLA), which requires employers with 50 or more employees to allow up to 12 weeks of unpaid leave for certain family and medical reasons, including childbirth, the adoption of a child, or assuming care of a foster child, during any 12–month period.

In addition, the FMLA makes provision for the care of a spouse, child, or a parent with a serious health condition, and it protects a worker who is not able to do her job because of her own serious health condition, including a pregnancy- or birth-related disability. To take disability leave, a woman must have worked for at least 1,250 hours for her employer, for at least 12 months. Certain kinds of paid leave, such as vacation or sick leave, may be substituted for unpaid leave, depending on what you can negotiate.

Under the provisions of the FMLA , you are entitled to the same position or to a similar one that provides equivalent benefits, salary, and other terms of employment, when you return to work. Although you can't lose benefits that you've already earned, salary and seniority benefits can't be accrued during your maternity leave.

Paternity leave

Paternity leave is rarely paid in the United States, although a few progressive companies offer new dads paid time off, ranging from a few days to a few weeks. In 2004, California became the first state to offer paid leave. If you work in that state, you may be able to take up to six weeks at partial pay to help care for your new baby. Paid family leave bills have been introduced in states other than California as well.

In the meantime, however, most fathers take vacation time or sick days when their children are born, and a growing number of dads are taking unpaid family leave from their jobs to spend more time with their newborn babies. To find out if you are entitled to unpaid leave, start by asking your company's human resources department. Many employers are required by federal law to allow their employees (both men and women) 12 weeks of unpaid family leave under the Family and Medical Leave Act (FMLA).

Birth certificates

Registering your baby's birth is mandatory for all children born in the US. The birth certificate serves as proof of citizenship and date of birth.Fortunately, when applying for a birth certificate, the hospital staff will do most of the work for you. After your baby is born and you've filled out a brief questionnaire, the staff will complete the certificate and send it to your local health department. The process of obtaining a copy of your baby's birth certificate varies, so ask the staff about the procedure in your area.

Rights and benefits summary

When	What you need to do	Why you need to do it
Before you are pregnant	Find out what your company's maternity leave policies are. If you are unemployed or sick, you may be eligible for government help. Ask your local health department.	To maximize your employee benefits.
12 weeks or after amnio results	If you are working, inform your employer.	To maximize your employee benefits.
About 12 weeks before due date	Discuss your maternity-leave plans with your employer.	To negotiate the best maternity-leave package possible.
About 10 weeks before due date	Give your employer a letter summarizing your maternity-leave plans and what you've agreed upon.	To clarify your expectations and your employer's. This gives both of you time to fine-tune points.
At least 30 days before leave begins	Inform your employer in writing.	To protect your rights under the Family and Medical Leave Act (FMLA).
One month before due date, or later	Leave work.	To give you time to rest and prepare for birth.
Immediately after your baby's birth	Register your baby's birth. Apply for a birth certificate and a social security number for your baby if the hospital has not done this.	To provide official proof of your baby's citizenship and date of birth. Required to apply for government services on your child's behalf.

✳ Healthcare professionals

You'll be cared for by a series of professionals.

Obstetrician

Most of the prenatal care and deliveries in the U.S. are provided by obstetricians. Your obstetrician will perform your prenatal checkups and will manage most complications, including cesarean sections. Obstetricians usually perform deliveries in a hospital and increasingly include midwives in their practices.

Certified nurse midwife

Midwives attend an increasing number of births. Many work as part of a team with obstetricians or family physicians. Their services, in this case, are often covered by insurance. You can select a midwife outside your obstetrician's practice, although coverage varies. Midwives attend low-risk deliveries and can provide much of your prenatal care.

✳ Other attendants

Family physician

Some women choose to see their family physician during pregnancy.

Perinatal specialist

Your obstetrician may consult with, or refer you to, a perinatologist if there are complications, or a pregnancy is high risk.

Doulas

Birth doulas, women trained and experienced in childbirth, offer support, companionship, and encouragement during labor and birth.

Health information

Your baby's health will be closely monitored so that any problems can be picked up as early as possible. A record of your pregnancy, labor, and delivery is kept, as well as anything from your medical history—or your family's—that could affect your child. Details of your baby's growth and development are recorded and updated at the regular checks.

   To protect your baby from certain illnesses, you will be advised to take her for a series of immunizations. Some parents are anxious about possible side effects; if you have concerns, talk to your pediatrician. The risk of complications in all cases is extremely small. The risk of harmful effects from the diseases themselves is much more serious. Your baby will not be immunized if she was premature or has a fever. Vaccines often have side effects, such as fever and crying or irritability in the first 24–48 hours. If your baby has had side effects from a previous vaccination, your pediatrician may delay or stop further immunizations, depending on the severity of the reaction.

✳ First immunizations

Age due	Vaccination	How given	Possible side effects
Two months	✳ Pneumococcal infection	✳ One injection	✳ Redness and swelling at injection site, mild fever; irritability, headache
	✳ Hepatitis B	✳ One injection	✳ As above
	✳ Diphtheria, tetanus, pertussis (whooping cough), polio, and Hib	✳ One injection	✳ A raised temperature, vomiting and/or diarrhea, a small lump at site that will disappear
	✳ Rotavirus vaccine	✳ Oral administration	✳ Rarely, diarrhea
Four months	✳ Diphtheria, tetanus, pertussis (whooping cough), polio, and Hib	✳ One injection	✳ A raised temperature; vomiting and/or diarrhea, a small lump at site that will disappear
	✳ Hepatitis B	✳ One injection	✳ As for Hepatitis B, above
	✳ Rotavirus vaccine	✳ Oral administration	✳ Rarely, diarrhea
Six months	✳ Diphtheria, tetanus, pertussis (whooping cough), polio, and Hib	✳ One injection	✳ A raised temperature; vomiting and/or diarrhea, a small lump at site that will disappear
	✳ Pneumoccocal infection	✳ One injection	✳ As above
	✳ Hepatitis B	✳ One injection	✳ As for Hepatitis B above
	✳ Rotavirus vaccine	✳ Oral administration	✳ Rarely, diarrhea
Around 12 months	✳ Hib	✳ One injection	✳ As for DTP and Hib above
	✳ Pneumococcal infection	✳ One injection	✳ As above
Around 13 months	✳ MMR (measles, mumps, rubella)	✳ One injection	✳ Fever; rash; slight risk of high fever and convulsions
	Varicella (chicken pox)	✳ One injection	✳ Fever; rash

Useful addresses

Labor and birth support

American Academy of Husband-Coached Childbirth (Bradley)
P.O. Box 5224
Sherman Oaks, CA 91413
(800) 422-4784
www.bradleybirth.com
Coaching information for parents

American College of Nurse Midwives
8403 Colesville Road, Suite 1550
Silver Spring, MD 20910
(240) 485-1800
www.midwife.org
Nurse midwives organization; provides
directory of practices

American College of Obstetricians and Gynecologists
P.O. Box 96920
Washington, DC 20090-6920
(202) 638-5577
www.acog.org
Obstetricians and gynecologists organization;
has informational pamphlets for the public

Maternity Center Association
281 Park Avenue South
New York, NY 10010
(212) 777-5000
www.maternitywise.org
Birthing center

Society of Obstetricians & Gynaecologists of Canada
780 Echo Drive
Ottawa, ON K1S 5R7
(800) 561–2416
http://sogc.medical.org

Lamaze International
2025 M Street NW, Suite 800
Washington, DC 20036
(800) 368-4404
www.lamaze.org
For parents and doctors interested
in the Lamaze method of childbirth

Support for you as parents

American Foundation for Maternal and Child Health
(212) 759-5510

Canadian Paediatric Society
2204 Walkley Road, Suite 100
Ottawa, ON K1G 4GS
(613) 526–9397
www.cps.ca

Cesareans/Support Education and Concern (C/SEC)
22 Forest Road
Framingham, MA 01701
(508) 877-8266
Cesarean birth information

Depression After Delivery (DAD)
P.O. Box 278
Belle Mead, NJ 08502-0278
(800) 944-4733
www.depressionafterdelivery.com
Information and support for PPD

First Candle/SIDS Alliance
1314 Bedford Avenue, Suite 210
Baltimore, MD 21208
(800) 221-7437
www.sidsalliance.org
Research Group provides information,
support services, and counseling

La Leche League International
1400 N. Meacham Road
Schaumburg, IL 60173-4808
(847) 519-7730
www.lalecheleague.org
Breastfeeding help and information

Multiple Birth Families
www.multiplebirthsfamilies.com
Online resource for multiple birth families

4Sitters.com
P.O. Box 52
Cottage Grove, MN 55016
(651) 254-9720
www.4sitters.com
An online directory of babysitters

Maternity rights

Family and Medical Leave Act
U.S. Department of Labor
200 Constitution Ave. NW
Washington, DC 20210
(866) 4-USA-DOL
www.dol.gov/esa/whd/fmla
An explanation of laws concerning
maternity rights

National Women's Health Network
514 10th Street NW, Suite 400
Washington, DC 20004
(202) 347-1140
www.womenshealthnetwork.org
Advocacy group for women's health and
rights issues

Canadian Women's Health Network
419 Graham Avenue
Suite 203
Winnipeg, MB R3C 0M3
(204) 942–5500
www.cwhn.ca
Advocates for women's health
and rights issues

Special needs

March of Dimes Birth Defects Foundation
1275 Mamaroneck Avenue
White Plains, NY 10605
(914) 428-7100
www.modimes.org
Campaigns for pregnancy and child health

Easter Seals Canada
90 Eglinton Avenue East
Suite 208
Toronto, ON
M4P 2Y3
(416) 932–8382
www.easterseals.ca
Provides programs and services for
children with physical disabilities

Learning Disabilities Association of Canada
323 Chapel Street
Ottawa, ON K1N 7Z2
(800) 238-5721
www.ldac-taac.ca

National Healthy Start Association, Inc.
P.O. Box 25227
Baltimore, MD 21229-0327
(410) 525-1600
www.healthystartassoc.org
Promotes community-based maternal and
child health programs

Parents of Premature Babies Inc. (Preemie-L)
www.preemie-l.org
Provides support to families and caregivers
of premature babies

Maternity Center Association Foundation for Blind Children
Rose Mofford Center
1235 E. Harmont Drive
Phoenix, AZ 85020
(800) 322-4870
www.the-fbc.org
Information on caring for blind children

Index

Acknowledgments

Picture library: Romaine Werblow
Proofreader: Alyson Silverwood

The publisher would like to thank the following
for their kind permission to reproduce their
photographs:

(Key: a-above; b-below/bottom; c-centre; l-left;
r-right; t-top)

Alamy Images: Bubbles Photolibrary 66; Janine
Wiedel Photolibrary 150; plainpicture 60; Peter
Usbeck 63; Corbis: LWA-Dann Tardif 13, 19, 23,
33tr, 39tr, 45tr, 47, 49, 51tr, 57, 59tr, 73, 82tl, 95tr,
101tr, 129, 135, 137, 141, 149, 171, 175tr; Larry Williams
46; Carolyn Djanogly: 6; DK Images: Courtesy of

Simon Brown 112; Getty Images: George Doyle
16-17; Studio Tec / ailead 126-127; Mediscan:
SHOUT 28; Mother & Baby Picture Library: 48,
52, 138, 146, 153; Photolibrary: Banana Stock 103;
Brand X Pictures 128b; Stockbyte 59bl; Larry
Williams 41; Science Photo Library: 32; Samuel
Ashfield 29; BSIP, Laurent 44; Ian Hooton 26

All other images © Dorling Kindersley
For further information see:
www.dkimages.com

The publishers would also like to thank the
following for modelling in this new edition:
Nicola Munn, Joe and Leo Hayward, Chloe and
Oscar Dunne, Mandeep and Ethan Kalsi, Louise
and Ruth Izod, Dharminder and Biba Kang,

Chloe Webb, Nicole Bheenick-Coe and
Lily Coe, Sheela Lomax and Lorenzo Lapinid,
Carrieann Austin and Emily Collis, Daniel and
Matilda Young, Roisin Donaghy, Elisa and Jolie
Margolin, Charlotte Seymour.